Honour, Violence, Wome

Why are honour killings and honour-related violence (HRV) so important to understand? What do such crimes represent? And how does HRV fit in with Western views and perceptions of Islam? This distinctively comparative collection examines the concept of HRV against women in general and Muslim women in particular. The issue of HRV has become a sensitive subject in many South Asian and Middle Eastern countries, and it has received the growing attention of the media, human-rights groups and academics around the globe. However, the issue has yet to receive detailed academic study in the United Kingdom, particularly in terms of both legal and sociological research. This collection sets out the theoretical and ethical parameters of the study of HRV in order to address this intellectual vacuum in a socio-legal context. The key objectives of this book are to construct, and to develop further, a theory of HRV; to rationalise and characterise the different forms of HRV; to investigate the role of religion, race and class in society within this context, in particular the role of Islam; to scrutinise the role of the civil/criminal law/justice systems in preventing these crimes; and to inform public policy-makers of the potential policies that may be employed in combating HRV.

Mohammad Mazher Idriss is a Researcher in Law, and was formerly Senior Lecturer in Law at Coventry University.

Dr Tahir Abbas FRSA is currently Honorary University Fellow at the Exeter Centre for Ethno-Political Studies.

Honour, Violence, Women and Islam

Edited by
Mohammad Mazher Idriss
and Tahir Abbas

Routledge
Taylor & Francis Group

a GlassHouse book

First published 2011 by Routledge
2 Park Square, Milton Park, Abingdon, Oxfordshire OX14 4RN

Simultaneously published in the USA and Canada
by Routledge
711 Third Avenue, New York, NY 10017

A GlassHouse book
Routledge is an imprint of the Taylor & Francis Group, an informa business

First issued in paperback 2011

© 2011 editorial matter and selection Mohammad Mazher Idriss and Tahir
Abbas, individual chapters the contributors

Typeset in Times New Roman by Taylor & Francis Books

British Library Cataloguing in Publication Data
A catalogue record for this book is available from the British Library

Library of Congress Cataloguing in Publication Data
Honour, violence, women and Islam / edited by Mohammad Mazher Idriss and
Tahir Abbas.
    p. cm.
1. Honor killings--Great Britain. 2. Honor--Religious aspects--Islam 3.
Violence--Religious aspects--Islam. 4. Muslim women--Violence against--Great
Britain. 5. Women--Violence against--Great Britain. I. Idriss, Mohammad
Mazher. II. Abbas, Tahir, 1970–
    HV6250.4.W65H665 2010
    364.152'3--dc22

                                                        2010003040

ISBN13: 978-0-415-56542-4 (hbk)
ISBN13: 978-0-415-69779-8 (pbk)
ISBN13: 978-0-203-84698-8 (ebk)

Contents

Notes on Contributors

Dr Tahir Abbas FRSA is currently Honorary University Fellow at the Exeter Centre for Ethno-Political Studies.

Dr Samia Bano is Lecturer in Law at the University of Reading.

Dr Anna Carline is Lecturer in Law at Liverpool John Moores University.

Dr Åsa Eldén is Researcher in the Swedish Research Institute in Istanbul, formerly at the Department of Sociology, Uppsala University.

Dr Aisha Gill is Senior Lecturer in the Department of Criminology, Roehampton University.

Sjaad Hussain is Lecturer at the Faizan al-Rasool Educational Institute, Birmingham, UK.

Rana Ahmed Husseini is a Jordanian journalist for *The Jordan Times* and is the author of *Murder in the Name of Honour*.

Mohammad Mazher Idriss is a Researcher in Law, and was formerly Senior Lecturer in Law at Coventry University.

Sadia Kausar is a Law graduate from Coventry University, currently employed at the Law Society, UK.

Zahira Latif is a doctoral researcher in the Institute of Applied Social Studies, School of Social Policy, University of Birmingham.

Veena Meetoo is Research Officer for the Centre for Rights, Equalities and Social Justice (CRESJ), Institute of Education, University of London.

Heidi Safia Mirza is Professor of Equalities Studies in Education and the Director for the Centre for Rights, Equalities and Social Justice (CRESJ), Institute of Education, University of London.

Joanne Payton is Information and Research Officer for the Iranian and Kurdish Women's Rights Organisation.

Dr Leylâ Pervizat is Lecturer in Gender Studies and Intra-Family Violence, at the Halic University, Istanbul, Turkey.

Geeta Ramaseshan is a Criminal Solicitor in India.

Nancy Kaymar Stafford is a legal consultant at King and Spalding, LLP, in Atlanta, USA.

Dr Suruchi Thapar-Björkert is Senior Lecturer in Sociology at the University of Bristol.

Chapter 1

Honour, violence, women and Islam – an introduction

Mohammad Mazher Idriss, LLB, LLM, Cert. Ed.
Senior Lecturer in Law

Why are honour killings and honour-related violence (HRV) so important to understand? What do such crimes represent? And how does HRV fit in with Western views and perceptions of Islam? This book provides a collection of scholarly essays and research papers examining the concept of HRV against women in general and Muslim women in particular. This introduction outlines the main objectives and rationale of this book, and its contributions to both socio-legal understanding and public policy in general.

The issue of HRV has become a sensitive subject in many South Asian and Middle Eastern countries, and it has received the growing attention of the media, human-rights groups and academics around the globe.[1] However, the subject has yet to receive detailed academic study in the United Kingdom, particularly in terms of both legal and sociological research. This collection of essays sets out the theoretical and ethical parameters of a study of HRV in order to address this intellectual vacuum. The key objectives of this book are:

- to further construct, and further develop, a theory of HRV;
- to rationalise and characterise the different forms of HRV;
- to investigate the roles of religion, race and class in society within this context, in particular the role of Islam;
- to scrutinise the role of the civil/criminal law/justice systems in preventing these crimes; and
- to inform public policy-makers of the potential policies that may be employed in combating HRV.

The concept of HRV has emerged in recent years, referring to acts of violence predominantly against women who are perceived to have transgressed a religious-cultural divide, particularly in matters relating to sexuality. Persecution in the name of honour affects many women, South Asian and Middle Eastern women in particular, in communities both in Western Europe and in the sending regions. Incidents of honour violence take place in all social classes, but in less developed South Asian and Middle Eastern communities it is men who are the main perpetrators and young, vulnerable women who are the most likely victims. One explanation for the preponderance of female victims is that men who have breached the honour code are more likely to be able to escape the wrath of the aggrieved family by fleeing to other parts of the country or finding sanctuary with other friends and family. Women, by contrast, have little or no refuge to resort to; their freedom, money and lives are controlled and placed in the hands of men, in deeply rooted patriarchal culture. Another explanation is that women are more frequently blamed for breaching the honour code than men, and to kill a male from another family may create feuds in community structures that regard men as more 'honourable' than women.

Many HRV cases go unnoticed by the police and the authorities as they are not reported; offenders therefore often go unpunished.[2] Incidences of honour killings and HRV in Western Europe have occurred in many social contexts, for example in relation to Turks in Germany and Kurds in Sweden (see in particular Chapter 9 by Åsa Eldén and Chapter 13 by Suruchi Thapar-Björkert in this volume). The patterns of HRV crimes are also remarkably similar. A typical example may involve a young Muslim woman falling in love with a man of another religion/caste/sect, and once the community hears of it, it is felt incumbent on the head patriarch to take action so as to avoid any 'shame' being placed on the wider family. In essence, HRV is seen as a mechanism to control female sexuality,[3] and in all the instances of HRV one is referring to groups who have arrived in host nations relatively recently and as such are still experiencing early concerns around cultural identity and multiculturalism, labour-market participation, their service needs and the role and impact of their 'roots back home'. These groups have a strong sense of group identity and loyalty, and in cases where these communities are Muslim, there is extra pressure placed upon young women to remain chaste until marriage, and even then to marry partners that are chosen by members of the wider family, including the head patriarch as well as the head matriarch. When this line is crossed, it is quite possible for men to act to 'punish' their wives, daughters or sisters in the most extreme of ways, and such actions are tacitly sanctioned or approved by members of the community, directly or indirectly. These include criminal damage, bodily injury and death.

There is strong anecdotal evidence to suggest that patterns of honour killings and HRV are on the increase in the United Kingdom. For example, in 2003 Shada Bibi, a young Muslim woman aged 23, was murdered on her wedding day by her cousin, who opposed her marrying her 'first love', a Pakistani man from the North. In September 2003 an Iraqi-Kurdish father, Abdalla Yones, cut the throat of his 16-year-old daughter, Heshu, after she embraced Western culture and began dating a young man. And in January 2006 Banaz Mahmod was killed for having a relationship outside marriage. It seems clear that men often kill women on the grounds of their illicit sexual relationships; very rarely are there cases of women killing men on the grounds of a man's illicit sexual relationship. It is also men who command 'honour' – women do not control 'honour' in the same manner nor can they require men to adhere to chastity and other similar moral values. However, there are other acts which may 'dishonour' a family name, other than illicit relationships. They include:

- women marrying men of their choice, or vice versa;[4]
- women divorcing abusive husbands (e.g. the well-documented case of Samia Sarwar, who was killed in 1999, at the request of her mother, at her lawyer's office where she was seeking a divorce);
- being raped;[5] and
- entering into homosexual relationships, whether male or female.

The growing incidence of such crimes in the United Kingdom is illustrated by the fact that the Metropolitan Police Service has investigated over 100 cases of suspected 'honour killings' over a period of approximately two years, although it never completed a final survey (see Chapter 15 by Aisha Gill in this volume). The existence of HRV in the United Kingdom might be due to ethnic minority communities, and in particular second generation migrants, finding conflict with the norms and values of the elder generation. Second generation migrants who have become more 'Westernised' may provoke the first generation to take physical action in order to 'remedy' the perceived shame created by their apparent transgressions. But why is there increased media interest in this phenomenon in Western societies?

Within the global context of Islamophobia, especially in the United Kingdom and the United States, many Western societies are preoccupied with barbarism and acts of cruelty carried out in the name of Islam, especially in the aftermath of 9/11 and 7/7. Furthermore, those in the West yearn for an understanding of concepts such as 'honour' and 'shame' as a moral code for a way of life for Muslim communities, as well as the impact that this has upon Muslim women. Understandings of complex notions such as patriarchy as well as the socio-legal approaches to combat HRV within Muslim communities are also sought. Consequently, there is now real demand to comprehend the reasons behind the persistence of 'honour crimes' in Muslim societies and in Muslim diaspora communities, including the role the legal system has in preventing these crimes.

Unfortunately, it is only when HRV occur in advanced Western European societies that greater notice is taken (and more efforts are made to tackle the issue more directly). The concepts of honour killings and HRV are found in almost all Muslim countries and Muslim-dominated communities. Indeed, in Pakistan, Jordan and Turkey there is considerable evidence of violence against Muslim women in patriarchal societies and social systems that do not sufficiently protect the rights of women.[6] However, there is also a common (misconceived) understanding that honour crimes occur mainly against Muslim women (and are mainly perpetrated by Muslim males) living in Muslim communities, and that HRV is expressly supported in Islamic scriptures and the Qur'an; this misconceived import is based upon a neo-Orientalist conception that Muslim men are violent, fundamentalist and irrational. However, this misconstrued understanding is supported by the bloodshed witnessed in Pakistan in the name of so-called honour. Not only do we witness vulnerable, isolated women targeted by the accusation of being *karo kari* (i.e. an adulteress), but men in Pakistan also direct their violence and anger towards other vulnerable minority groups, including Christians and Shias.' It will therefore be demonstrated through detailed analysis within the context of Islamic theology that the concept of honour and HRV is not specifically a Muslim phenomenon nor is it limited to Muslim societies; sociologically, the concept of honour affects all societies, classes and religions. The concept of honour can even be said, in one sense, to be practised by Western societies and dominant groups.[7] It is important to remain aware that the notion of HRV is neither confined to Muslim societies nor to South Asia; rather it should be viewed as an international women's human-rights issue.[8] Nevertheless, such acts of violence forced The Muslim Council of Britain in 2004 to issue a statement that honour killings and HRV are against Islamic Law, although they acknowledged that they do exist 'within a very small section of the British Muslim community'.

This collection of essays aims to assist in the transformation of conventional assumptions about Muslims and their supposed support of HRV, based on an analysis of Islamic scriptural teachings that clearly do not support HRV. Furthermore, the essays provide a very distinctive comparative dimension in relation to HRV, presenting not only an examination of the phenomenon in Muslim and other ethnic communities living in the United Kingdom, but also an examination of the phenomenon in a number of non-Muslim-dominated societies (including Sweden, India and sub-Saharan Africa) as well as in traditionally Muslim-dominated countries (including Jordan, Pakistan and Turkey).[9] The editors believe that it is vital to show the dynamics of HRV in both Muslim and non-Muslim societies, for it helps to reveal that HRV permeates all religions and social classes, as well as importantly rebutting the assumption that HRV is entirely foreign to Western societies and cultures; it is a 'world-wide phenomenon'.[10] There is a clear need to understand the dynamics of integration by immigrant and ethnic minority communities, the processes of assimilation and the issues surrounding exclusion within this context; there is also a genuine case for analysis of the difficulties surrounding the transformation of religious and cultural beliefs held by immigrant communities living in Western societies, and of the tensions between respect for cultural and religious diversity on the one hand and the legal-rational organisation of Western civil society on the other.

The editors believe that there is a dearth of research in relation to the phenomenon of HRV and this collection of essays attempts to address some of these issues. Despite many books having been written on this topic (see most recently Thiara and Gill's (2010) *Violence Against Women in South Asian Communities)*, there is – to the knowledge of the editors – no single text covering the issues of honour, violence, women and Islam from the socio-legal perspective adopted here, written by lawyers, sociologists, criminologists and Islamic theologians. This collection of essays contains the work of nationally and internationally distinguished academics, professionals and practitioners in law, sociology and criminology, as well as human and women's rights activists. It provides expert analysis on the discussion associated with HRV nationally and internationally and pushes the debate in relation to how government agencies can best begin tackling the problem. Undoubtedly, one of the main books in this area of study is that edited by Welchman and Hossein (2005), *Honour: Crimes, Paradigms and Violence against Women*. While this is an excellent book to read concerning honour crimes, there is only one chapter in it that deals with the United Kingdom specifically and offers some criticisms about the law. This collection of essays goes much further in its analysis of English law and society, and in proposing reforms in Western societies that could help in the fight against HRV.

Structure of the book

The aim of this collection of essays is to confront the challenges presented by crimes of honour and to present them clearly to those teaching and researching sociology, law and criminology and, in particular, to those with research or practical interests in these fields. Throughout, the significance of legal and social reform on the issues covered will be clearly drawn out. To that end, the role of lawyers, of sentencing and of public policy generally, as well as the role of the police in the investigation of such crimes, will seek to introduce proposals for and subsequently analyse important reforms, highlighting their application to crimes of honour.

Each chapter is explored with a view to providing the reader with a broader appreciation of the development and contemporary relevance of crimes of honour and how social and legal reform can combat this trend. HRV is a topic which is as much about sociology, criminology and religion as it is about law, so a full understanding of the topic cannot be gained without an appreciation of all these aspects of the dynamic. This book includes greater emphasis on the perspective of women and the religion of Islam, and while it intends to provide a focus that cuts across the United Kingdom position, many of the essays address HRV specifically in Muslim communities inside and outside the United Kingdom. The focus of this collection should therefore appeal to a large audience interested in

Islamophobia and HRV in relation to Muslim women living in Muslim communities in both Western and non-Western societies. By maintaining a strict focus on these topics, which are at the heart of this fascinating subject area, the editors have been able to produce an important and necessary text that will appeal to a wide body of readers.

Chapter 2 by Dr Tahir Abbas provides a focus on Britain and the nature of the problem of HRV among British-born Muslim men, in the context of post-war post-colonial societies. It explores the ideas of assimilation, integration, multiculturalism and the (re)turn to Islam among second and third generation Muslim minorities, as well as the desire by nation-states to perpetuate the myth of the Oriental Other in the wake of the 'war on terror.' The question of honour in Islam is explored with reference to the concept of hegemonic masculinity, and how it has evolved in pre- and post-colonial multicultural contexts. Chapter 3 by Zahira Latif examines the experiences of Pakistani/Muslim women in the United Kingdom who are in violent relationships, identifying the 'cultural factors' preventing women from 'speaking out' against abuse and seeking help. Chapter 4 by Veena Meetoo and Professor Heidi Mirza concludes that the term 'honour' is a misnomer, since honour crimes are essentially about domestic violence and regulation of women's sexuality through the ideology of 'honour and shame'. The chapter explores how the concept of 'honour' is invoked within a multicultural context as a motivation for the perpetration of domestic violence, highlighting the inadequate responses to women's needs by the state and service providers, social services, the police and GPs.

Chapter 5 by Joanne Payton examines the case of Banaz Mahmod, who was murdered in what police termed an 'honour killing' in January 2006. It points out the specific failures in the case, showing that the police failed to protect Banaz and that, while police detection was committed and professional, more could have been done to bring the other perpetrators to justice. Chapter 6 by Dr Anna Carline examines crimes of passion and contributes to the debate on honour and violence, illustrating how concepts of honour and shame are not only deeply entrenched within the criminal law's response to domestic homicide, but also constructed according to certain conceptions of gender and culture. The chapter provides analysis of honour and shame with a focus on the 'cultural defence' in English cases, whereby a woman is killed due to her 'shameful' behaviour in order to protect the family's honour. It argues that notions of honour and shame are not restricted to 'cultural defence' cases but operate within the majority of cases involving domestic homicide, including 'honour killings' committed by the dominant group within society (i.e. by white Western males). It argues that the provocation argument has not proved so successful (within the jurisdiction of English law) for 'honour killings' committed by minority groups. Chapter 7 by Sadia Kausar, Sjaad Hussain and myself encompasses the whole dimension of social interaction between the genders in Islam and argues that domestic violence is a universal condition, present to an equal extent in Muslim and non-Muslim societies. It argues that traditional interpretations of Qur'anic injunctions, amongst others, perpetuate a patriarchal system not intended by the Qur'anic world view in its genesis and (incorrectly) serve as justification for the oppression of women in Muslim societies, whether in the East or West. Chapter 8 by Geeta Ramaseshan examines the construction of the term 'honour' within statutes found in Indian criminal law. In particular, it examines three Indian statutes, the Penal Code, the Criminal Procedure Code and The Evidence Act, and their relationship to the term 'honour' within the context of sexual offences. Chapter 9 by Dr Åsa Eldén examines the role of women in HRV cases, arguing that close female relatives of victims often act in opposition to them. In order to truly understand the meaning of HRV, it is important to study the multifaceted relationships between different victims and to see a comprehensive picture in terms of both women's victimisation and women's agency in crimes of honour. Chapter 10 by Dr Leylâ Pervizat explores the idea that crimes of honour are very complex and multidimensional, and argues that an analysis of this issue requires multiple and interdisciplinary approaches with different strategies in mind. The chapter approaches the issue of honour killings in Turkey and the fact that such cases are not diligently prosecuted by the Turkish authorities. It examines recent Turkish reforms and the reform of the Turkish Penal Code and its impact on dealing with crimes of honour. Chapter 11 by Rana Husseini explains that in Jordan and Syria those who commit crimes of honour can escape punishment, serving as little as three months in prison for killing a sister or daughter. It explores numerous successful initiatives, including a group of young migrant men who toured Jordan to encourage their male peers to refrain from practising HRV against their female relatives. Chapter 12 by Nancy Kaymar Stafford examines the violent practices within several sub-Saharan countries, and related legislation, and provides an examination of what is working, with recommendations for moving forward. It argues that ending behaviour embedded in tradition is not simple – cultural practices die a long 'hard death' and enacting laws to prohibit these crimes is not enough. It concludes that steps must be taken to address these issues through a comprehensive approach involving legal reform, social services and public education. Chapter 13 by Dr Suruchi Thapar-Björkert critically engages with debates on forms of gendered violence in the United Kingdom and Sweden. The central argument looks at various subject positions that men can occupy in relation to HRV: as perpetrators, as victims and as combatants. It engages critically with the Sharaf Heroes Project in Sweden – a preventative men's project that works to change attitudes towards HRV – and argues that, comparatively, while state institutions in the United Kingdom lead on research on men as perpetrators of violence, they are hesitant to engage men in combating HRV. Chapter 14 by Dr Samia Bano critically analyses the relationship between law, multiculturalism, the community and the state in order to critique the practice and process of challenging 'crimes of honour' in the United Kingdom. It examines how English law currently deals with the concept of honour and forced marriages under the Forced Marriage (Civil Protection) Act 2007. It also questions the issues the legislation raises in relation to the treatment of minority ethnic women who may be subject to such practices, including whether the 2007 Act should have criminalised forced marriages instead of making them a civil issue with an injunction the only main remedy. Finally, Chapter 15 by Dr Aisha Gill considers the definition of HRV and provides discussion on 'what must be done' in order to eliminate crimes of honour and honour killings.

Reforms

While this collection of essays will be of benefit for students and academics interested in HRV, it will also be of great interest to public policy-makers, government agencies and law-reform bodies. Therefore, it is believed that this book is timely, not only in terms of its topicality, but also because reform of the law of murder has been proposed by the Law Commission and undertaken by the Coroners and Justice Act 2009.[11] This book informs the reader of the various policies and strategies that have been (or may be) employed by European and international countries in order to combat HRV and to provide adequate protection to victims through social and government institutions.

The suggestions for reform can be classified under three particular headings: (a) Legislative and Other Legal Reforms; (b) Preventative Reforms; and (c) Protective Reforms. Some of the reforms mentioned below have been explored by Ali (2001: 39–47). However, an effort has been made here to elaborate on some of the issues in more detail within the context of the United Kingdom's unusual constitutional structure, in terms of legislation creation and law enforcement.

Legislative and other legal reforms

The characteristics of the United Kingdom legal system mean that there is no single codified constitutional document signifying the legal rights of those living within its borders. There is no special constitutional document of legal sanctity providing the rights, roles and responsibilities of the state, state organs and the individual. Rather, the rules of the constitution may be found in a variety of sources; some legal, others not. In terms of legal sources of the United Kingdom constitution, Acts of Parliament and case law are the two main legal sources that make up the constitutional rules. In this respect legislative reform in the shape of the creation of Acts of Parliament is vital in the fight against HRV, at least as an initial step. The editors believe that there should be a suitably named Bill presented before the bicameral UK Parliament in order to address the issue of HRV. Such a Bill might be appropriately named the Prevention of Honour Related Violence Bill. Within a democracy such as the United Kingdom, the rule of law prevails, which includes notions of fairness, equality before the law and respect for human rights. Although there is already a Sex Discrimination Act 1975 which aims to provide equality between men and women, the legislation is concerned with equality in employment and education; it was not designed with the intention of dealing with HRV within a criminal context. Therefore, the first provision within the Bill should make a declaratory statement in relation to the rule of law and HRV that citizens, both men and women, shall be treated equally before the law and shall have equal right to the pro-tection of the law in relation to HRV. The important declaratory statement behind this provision would explain that women have rights and that they should not be subjected to physical abuse and/or death in the context of HRV. It would help convey the message that vulnerable women, many of whom will come from minority ethnic groups, will have the support of the state and the law and that the state is perceived as taking a very serious role in its duties and obligations in tackling HRV.[12]

The second provision within such a Bill should make it illegal to commit HRV,[13] be it criminal damage, assault or murder, through the imposition of tougher penalties for existing laws on domestic violence. Akin to provisions found in the Crime and Disorder Act 1998 (as amended by the Anti-Terrorism, Crime and Security Act 2001) that deal with racially and religiously aggra-vated offences, it is suggested that a Bill combating HRV should include provisions that enable the courts to impose higher maximum penalties for offences committed in the name of honour. Such provisions may be aptly termed 'HRV Aggravated Offences'. By creating higher penalties for crimes of honour, this will not only deter would-be offenders contemplating com-mitting honour crimes, it would also enable sentencing judges to impose tougher sentences upon those convicted of HRV crimes. It would help explain that HRV crimes are aggravated crimes and much more serious (and devastating to their victims) in comparison to those crimes which are not aggravated.

The third provision within a Bill drafted on HRV should include HRV and its relationship to the law of murder. A provision should be included within the Bill that clearly states that honour killings are no different to murder with a direct intention to kill a victim.[14] In this context, a mandatory sen-tence of life imprisonment would be served upon an offender who is found guilty of a murder in the name of honour. However, in recognition of the reforms described above, a tougher sentence could be imposed on a person convicted of such a murder. While currently the average sentence for murder is approximately 14 years in the United Kingdom, judges would be at liberty to increase the tariffs of convicted honour killers, as perpetrators of an aggravated crime. However, a hugely controversial amendment to the law of murder would be a reformation of the law on provocation. Currently, in the United Kingdom, provocation (or 'loss of self control' as it is now under the Coroners and Justice Act 2009) is a partial defence (excuse) for murder, in that a defendant who successfully raises the defence is able to mitigate the offence of murder and receive a conviction of manslaughter instead. When the provisions come into force, under sections 54 and 55 of the 2009 Act, loss of self-control will be a statutory defence for murder alone (it is still currently governed by section 3 of the Homicide Act 1957 until the provisions of the 2009 Act come into effect); it is not a defence for other crimes, although it might be a mitigating factor in relation to sentencing. Should the partial defence of loss of self-control (i.e. in this context the 'cultural defence') be unavailable in murders committed in the name of honour? Should a Bill dealing with HRV expressly forbid recognition of the loss of self-control defence in the context of honour killings?

An argument in favour of this approach would be that a criminal who, with evidential proof, has committed a murder in the name of honour may wish to 'take advantage' of the law by pleading the loss of self-control defence, arguing that his characteristics and culture drove him to the killing. The danger is that, if the loss of self-control defence is recognised, offenders may mitigate homicides based on cultural and oppressive attitudes towards women and receive the lesser conviction of manslaughter as opposed to murder. On the other hand, English criminal law has rarely accepted the 'cultural defence' (and this still appears to be the position under the 2009 Act), and therefore provisions forbidding the loss of self-control defence may be unnecessary (see Chapter 6 by Dr Anna Carline on these issues). At this juncture, it should be pointed out that the recent reforms under the Coroner's and Justice Act 2009 appear to have a major impact on HRV. For example, section 54(4) of the 2009 Act states that the loss of self-control defence 'does not apply if, in doing or being a party to the killing, D acted in a considered desire for revenge'. The use of the word 'revenge' appears to rule out some or many cases of honour killings where the offender killed in an act of revenge in order to restore familial 'honour' perceived to have been lost by some act of the victim. Also, section 55(6)(c) states that (within the context of loss of self-control) 'the fact that a thing done or said constituted sexual infidelity is to be disregarded'. The control of sexuality and a woman's (actual or perceived) infidelity is therefore expressly excluded as a factor to be considered under the defence. Sexual infidelity (one of the classic hallmarks of HRV cases) is no longer a relevant factor in loss of self-control cases and cannot be relied upon by an offender when seeking to plead the defence. This reform is welcomed and should therefore be viewed as a shift in attitude towards the treatment of women in English law and society, as highlighted by Dr Carline in Chapter 6.

Preventative reforms

Connected to the above-mentioned reforms, the various actors within the criminal justice system, the police, healthcare professionals, the Crown Prosecution Service (CPS), lawyers, judges and other public servants must have full knowledge of HRV, of honour killings and of the law relating to HRV.[15] There needs to be established full educational programmes to draw attention to HRV issues in order to successfully combat the phenomenon. Perhaps most importantly, educational programmes must begin with police forces and healthcare professionals, as they will most often be the first point of contact victims of HRV will use (see Chapter 5 by Joanne Payton). In particular, police forces and police officers must begin to take special notice and file special reports in cases where they suspect victims may be subjected to HRV, or where a victim has specifically raised an allegation of HRV. These reforms are unfortunately harsh lessons learned after the deplorable case of Banaz Mahmod, in which the police did not take her cries for help seriously. Police forces must ensure that allegations by victims of HRV are thoroughly investigated and brought before the courts for trial. Ali recommends that there should be an independent body specifically designed to monitor the handling of complaints relating to HRV made by victims to the police.[16]

The role of female police officers in the investigation of HRV cases should also not be underestimated. There needs to be a drive to recruit more female officers, and more from minority ethnic backgrounds, to deal with complaints of HRV and to help assess the likely risks in their assessments of those victims who make a complaint. Language and culture may prove to be obstacles so there needs to be a drive to recruit female officers from a variety of backgrounds who can appreciate the cultural and language difficulties that complainants face, as well as helping to identify cases which are not related to HRV. It is accepted that the latter will prove difficult to assess and so it is imperative that the police view initial complaints made by HRV complainants as coming from 'high-risk' victims, at least until further investigations are made. The lesson to be learned from the death of Banaz Mahmod demonstrates the need to register and investigate all honour killings and all incidences of HRV at the earliest opportunity. If there are allegations of HRV, police forces as well as healthcare professionals need to react quickly. As such, there needs to be appropriately drafted guidelines on intervention by police and/or healthcare professionals in cases of HRV.[17] Although there is little space in this introduction to cover these issues, some of the more important intervention strategies for healthcare professionals may be explained as follows.

In the United Kingdom, efforts to tackle domestic violence appear to be driven by women's and human-rights organisations, as well as actions taken by the police. While this is no doubt correct and understandable, tackling domestic violence and HRV needs to be undertaken much earlier. Indeed, in many cases the invocation of these organisations will only happen in extreme cases; it is a well known fact that the police are reliant on other organisations for information and will not investigate the majority of domestic violence cases. Healthcare professionals are in an ideal position to identify women who may be at high risk from HRV, simply because they are at the front line in terms of contact with patients who suffer illness, injury and HRV abuse. Their relationship (and communication) with the police is therefore vital because healthcare professionals will be able to identify and refer victims of HRV abuse to the relevant agencies (e.g. the police) before circumstances become serious or life-threatening. Healthcare professionals must therefore take an active step in making enquiries about patients who have suffered injuries or illnesses; healthcare professionals, when confronted with suspected victims of domestic violence, must ask them what the causes of their injuries are, especially if the patient matches the profile of an 'at high-risk victim'. In this context the training of healthcare professionals is vital. They must receive the appropriate guidance, information, time and support in order to successfully intervene in HRV cases at a community-wide level. If healthcare providers do not, there is a chance that the failure to deal with a case appropriately may result in death or serious injury.

The obvious initial method of identification for healthcare professionals is if victims of HRV disclose their abuse. While this is the most obvious form of identification, it is arguably the least productive because very few victims of HRV will openly disclose their abuse. The second method of investigation relates to the identification of symptoms and signs of HRV abuse. This method requires a competent level of training on the part of healthcare professionals to diagnose and recognise indications of potential abuse, although caution must be taken as not all injuries and illnesses will be firm indicators of HRV abuse. The third and most productive method of investigation would be to monitor and question HRV amongst potential victims matching the profile of 'at high-risk victims' (e.g. South-Asian Muslim women with a history of abuse). The varied nature of HRV and the fact that victims cut across all social classes, cultures and religions could result in this method of inquiry having more or less the same low success rate as the other two. However, careful and considerate observations undertaken at hospital emergency wards may show a higher number of patients at high risk entering hospitals than visiting their GPs. The other alternative might be to undertake routine enquiries and screening into domestic abuse for *all* patients, whether or not they show or demonstrate signs of abuse. Indeed, this is actually recommended by the Department of Health in its most recent Report issued in 2005,[18] which not only provides best-practice guidance on the methods to adopt when undertaking routine enquiries with all patients but how best to respond and advise patients if they disclose abuse (including sections on how to ask about domestic abuse; that caution should be given to the recommendation that victims leave their abusive partners immediately; what domestic abuse support services are offered locally; risk assessment and the creation of 'safety plans' for victims when they face an emergency). Records kept by healthcare professionals are also vital: the logging of incidences of domestic abuse is essential, not only in terms of keeping an eye on the patterns of abuse of victims, it may also serve as a vital evidential tool in a court of law if and when healthcare professionals are called to give evidence. Using the victim's own words ('Patient states she was kicked in the stomach twice by husband for dishonouring family'), drawing diagrams of injuries to the body and showing photographs are also crucial. Poorly kept records may hinder the chances of a successful prosecution.

Education on a national scale is also required if public awareness in relation to HRV is to be raised. Education on a national front, with the aim of educating both men and women, should be undertaken at all levels, including in schools, colleges and universities, and via GPs and the media. Medical leaflets and pamphlets should be printed and distributed to GPs and hospitals explaining the notion of HRV, the help and support victims may receive from state institutions, and 'key steps' that may be pursued by victims if they ever find themselves in an emergency (e.g. if they believe they are about to be physically attacked or killed). Various human and women's rights organisations should also be involved in the dissemination and delivery of this education. The education should explain the legal rights of victims; the law relating to domestic violence and HRV; and the availability of state resources, help and legal aid in certain areas of the law (e.g. criminal law, family law, child law, human rights, and so on). Educational programmes should also be established for members of the judiciary, the CPS [Crown Prosecution Service], social workers, housing officers and other public servants.[19]

Protective reforms

Information about government-funded support shelters or safe havens, such as Karma Nirvana, should be created and/or advertised further in relation to HRV, with the aim of providing support to victims should they flee their homes in fear of an attack. Legal aid must be advertised and made freely available to victims of HRV. One particularly important reform also relates to the role of men within society and more specifically within minority ethnic communities; while men are viewed (negatively, but often correctly) as the main perpetrators of honour crimes and HRV, this book examines those activities and social programmes that positively and innovatively use men to address their male peers and educate them, in order to prevent them from practising any form of HRV in the name of 'honour' (see Chapter 13 by Suruchi Thapar-Björket).

In fact, this book enlists the help of men to tackle HRV. The editors (both of whom are South Asian Muslims) are two men positively and actively taking an interest in combating HRV. Who said that men cannot be used in such a positive way in order to tackle HRV? Who said that HRV as a subject matter remains the monopoly of women and female activists? In reality more men are needed in order to continue the fight against HRV. The presence and participation of men in this context will have huge benefit, especially in relation to the reformation of ideologies and attitudes held within ethnic communities, as well as within the context of law and public policy. It is hoped that this collection of essays takes that small step in a positive direction in the fight against HRV.

Notes

1 See, for example, Goodwin (1995); Al-Sayyid-Marsot (1979); Arvind and Young (1999); Afshar and Maynard (1994); Barot et al. (1999); and Brooks (1995).
2 See Ali (2001).
3 See generally Goodwin, n.1 above.
4 See Anwar (1998: 99) on the issue of 'respect' and 'prestige' within traditional Asian family structures.
5 See Quraishi (1997).
6 See An-Na'im (1993: 167). In some Muslim countries, the legal system adopts methods to purge criminal sanctions for husbands who kill their wives: see Spatz (1991). However, there is recognition of the 'cultural defence' in Western societies, such as the United States: see Volpp (1994). The issue is also pertinent in the United Kingdom – see for example Chapter 6 by Dr Anna Carline in this volume; Phillips (2003); and Herring (1996).
7 See Spierenburg (1998). See also Chapter 6 by Dr Anna Carline in this volume on the 'cultural defence' issue.
8 Asamoah-Wade (1999/2000).
9 See, for example, Pervizat (January 2002). Dr Leyla Pervizat is also a contributor to this collection of essays.
10 See Baker et al. (February 1999).
11 The 2009 Act received the Royal Assent on 12 November 2009, though a number of provisions are yet to come into force, including ss52–58 of the 2009 Act, dealing specifically with the subject of homicide. On the issue of provocation/crimes of passion and the law in the West, see generally Chapter 6 in this volume; Abu-Odeh (1997); and Leader-Elliott (1997).
12 See Ali (2001: 42).
13 Ibid.: 43.
14 Ibid.
15 Ibid.
16 Ibid.
17 Ibid.: 44.
18 Department of Health (2005).
19 See Ali (2001: 45).

Bibliography

Abu-Odeh, L. (1997) 'Comparatively Speaking: The "Honor" of the "East" and the "Passion" of the West', *Utah Law Review*, Vol. 2, 287.

Afshar, H. and Maynard, M. (1994) (eds) *The Dynamics of 'Race' and 'Gender'*, London: Taylor and Francis.

Ali, R. (2001) *The Dark Side of 'Honour': Women Victims in Pakistan*, Lahore: Arqam.

Al-Sayyid-Marsot, A. L. (1979) (ed.) *Society and the Sexes in Medieval Islam*, Malibu, California: Undena.

An-Na'im, A. A. (1994) 'State Responsibility under International Human Rights Law to Change Religious and Customery Laws', in Cook, R.J. (ed.) *Human Rights of Women: National and International Perspectives*, Philadelphia: University of Pennsylvania Press.

Anwar, M. (1998) *Between Cultures, Continuity and Change in the Lives of Young Asians*, London: Routledge.

Arvind, S. and Young, K. (1999) (eds) *Feminism and World Religions*, New York: State University of New York Press.

Asamoah-Wade, Y. (1999/2000) 'Women's Human Rights and "Honor Killings" in Islamic Cultures', *Buffalo Women's Law Journal*, 21.

Baker, N. V. et al (February 1999) 'Family Killing Fields: Honour Rationales in the Murder of Women', *Violence Against Women*, Vol. 5, No. 2, 164.

Barot, R. et al (1999) (eds) *Ethnicity, Gender and Social Change*, London: Macmillan.

Brooks, G. (1995) *Nine Parts of Desire: The Hidden World of Islamic Women*, London: Penguin.

Department of Health, *Responding to Domestic Abuse: A Handbook for Health Professionals*, 1 December 2005, 5802.

Goodwin, J. (1995) *The Price of Honour: Muslim Women Lift the Veil of Silence on the Islamic World*, London: Warner Books.

Herring, J. (1996) 'Provocation and Ethnicity', *Criminal Law Review*, 490.

Leader-Elliott, I. (1997) 'Passion and Insurrection in the Law of Sexual Provocation', in Naffisen, N. and Owen, R. J. (eds) *Sexing the Subject of the Law*, Sydney: Sweet and Maxwell.

Pervizat, L. (January 2002) '"Honour Killings" in Turkey: Stories of Extra-Judicial Executions', *International Children's Rights Monitor*, Vol. 15, No. 1, 18.

Phillips, A. (2003) 'When Culture Means Gender: Issues of Cultural Defence in the English Courts', *Modern Law Review*, Vol. 66, 510.

Spatz, M. (1991) 'A "Lesser" Crime: A Comparative Study of Legal Defences for Men Who Kill Their Wives', *Columbia Journal of Law and Social Problems*, Vol. 24, 597.

Quraishi, A. (1997) 'Her Honour: An Islamic Critique of the Rape Laws of Pakistan from a Woman-Sensitive Perspective', *Michigan Journal of International Law*, Vol. 18, 287.

Spierenburg, P. (1998) *Men and Violence: Gender, Honour and Rituals in Modern Europe and America*, Columbus: Ohio State University Press.

Thiara, R. and Gill, A. (2010) *Violence Against Women in South Asian Communities – Issues for Policy and Practice*, London: Jessica Kingsley.

Volpp, L. (1994) '(Mis)Identifying Culture: Asian Women and the "Cultural Defense"', *Harvard Women's Law Journal*, Vol. 17, 57.

Welchman and Hossein (2005) *'Honour': Crimes, Paradigms and Violence against Women*, Zed Books.

Chapter 2

Honour-related violence towards South Asian Muslim women in the UK

A crisis of masculinity and cultural relativism in the context of Islamophobia and the 'war on terror'

Dr Tahir Abbas FRSA
Honorary University Fellow, Exeter Centre for
Ethno-Political Studies, University of Exeter

Introduction

This chapter provides a focus on Britain and the nature of the problem of honour-related violence (HRV) among British-born Muslim men and Muslim women in the context of post-war post-colonial societies. It explores the ideas of assimilation, integration, multiculturalism and the (re)turn to Islam among second and third generation Muslim minorities on the one hand, and the desire by nation-states to perpetuate the myth of the Oriental 'Other' in the wake of the 'war on terror' on the other, both of which provide the context for the emergence of HRV among Muslim men – however, the essential dynamics of patriarchy and a crisis of masculinity also exist at the heart of the patterns found. The experiences of British Muslim minorities are analysed in the post-war period, with a particular focus on immigration, settlement, adaptation and institutionalisation of Islam into Britain, as well as other gender differences. The author considers how notions of honour and violence permeate the psychological, ideological and cultural premises behind the actions taken by not just men but also elder women in the household in an attempt to discern the nature of how such violence is related to attempts to maintain honour in a secular Western European context. The chapter defines notions of honour among Muslim men, incorporating sociological, criminological, theological and philosophical understandings, historically and contemporaneously derived, and using the notion of the decline of masculinity to identify how men relate to others, especially Muslim women, in this context.

The concerns emanating from issues of HRV have come to the fore more and more, with new criminological questions raised in relation to the deaths of young Muslim women that were previously unexplained. As society has become more aware of this issue, academics have also determined it as an important field of enquiry. In the context of post-7/7 Britain, the focus on Islam and Muslims has been greater than ever, and while there is a degree of concentration on political and social matters, the cultural issue also becomes significant in discussions of the 'good multicultural society'. An aspect of the cultural dynamic relates to questions of gender and, in particular, the nature of power relations between men and women in the context of questions of sexuality, equality and diversity. This chapter provides a discussion of the ways in which honour permeates critical cultural discourse and how concerns in relation to masculinity have also impacted on the wider sociological phenomenon of HRV towards Muslim women. But, crucially, many of these acts of violence towards women are not just a function of men, first and second generation, but also of the elder women in the household who see their own honour at stake because of their daughters' behaviour. This is an important issue to understand. If the violence is perpetuated by men, it is not the case that only men are involved in its design or are party to its execution – elder women in the household sometimes have a role in sanctioning murder (*Observer* 2009).

First, this chapter provides a sociological overview of the history of migration and the settlement of Muslims in Britain, emphasising the nature of the idea that there are many rural and subsistence-level communities which have arrived in complex urban metropolises and held intact notions of 'honour' and 'respect' (*izzat* and *ghairat* in the South Asian sense) which are at odds with the wider sexual freedoms and liberties of majority societies. Second, the policies of integration are examined, and how, in effect, ignoring aspects of the cultural dynamics of communities and their practices, or rather letting them pass by undetected underneath the radar, has given space and almost a tacit acknowledgement of the issues. Third, the nature of the question of the breakdown in masculinity among Muslim men is explored, in the context of the inter-generational disconnect. Although this gap has many deep chasms, notions of honour and respect have remained intact, in particular in relation to how women in the family ought to be 'protected from themselves'. Women, particularly in Middle Eastern and South Asian families, are seen to be the holders of moral uprightness within those communities, and if a woman is seen to have left the flock the entire community is made to feel shame and embarrassment. In the remote villages of Iraq, Afghanistan, Pakistan and Bangladesh, from where the largest diaspora communities in Britain have come, ideas of honour and revenge are everyday. Finally, the ways in which society views notions of HRV have their own misconceptions and complex issues relating to identity and representation, particularly in the media. In a climate of post-9/11 Islamophobia, Muslim communities are homogenised and stereotyped in general, and routinely objectified as the 'enemy other', particularly in the context of terrorism and as part of wider geopolitical East–West tensions. The risk here is that while a significant issue has finally caught the attention of authorities and has led to greater focus and attention, which is important and necessary, it is being carried out in the context of widespread anti-Muslim sentiments among the wider public and in social and media discussions. It is necessary and important to begin to treat the many cases as criminological phenomena rather than ones which are seen to be culturally generalisable.

Muslim migration and settlement

According to Ceri Peach, the size of the Muslim population in Britain was the subject of much controversy during the 1980s and 1990s. Today, as a result of the 2001 Census, it is possible to show how the official 1.6 million population of Muslims in Britain is highly concentrated in a small number of large urban areas: in particular, London (607,000), the West Midlands Metropolitan County (predominantly Birmingham – 192,000), Greater Manchester (125,219) and the West Yorkshire Metropolitan County (the Bradford–Leeds urban area – 150,000). Ten of the 20 local authorities with the largest numbers and highest proportions of Muslims in England and Wales are London boroughs. Tower Hamlets, in the East End of London, has the highest percentage of Muslims of all the local authorities in Britain (36 per cent) and is also the third largest in size. It is the centre of the Bangladeshi population in Britain, and the borough contains nearly a quarter of the total Bangladeshi population in the country. Despite growing by 66 per cent between 1991 and 2001, the percentage of Bangladeshis living in Tower Hamlets has remained consistent (Peach 2006a). Furthermore, in the urban areas in which they settled, Pakistanis and particularly Bangladeshis show high rates of residential clustering (or 'segregation'). This is a highly contentious subject as it tends to be politically and culturally charged as well as being a genuinely difficult concept for statisticians and geographers to fully determine. Using the 2001 Census, on a scale from 0 (no segregation) to 100 (complete segregation), Pakistani segregation from white Britons averages 54, while Bangladeshis average 65. Bangladeshis show the highest degree of segregation of any ethnic-minority population in Britain in the 1991 Census (Peach 1996). They show a relatively high level of segregation from the Pakistanis (46), while Pakistani segregation levels compared with Indians is lower than with Bangladeshis (39 versus 46). Thus, even though Pakistanis and Bangladeshis share a religion and once shared a nationality, ethnicity appears to be a stronger bond than religion among these groups of South Asian Muslims.

The 2001 Census shows that 72 per cent of the population of the UK considered themselves Christian (around 42 million people). Muslims were the second largest religion with 2.7 per cent (around 1.6 million). Hindus accounted for 1 per cent, Sikhs for 0.6 per cent, Jews for 0.5 per cent and other religions for 0.3 per cent; just under a quarter of the population had 'no religion' or did not state one. The 2001 Census also shows that 68 per cent of the Muslim population were South Asian. Pakistanis alone account for 43 per cent of the Muslim population and are the single dominant group. The number of white Muslims in England and Wales (179,000) was higher than expected, with a third defined in the Census as 'white British' (around 61,000 people). The other two thirds are described as 'other white'. These include Turks (see Küçükcan 2004), Bosnians, Kosovans and Albanians, but also those originating from North Africa and the Middle East. The religion-by-birthplace data suggests that 60,000 Muslims were born in Eastern Europe. These groups are assumed to be largely Bosnian and Kosovan refugees. Moreover, 36,000 Muslims were born in North Africa, and 93,000 Muslims were born in the Middle East. It is thought that many of these would have been counted among the 'white' population and therefore of the 116,000 'other white' Muslims. There were also found to be 96,000 Black African Muslims in England and Wales, but there were only 7,500 Nigerian-born Muslims and a further 11,000 from 'other central and west African countries'. It is suggested that a substantial part of the Black African Muslim population is of Somali origin (Peach 2006b). While Pakistanis accounted for 43 per cent of British Muslims, only 13 per cent of the Indian population were Muslim. It confirms that around half of the South Asian population, taken as a whole, is Muslim. Two out of three of all South Asian Muslims are Pakistanis (750,000), with approximately three out of four Pakistanis of Azad Kashmiri origin (approximately 550,000). It can be estimated that almost one in three of all British Muslims are quite probably Azad Kashmiri in origin.

The ethnic composition of the Muslim population, as revealed by the 2001 Census, permits a calculation of its estimated growth. This is achieved by applying the 2001 percentages of the different ethnic groups to the estimated ethnic composition of the population in the Census years 1951 to 1991. It is an approximate method since the ethnic diversity of the Muslim population of Britain has grown in the past decade due to the arrival of refugees and asylum seekers from Afghanistan, Iran, Iraq, Somalia and the former Yugoslavia. Nevertheless, the proportions originating from non-Asian or African sources should not distort too greatly given the relatively small size of the ethnic-minority population between 1951 and 1981. Based on this analysis, the Muslim population of the UK rose from about 21,000 in 1951 to 55,000 in 1961, a quarter of a million in 1971, nearly 600,000 in 1981, 1 million in 1991 and 1.6 million in 2001. The rate of growth is rapid while the population remains, on average, relatively young.

It is true that British Muslim communities have remained concentrated in the inner-city areas of older towns and cities. It is an indicator of how they have not benefited from the levels of social mobility enjoyed by other immigrant communities, past and present, but also of their inability to move out of areas facing high levels of social tension and economic deprivation as well as direct discrimination, racial hostility and cultural exclusion (Ameli et al. 2004). The Islamic Human Rights Commission has extensively mapped the physical, racial and cultural discrimination and violence experienced by Muslims in Britain in all spheres of social life, including in relation to health, education and policing services as well as in how Muslims have been attacked by random members of majority society. Birmingham, located at the centre of the West Midlands region, is a post-industrial city in which many of the challenges faced by Muslims across the country are typified. The experiences of Birmingham Muslims bring into sharp focus the fact that economic opportunities have tended to bypass these communities, even when others have prospered. Where other cities with large Muslim populations, such as Bradford, are trapped in economic decline, the economic performance of Birmingham has been favourable. Despite the decline of its manufacturing and engineering sectors, the city is undergoing regeneration, with considerable expansion in service (retail) and commercial sectors. These opportunities, however, have largely evaded most Muslims, and they may have even entrenched some of the barriers faced by this group. While most of the white British indigenous population has moved out of the inner cities through 'white flight', many South Asian Muslims have failed to move beyond the inner-city areas to which they originally migrated. These areas have become further disadvantaged, with new employment created elsewhere and in other economic sectors (Owen and Johnson 1996).

What this suggests is that in certain urban localities there are significant concentrations of Muslim groups, many of which have emerged from rural origins in the sending regions and have maintained to a considerable degree a range of cultural, social and religious practices that may be seen to be at odds with the majority society. Given the physical boundaries that have kept these Muslim communities concentrated, certain cultural practices have existed without any real modification and adaptation to majority society. In the context of questions of HRV, where there is patriarchy and the control and management of public spaces occupied by Muslim women, problems can remain undetected and have done until recently. This applies to communities within the range of South Asian and Middle Eastern origins. While there is a thousand years of history of Muslims in Britain, it is the post-war period that has witnessed the significant growth of the population. This migration has been linked to the experiences of Muslims in the Second World War, but the 'pull' also needs relating to employment in certain industrial sectors of the economy. These jobs were invariably found in the inner areas of older towns and cities, and this is where communities first gravitated towards and ultimately settled. However, as these communities have grown so have the challenges in relation to integration. Where groups have retained a distinctively cultural profile, largely based on patriarchal relations, it has also impacted on attitudes and behaviours towards Muslim women. The experience of immigration and the socioeconomic context of lived realities has intensified patterns of alienation, exclusion and disenfranchisement, but at the same time also re-emphasised traditional cultural norms – in particular hegemonic masculinity, which, as shall be seen, has regressed further under pressure.

Integration and multiculturalism

Responding to the failure of assimilation in the late 1960s, multiculturalism emerged as a policy that permitted the recognition of ethnic diversity in places such as the United Kingdom, Germany and the Netherlands. The idea of multiculturalism provided a framework within which ethnic diversity could be recognised by policy-makers and respect for different cultures encouraged between individuals. Thus, the identities and needs of ethnic minorities have tended to be shaped in a political process where difference is the perceived problem. However, throughout the late 1970s and into the mid-1980s multiculturalism was criticised by members of ethnic-minority communities who deeply resented its implicit paternalism. At the beginning of the 1980s, anti-racist strategies emerged as an alternative to multi-culturalism. This model recognised the conflict of interest within multi-ethnic nation-states and aimed to address systematic processes of inequality within institutions. It developed its insights from the concept of institutional racism and promoted the idea that perfectly ordinary people may be involved in generating discriminatory outcomes through their everyday professional practices. As a model for responding to inequalities and discrimination within a multi-ethnic society, anti-racism is a direct challenge to members of the indigenous dominant white majority community who feel comfortable with the nation's tolerant credentials. The movement started a considerable debate in political and governmental circles. It also, however, attracted criticism from many on the Left and from ethnic-minority communities, who found it strong on rhetoric and weak on delivery.

In the United Kingdom, since the 1960s governments have shaped policy and practice in relation to ethnic-minority groups around various strategies of anti-immigration and anti-discrimination legislation on the one hand, with a programme of assimilation, integration and, latterly, multiculturalism on the other. However, what permeates policy and practice is the underlying assumption concerning the inevitable assimilation of immigrant groups. In relation to Muslims, this has not taken place to the extent envisaged, partly as a function of racist hostility affecting the potential to positively integrate into the dominant economy and society, but also because of a lack of appreciation of the extent to which ethnic-minority communities have come to rely upon group religious, class and ethnic resources to mobilise the limited economic and social development that they can achieve. In effect, Muslims often have little choice but to retreat into their communities; however, where this has taken a social, political and economic manifestation which is seen to be a function of a limited opportunity structure, there has also emerged a cultural relativism which is regarded as particularly problematic.

Even before the events of 9/11, questions in relation to 'loyalty' to a cultural national identity were being asked of British Muslims. The publication in 1988 of *The Satanic Verses* by Salman Rushdie placed the concerns of British South Asian Muslims firmly on the political, cultural and social landscape. Issues of civic engagement, blasphemy laws, multicultural philosophy, the nature and orientation of certain religio-cultural norms and values, cultural hybridity and socioeconomic exclusion and marginalisation dominated rhetoric, policy and practice throughout the 1990s. The experience of, and dominant attitudes towards, British Muslims at this time reflected the entire range of debates and discussions in this area. In 2006 the culture editor of the Danish daily newspaper *Jyllands-Posten*, Flemming Rose, attracted as much attention as Salman Rushdie in 1989, but this time much of the wider Islamic world conflated its anger against the editor, the magazine and the country of Denmark. In both cases, Muslim leaders expressed sentiments ranging from general disquiet to outright death threats (e.g. the 1989 *fatwa*, or edict, of Ayatollah Ruhollah Khomeini imposing the death penalty on Rushdie and the many *fatwas* of 2006) and aggressive protests on the streets ('book burning in Bradford' in 1989 and the demonstrations organised by the Islamist group al-Ghuraba – Saviours Sect – in London in February 2006). Following these events the media questioned the compatibility of Islam with Western values and accused Muslims of being averse to the basic tenets of freedom and democracy.

Thus, the experience of Western European Muslims allows the debate in relation to multiculturalism to be realised in its fullest form. After 9/11, the international agenda has dominated domestic politics, with a tightening of security and anti-terrorism measures and 'citizenship tests' for new immigrants. It is important also to consider the disturbances in the North of England in 2001 and the civil unrest in France in 2005, as government reactions to them have direct and lasting implications for young South Asian Muslims in the United Kingdom and Muslims of North African origin in France. Young Western European Muslims are increasingly finding themselves in the precarious position of having to define their loyalties, with radical political Islamism on the one hand and developments to national multicultural citizenship on the other. This creates tensions and conflicts, encouraging some to take up the Islamic 'struggle' more vigorously, while others seek to adopt explicitly Western values.

From assimilation to multiculturalism, the adaptation of certain immigrant and ethnic minority communities to the 'host' society has remained an issue. Importantly, what it has also done is to generate a particular intergenerational gap between traditional first generation norms and values and those of the second and subsequent generations. Conflicts and tensions between different sets of expectations have created a chasm in relation to identity politics and certain cultural norms, values and practices. Where multiculturalism remains more of a 'philosophical tool' (Parekh 2005) and less of a dedicated policy action, the space created by difference is differentially conceptualised and propagated. While London is regarded as a global city where diversity is an asset, many of the Northern towns are seen as monolithic, mono-ethnic communities where acute concentrations of a particular kind of difference are seen as a disadvantage, and more specifically a liability. In London, ethnic differences are commodified and presented as beacons of economic success. In the North, difference is seen as a sign of crime, regressive cultural practices or backward-looking communities seeking to isolate themselves from wider society. In the context of post-Islamism, they are also thought to be a threat to cohesion and, in some senses, the security of the nation.

A crisis of Muslim masculinity: hegemonic patriarchy and the public space

In the current period, much has been discussed in relation to the idea of a crisis of masculinity. It is a phenomenon that has received considerable attention and in the current analysis it has implications for Muslim men in the diaspora. This crisis has at its heart an economic explanation with implications for societies, communities and families. As the traditional industries have collapsed in the post-war period, men are no longer guaranteed a 'job for life'. With de-industrialisation, the internationalisation of capital and labour and the introduction of new technologies in the workplace (Massey and Meegan 1982), working-age men no longer have access to the kinds of employment they previously tended to find. Moreover, with the introduction of equalities legislation in the early 1970s, women are now also able to compete for employment in non-industrial sectors, and since the 1990s their educational achievements have slowly been surpassing those of men, making them more marketable. As the number of women in the most senior posts continues to increase it adds considerable confidence to an already confident generation of women in post-industrial liberal societies. All of these shifting industrial and cultural processes have squeezed men out, adding to their existing and growing sense of malaise. South Asian Muslim women are increasingly finding themselves in well-paid professional employment, realising a range of educational and professional aspirations and expectations (Basit 1997).

For South Asian Muslims, forming communities in the wake of the 1968 Commonwealth Immigrants Act, effectively ending primary migration and replacing it with family reunification, there is an even greater frailty.

Originally employed in the declining economic sectors, these minorities were disproportionately impacted by economic downturn. Hyper-cyclical patterns of employment for ethnic minorities mean that at times of recession these groups experience greater disadvantage. By the late 1970s, while family reunification continued unabated, with implications for increasing trans-national marriages and the outcome of high birth rates, concentrated communities of disenfranchised Muslim background formed strong local religious, social and cultural infrastructures. One implication was in relation to attitudes towards Muslim women in wider society. Given the nature of South Asian patriarchy in the sending regions of Kashmir, Pakistan, Sylhet and parts of the Middle East, Muslim women began to be seen to be an ever greater asset that required protecting in what was regarded as an alien, non-Muslim society; that is, from perceived threats of permissiveness, alcoholism and wider societal decadence. The concept of *izzat* is important to bear in mind; it relates to notions of respect and respectability in the community. The idea of *ghairat* is also seen to be important: 'meaning honour, jealousy, courage, modesty *and* shame, [it] is a complex concept which applies to both men and women' (Werbner 2005: 17).

In traditional Muslim societies in the Middle East and South Asia, women are regarded as possessions. In the Middle East, where Islam first emerged, sex is a private matter. The openness of the sexes is seen to lead to social disorder and this is why public segregation of the sexes still goes on in parts of the Middle East. In reality, what it does is to reinforce the view that women are merely the object of Muslim male sexual consumption – hegemonic masculinity is what this is. Thus, Muslim women who transcend these boundaries are regarded as a threat to masculinity where it is perceived that women are no longer under the control of men. For a Muslim woman to have been touched by another man is seen as a violation of property, which for Muslim men is a degradation. What is even more inter-esting is that when an illegitimate sexual union, perceived or actual, has occurred, it is seen to be the fault of the woman and not the man. Apart from the notion that 'it takes two to tango', in traditional societies men tend to be wholly dominant. Taking advantage of their dominant situation in relation to women, they punish them with violence.

Not only therefore are gender relations set up in this way, women are also expected to be regulated by them. Apart from regulating opportunities for sex, there is also control of how women can look, what they wear and what spaces they can occupy in public life. For example, in Saudi Arabia, women cannot vote or drive a car, but they can fly planes as pilots, if they are taken to and from the airport in a car by a known male driver. Although control is one aspect of this regime, punishment is also part of the arrangement in cases where Muslim women have transgressed these boundaries. When a decision is made to carry out an act of HRV, it is often from a male-centred perspective, even if sometimes elder women in the household are complicit in the decision-making. In the villages of South Asia, this form of punishment can take the form of acid-burning, cutting off the nose, orchestrated gang-rape and even cold-bloodied murder ('femicide'). There are implications here for marriages, often arranged by fathers who trade their possessions – in this case daughters – and where respectability is measured by the chasteness of those daughters. Hence, virginity is the most significant asset Muslim women are felt to possess, and if it is in any way violated this serves as the basis of male retribution for bringing dishonour to the community. 'Honour killing' is the embodied extension of this expression of a loss of control over women, and also therefore status in the community.

When such traditional and rural values are found in the West embedded within diasporic Muslim communities, they are sometimes imbued with religious justification, although it is known that this is not religious but indeed cultural, and where no Islamic religious authority has given it any validation. Given the ways in which Muslim communities are concentrated in certain localities, where the ability to integrate into society is sometimes structurally constrained for the greater part, a greater reliance on cultural and ethnic resources has meant that the issues of HRV towards women have until recently remained relatively hidden. A number of high-profile cases across Western Europe and in Britain have made it palpably clear that this phenomenon goes on, and it may well have been going on for quite some time under the guise of missing persons or the apparent high rates of suicide among Muslim women, as the policing services and certain third sector organisations have come to understand in recent periods.

Over the years, as South Asian communities have remained trapped in the inner-city areas in which they first arrived, a 'heritage bubble' has ensured that traditional practices have remained intact, even those considered to be wholly problematic, such as HRV towards women. As minority and majority communities continue to become divided communities, a significant proportion of Muslims are being left behind. As the gap between the generations becomes ever more acute due to differences in relation to attitudes towards majority society, the one significant gap in relation to sexuality appears most resistant. Muslim women experience high rates of unemployment or are simply excluded from the labour market under the premise of domestic responsibilities. While wider society experiences globalisation through the proliferation of global communication technologies such as the Internet and the deregulation of television media, the tensions between the generations intensify and become even more charged than usual. Muslims in Britain live in a society that has witnessed the highest rates of teenage pregnancies in Western Europe for over two decades – sexual permissiveness is seen as a major threat. Moreover, in the context of rising post-9/11 and post-7/7 Islamophobia and anti-Muslim racism, the belief in the need for Muslims to protect themselves from the ills of wider society becomes greater. While this goes on, hegemonic patriarchy remains unchallenged, and perhaps even grows, as seen in the number of cases where fathers as well as sons have been implicated in violence towards daughters and sisters as a result of seemingly transgressing the limits of sexuality. The pressures on the wider communities of Muslims in society, given the nature of these Muslim communities, mean that there are greater menaces potentially awaiting women who apparently cross acceptable lines of sexuality, identity or even participation in dominant society.

Concluding thoughts: locating between criminality and Islamophobia

The concept of Islamophobia has become established academic, practitioner and societal parlance over the last two decades, developing an especially malevolent form after the end of the Cold War and the beginning of the 'clash of civilisations' thesis. In Britain, the term took on a well-accepted meaning and application after the events of 'The Rushdie Affair' of the late 1980s and developments to state-orchestrated analysis of social and cultural exclusion facing ethnic minorities, differentiated by virtue of 'race', ethnicity, class, gender and religion in the mid-1990s. In the post-9/11 and post-7/7 climate, Islamophobia has gathered pace as a lived experience but also in the way it is utilised as an analytical concept in various research and policy-development arenas, instrumentalised both negatively and positively depending on the predilection of the definers.

As part of this analysis, it is important to explore the ways in which the state relates to its citizens and defines its roles and responsibilities in relation to them. That is, how is the problem of Islamophobia stated, and what are its precise characteristics? What can be done to alleviate it? To this end, the 1997 Runnymede Trust Commission into Islamophobia can be used as a starting point. Case studies based on the publication of the *The Satanic Verses* by Salman Rushdie in 1988, the more recent Danish cartoons controversy of 2006, and the 2006 comments and debate made in relation to the veil by former Home Secretary Jack Straw, demonstrate the ways in which the discourse has shifted over this time period. It is argued that there are changing notions in relation to the ways in which ethnicised and racialised minorities are now regarded, with religio-cultural characteristics at the fore in how they are 'othered' by wider society. In this regard, Islam and Muslims have the greatest exposure. This experience has implications for human social relations in the context of a flailing global 'war on terror', developments in international information and communication technologies and the ways in which the state (through 'elite racism', after Dijk (1993)) regards its minority citizens in the context of devolution, Europeanisation and 'the problem' of Muslim minority youth radical identity politics. This new racism takes the form of an assault on groups through the lens of culture and language, rather than direct forms of colour discrimination (Blackledge 2006). It is subtle yet sophisticated, new yet age-old.

Although anti-Muslim discrimination, Islamophobia and the impact of the 'war on terror' have severely increased in recent periods, it is important to look at certain characteristics of South Asian Muslim communities from within. As a male second-generation Muslim academic, I am uniquely placed to discern the nature of the social concerns in relation to this matter. It is quite clear that in the last two decades there has been an increasing awareness in relation to the idea of HRV, whereas little or no attention was paid to this menacing issue before. While I am sensitive to the need to concentrate energy and resources on a major problem, it needs to be set in the context of growing Islamophobia in society and the need to perennially 'other' the most 'othered of others' currently in society in an attempt to support the status quo. Domestic violence afflicts members of wider society, and there is recognised violence and abuse within the home; but it does not generate that same sharp focus as Islam and Muslims do in the current period in relation to HRV. What the chapters in this important collection testify is that HRV is a cultural phenomenon affecting a range of traditional communities in the diaspora, whether in parts of Western Europe more generally or in Britain in particular. Moreover, it is an issue of criminality and therefore it is necessary to apply the same set of logical conclusions to investigative matters, but because it is a cultural phenomenon, cultural education becomes imperative, particularly through notions of citizenship education. A particular combination of patriarchy, declining masculinity and the liberalising of sexuality in wider society is negatively impacting on the Muslim male psyche, which feels under threat in the context of wider social and cultural pressures on this community in Britain. The balance is precarious and so are the solutions to the problems, which require degrees of sophistication that adequately tackle both the structural *and* the cultural dynamics at play. The danger to Muslim women will remain in the context of these forces.

Bibliography

Ameli, S. R., M. Elahi and A. Merali (2004) *British Muslims' Expectations of the Government Social Discrimination: Across the Muslim Divide*, London: Islamic Human Rights Commission.

Basit, T. (1997) *Eastern Values, Western Milieu: Identities and Aspirations of Adolescent British Muslim Girls*, Aldershot: Ashgate.

Blackledge, A. (2006) 'The racialization of language in British political discourse', *Critical Discourse Studies*, Vol. 3, No. 1, 61–79.

Dijk, Teun A. van (1993) *Elite Discourse and Racism*, London and New York: Sage.

Küçükcan, T. (2004) 'The Making of Turkish-Muslim Diaspora in Britain: Religious Collective Identity in a Multicultural Public Sphere', *Journal of Muslim Minority Affairs*, Vol. 24, No. 2, 243–58.

Massey, D. and R. Meegan (1982) *The Anatomy of Job Loss: The How, Why and Where of Employment Decline*, London: Methuen.

Observer (2009) 'Ending the silence on "honour killing"', *The Observer*. Available at http://www.guardian.co.uk/society/2009/oct/25/honour-killings-victims-domestic-violence. Accessed 11 November 2009.

Owen, D. and M. Johnson (1996) 'Ethnic Minorities in the Midlands', in P. Ratcliffe (ed.) *Ethnicity in the 1991 Census, Vol. III: Social Geography and Ethnicity in Britain: Geographical Spread, Spatial Concentration and Internal Migration*, London: HMSO, 227–70.

Parekh, B. (2005) *Rethinking Multiculturalism: Cultural Diversity and Political Theory*, Basingtsoke: Palgrave-Macmillan.

Peach, C. (2006a) 'Islam, Ethnicity and South Asian Religions in the London 2001 Census', *Transactions of the Institute of British Geographers*, Vol. 31, No. 18, 353–70.

——(2006b) 'Muslims in the 2001 Census of England and Wales: Gender and Economic Disadvantage', *Ethnic and Racial Studies* Vol. 8, No. 4, 629–55.

Peach, C. (ed.) (1996) *The Ethnic Minority Populations of Great Britain, Vol. II: Ethnicity in the 1991 Census*, London: ONS and HMSO.

Werbner, P. (2005) 'Honour, Shame and the Politics of Sexual Embodiment Among South Asian Muslims in Britain and Beyond: An Analysis of Debates in the Public Sphere', *HAGAR International Social Science Review*, Vol. 6, No. 1, 17.

Chapter 3

The silencing of women from the Pakistani Muslim Mirpuri community in violent relationships

Zahira Latif

Doctoral Researcher in the Institute of Applied Social Studies, School of Social Policy, University of Birmingham

Introduction

There have been several studies in the UK examining South Asian women's experiences of domestic violence (see Mama 1989; Choudry 1996; Rai and Thiara 1997; Adams 1998; Chantler et al. 2001; Batsleer et al. 2002; Minhas et al. 2002; CSPR 2004; Gill 2004). These studies have highlighted many of the main issues affecting women from South Asian communities who experience domestic violence. First, a common theme emerging from the literature is the impact of cultural practices on the lives of South Asian female victims of domestic violence, particularly the role of honour on women's ability to disclose violence. The impact of honour on South Asian female victims of domestic violence is more complex than initially envisaged by culturist perspectives. It is clear that not all South Asian women are 'equally affected by honour' (Minhas et al. 2002: 56) and, more importantly, not all women from the South Asian subgroups are equally affected.[1] Second, existing studies have tended to explore the experiences of women who have either temporarily or permanently left their abusers. The voices of women who make no real attempt to leave, or have no intentions of leaving perpetrators, are largely absent from current discourse. Yet the vulnerability of this cohort of women suggests that there is urgency in developing an understanding of their needs.

This chapter is concerned with developing an understanding of the experiences of domestic violence from a subgroup of Pakistani communities, the Mirpuri community. The Pakistani Muslim Mirpuri community in the United Kingdom originates from the Azad Kashmir[2] region of Pakistan, near and around the district of Mirpur (Shaw 1988; Ballard 1991). Peoples of this area are normally referred to as 'Mirpuris' (Shaw 1988).[3] This chapter is based on the first stage of doctoral research (Latif forthcoming) and explores the nature and dynamics of domestic violence in the Mirpuri community.

The study draws on the experiences of five Mirpuri women living in violent relationships and examines the impact of domestic violence on their lives.

An overview of the nature of domestic violence in South Asian communities

I grew up in the diasporic South Asian community in the UK and have seen close relatives, friends and family friends go through terrible ordeals which were never discussed. Even within women's circles, domestic violence was a taboo. This is not to suggest that domestic violence is more prevalent in the South Asian communities or that the communities are not aware of it. However, domestic violence is certainly an extremely sensitive and complex issue, which is compounded by the communities' 'reluctance to acknowledge its existence' (Adams 1993: 3). There are various reasons for this silence, including efforts by communities to maintain patriarchal relationships, safe guard the concepts of the 'nuclear' family and kinship groups, and reduce interference from the mainstream community. Yet the role of community and the family is pivotal in reducing, and perhaps even preventing, domestic violence. In societies where the community and family feel that it is their right and obligation to intervene (if they are aware of abuse), rates of domestic violence are lower than in societies where domestic violence is considered a private matter (Heise 1998). South Asian communities may condemn domestic violence in the public realm, yet in the private sphere the picture is different. South Asian women in violent relationships are often persuaded by family, friends and the religious community to be patient and to 'make her husband happy' (Ayyub 2000). Women who decide to leave violent relationships are often placed under excessive pressure from their families to return to their partners (Mama 1989; Choudry 1996; Singh et al. 1999; CSPR 2004).

Women who decide to leave their abusers may find themselves alienated from family and 'outcasts' from the very communities that formed a significant part of their social networks (Gill 2003). It is not uncommon for women who leave marital relationships, even when the cause is violence, to be branded by the community as dishonourable and then abandoned (Choudry 1996; Mama 1989; Singh et al. 1999; CSPR 2004; Batsleer et al. 2002; Minhas et al. 2002; Gill 2004). Most women experience some degree of rejection, though this varies from individual to individual. Rejection has a potential detrimental effect on the 'move-on' process, hindering efforts to build a new life, affecting women in numerous ways. A combination of their dishonourable status and the presence of children from the previous relationship means remarriage potential is bleak. Dishonourable women who live in the community without male protection are perceived as deviants and 'fair game' for other men (Wilson 2006). In extreme circumstances women will face the possibility of 'life on the run' from the perpetrator, or death if they are found. A successful marriage is synonymous with a 'good family life' and in particular is the responsibility of women. In cases where marriages have failed, families may find that their chances of finding suitable partners for girl children are affected (Choudry 1996).

Domestic violence in the Mirpuri community – the research participants

This chapter draws on an ethnographic study which was conducted with five women who had experienced domestic violence, but not left home.[4] The women – Shanaz, Sakina, Kouser, Tazeem and Asiya – lived in the city of Birmingham in the United Kingdom. The participants were all Mirpuri women, between the ages of 45 and 60, and had on average four children each. The women belonged to the *Sunni* sect of Islam and the *Braelvi*[5] school of thought and were members of what would be constituted as high castes,[6] *Gujar* and *Jat*. The study was conducted from January 2005 to November 2005 (inclusive) and access to the participants was gained through personal networks. An in-depth discussion of the methodology is available elsewhere (see Latif forthcoming).

During the period of the study the participants were in marital relationships living with the main perpetrators of domestic violence, their husbands. All the research participants had no immediate intentions of leaving their marital relationships. On average their marriages ranged from twenty to forty years, during which period they had endured not only systematic physical violence but also psychological, emotional and economic/financial abuse. The women arrived in the UK to join their spouses as dependants, and their period of residency varied from between twenty and thirty years. The arrival of the women as dependants of UK citizens is reflected in their dependency upon their husbands. The dependency culture was further exacerbated by the women's poor literacy skills. The women could communicate very effectively in their 'mother-dialect', *Mirpuri,* but their command of *Urdu*[7] and the English language was poor.

Research findings

The Mirpuri community like other South Asian communities embraces the notion of honour, particularly the concept of familial honour (Azam 2006). Though each family member has a responsibility and an obligation to protect this honour, women are expected to act as 'guardians' of the family or *khandaani* honour, and men as protectors of the guardians (Afshar 1994: 129). This was centrally the case in the five families that were my case studies. Although such a social order may seem overly simplistic, it provided domestic violence perpetrators with an opportunity to enforce a culture of submission upon their victims. When notions of honour did not have the desired effect perpetrators sometimes turned to spiritual abuse to further their aims. The manipulation of religious texts to instigate spiritual abuse helped to maintain dominance over their victims.

The context of spiritual abuse

Asiya, a woman in her early fifties who had been married for thirty years, living with her husband and four children, and Sakina, a woman in her late fifties living with her husband and two children, commented that the Urdu term *Majazee Khuda* (*Temporary God*) was used regularly by their respective husbands to explain a divine superiority over them. Sakina's husband told her that if she did not obey him, she would go to Hell. He often quoted Qur'anic verses and Hadiths,[8] chosen to reinforce the culture of submission and fear already created by the perpetrator. Verses appeared to have been taken out of context and manipulated to suit the perpetrator's objectives. Sakina explained how she was illiterate and largely relied on her husband's interpretation of the Qur'an. Asiya stated that her husband had '*socialised her and her children into believing that whatever he wanted the family to do is what Allah wants them to do*'. This kind of behaviour by the perpetrator of domestic violence suggests that he is 'something of a God'.

Women who observed the practices of this perceived social order were likely to be offered key benefits of status and respectability (Ayyub 2000). However, those who were perceived as having challenged the system were likely to face its wrath, the punishment for not fitting prescribed roles (Ayyub 2000; Wilson 2006). The good/bad woman dichotomy (Takhar 2005; Sahgal 2000) supports the notion that 'good' women conform to social ideals, whilst 'bad' women are deviants and are likely to be the downfall of the social order and thus need to be punished (Takhar 2005). Within this perceived social order the subordinate role of susceptible women and micro-family politics create an environment where the vulnerable can be seriously manipulated and further disadvantaged.[9]

In the Mirpuri community, an important part of the micro-family environment is the 'popularity' of cousin marriages (see Shaw 2001 for a discussion on cousin marriages in the Pakistani community).[10] Unlike many other South Asian communities, within the Mirpuri community consanguineous marriages are desirable. Such marriages represent the pinnacle of respectability and reduce somewhat the complexity involved in finding appropriate suitors. However, when the system is abused and relationships break down, they have the potential to act as catalysts for the types of domestic violence manifested in the South Asian communities, for example so-called honour-killings (Richards 2004), forced marriages (Anitha and Gill 2009) and violence/abuse from extended family and in-laws (Fernandez 1997).

The role of marital practices

All the women in the study were in consanguineous marriages. Tazeem, a woman in her mid-forties with five children, and Kouser, a woman in her late fifties with two children, had married either first patrilateral or matrilateral cousins. Kouser explained that the struggle between her and her husband was not helped by external influences from in-laws, particularly her mother in-law. Her mother-in-law desired to control Kouser in order to secure the patrilateral cousin marriages of her children. Tazeem further explained that it is not uncommon for children to be betrothed to cousins at birth. Preference is given to parallel patrilateral cousin marriages with the ideal being where a son marries his father's brother's daughter. Although the existence of accepted marital practices is common, the complications of the micro-family political environment play a significant role in how marriage choices are negotiated.

Mirpuri women in this study agreed that generally within the Mirpuri community exogamous marriages were discouraged. Where individuals were involved in such marriages, the non-related partners were commonly referred to as outsiders or *baar-aale*. In the community such marriages were a sign of bringing dishonour or shame upon the family. They were perceived as tainting the family bloodline and hence disseminating the family or *khandaani* honour. Exogamous marriages had the potential to socially isolate families and bring fewer suitable suitors for other siblings, particularly girl children. They also had the potential to create problems for married siblings. Although exogamous marriages were generally discouraged, their existence in Mirpuri communities is not a relatively new or even a diasporic phenomenon. As suggested by Shaw (2001: 318), *'marriage choice and negotiations that surround it must be understood in terms of strategies adopted by different participants, rather than in terms of any rule or preference'*. Marriage strategies generally encouraged consanguinity. Whilst consanguineous marital practices are open to abuse, the potential for abuse through *watta satta* marital practices is more complex. *Watta satta*[11] marriages involve the exchanging of brides and are the simultaneous marriages of a brother–sister pair from one household to another (Hassan 1995). These marriages create an environment where those who are most susceptible to abuse through them are further pressured into a culture of social isolation and dependency.

Tazeem and Kouser were directly involved in *watta satta* marriages and were in a position where they were affected by the potential abusive elements of the practice. Tazeem, with four children of 'marriageable age', was subjected to tremendous pressure by her in-laws. Her in-laws desired to arrange the marriage of her daughter to the child's patrilateral parallel cousin, whilst simultaneously accepting the hand in marriage of the cousin's sister for her son – a *watta satta* marriage. When Tazeem refused, her husband was encouraged by his mother to 'discipline' his wife. Though physical violence by Tazeem's husband was almost immediate in the marriage, Tazeem was not prepared to put her children through the marriages, but she believed she had no real alternative. Asiya, a woman in her mid-forties, was involved in a *watta satta* marriage to her matrilateral parallel cousin. Her husband's sister was the wife of one of Asiya's brother's – Khadim. Khadim was never in agreement with the two marriages, particularly his own. Inevitably this component of the double cousin marriage was an unhappy one, and the effects were evident in Asiya's relationship with her husband. Asiya's husband was physically and emotionally abusive to her, encouraging her to talk to her brother and per-suade him not to end the marriage as his family's honour was at stake.

In the name of honour

Culturist perspectives on domestic violence in the South Asian communities explore the notion of honour as a dominant force in the process of silencing women in violent relationships (Gill 2004). The causative relationship between honour and the silencing of South Asian women experiencing abuse is far more complex than envisaged by Western discourse. Although the use of 'pre-emptive measures' including violence is not uncommon in safe-guarding familial honour (Imkaan 2003: 6), how notions of honour and shame are negotiated varies between social actors (Bano 2010). Some South Asian women may accept their roles in the social order not because they cannot see an alternative but because they see it as 'natural and beneficial' (Minhas et al. 2002: 34), whilst others may challenge, negotiate and renegotiate their position in the order.

Mirpuri women in my study also attributed their position in the social order to *kismet* (destiny), which played a significant role in their lives. The notion of *kismet* was raised frequently in conversations with the Mirpuri women. It was normally used to understand predicaments which did not make sense or were against the natural order, particularly in situations where no blame could be easily attributed to a single party involved. The commu-nity generally sympathised with women whose transgression could be atoned for with *kismet*. Dishonourable women, whose conduct was not as easily justifiable, were blamed for their own predicaments. The treatment of what seems on the surface as classifying women into 'deserving' and 'undeserving' (Johal 2003: 30), despite honour being at stake in both cases, raises the question: What constitutes honourable conduct? Honour is highly con-tentious, with little in-depth understanding of the intricacies and nuances surrounding it, and of the impact these have on the lives of women from the different South Asian communities.

Which honour?

The concept of honour has been prevalent in most cultures at some point of a civilisation's evolutionary cycle (Gill 2004). The most popular and often brutal manifestation of honour in Western society has been the 'gentleman' duels of the fifteenth century, which formed a considerable part of the social order. These duels were conducted by way of a challenge on the basis that one party had in some way dishonoured the other; resolution was normally through a 'fight to the death'. The goal of the duel was often not so much to kill the opponent as to gain 'satisfaction', that is to restore a gentleman's honour by demonstrating a willingness to risk their life for it. Honour in these instances was not explicitly defined, nor were duels legal; but they were instead accepted as part of wider social practices. This particular practice also highlighted an important element of the social order, the interplay between honour, violence and death.

Themes of honour and death play a significant role in much of the litera-ture of medieval England. The most popular tragedies by William Shake-speare are based on the underlying theme of honour. In *Julius Caesar*, Brutus captures eloquently the relationship between honour and death when he suggests, '*Set honour in one eye, and death i' th' other,/ And I will look on both indifferently*' (Act 1, Scene 2). In his plays, Shakespeare's concept of what constitutes honourable is synonymous with what is described by Gill (2004: 475) using the work of Cohen (1997) as 'integrity, virtuous behaviour, good moral character and altruism', themes that are echoed by most civili-sations. However, despite these perceived similarities that have transcended time, honour is somewhat more complex. The meaning of terms like 'vir-tuous behaviour' and 'good moral character' are culturally context-driven. Shakespeare's model of what constitutes a person of good moral character and virtuous behaviour is likely to be rather different to modern-day inter-pretations of these terms.

Though Gill (2004: 475), using the work of Vandello and Cohen (2002), attributes further meanings to honour, which include 'respectability', 'status' and 'standing in the community', these terms merely represent socially con-structed rewards for behaving honourably. Research on South Asian Women experiencing domestic violence (CSPR 2004) suggests that the term *izzat*, often synonymous with honour, is constantly in flux. The terms of respect-ability, status and standing are also often synonymous with *izzat*, and it is these latter definitions of honour which are changing, as opposed to honour itself. *Izzat* is again equated by Ballard (1994: 15) as standing and status in the community and has no 'permanence'. He suggests further that *izzat* is a matter of 'relative standing which generates constant competition, both between individuals and even more between closely related families' (Ballard 1994: 15).

Mirpuri women in this study tended to live in an environment where *izzat*, particularly female *izzat*, needed to be protected. Kouser described female *izzat* as not only synonymous with virginity, chastity and fidelity, but also with other attributes which are associated with femininity: long hair, being softly spoken and lowering and covering one's head in the presence of elders and/or men. She continued to explain that *izzatdar*[12] women were not only fulfilling their prescribed roles but were fulfilling them in an appropriate and acceptable manner. Women's femininity also impacted upon women's reputation, standing and status in the community. Honourable women were normally married and displayed certain key features of femininity, which supported Guru's (2003) interpretations of femininity in the Punjabi community. These included being softly spoken, covering the head, particularly in the presence of elders, and wearing traditional clothing. In the Mirpuri community the *shalwar kameez*[13] was a sign of respectability. Women who wore the *shalwar kameez* received recognition from the community as being chaste and were upholding cultural values and beliefs. Sakina explained although there are expectations from the community which place a higher value on moral conformity for women, moral conformity has become a matter of perception as opposed to reality.

Perceived moral conformity

Sakina, Asiya and Kouser believed that the public face offered by many so-called honourable women is different from the face that is presented in private. In private, women were engaged in activities that were not acceptable for a respectable woman. Asiya explained how Mirpuri women and men were what she termed as *playing the game*.[14] *Playing the game* involved being perceived as 'honourable' in order to secure family and hence individual respectability. In contrast the private lives of individuals may not be as honourable as their public lives. Ballard (1994: 15) attributes the need to *'play the game'* to the existence of fierce *izzat* competition in the Mirpuri community. Asiya reluctantly explained how the *game* had now come to a point where very few families existed without their own dishonourable scandal. She believed that in order to achieve status and respectability people were bypassing the essentials of honourable conduct and were instead more interested in being perceived as *izzatdar*.

Sakina presented some anecdotes of Mirpuri mothers being very keen to find suitable partners for their daughters. Some mothers had resorted to educating their daughters in the art of seducing a man. It was then assumed that the man would place excessive pressure on his parents to accept his choice of marital partner. The importance of chastity and virginity were sidestepped in order to achieve the zenith of respectability: marriage. Sakina termed this 'the Mrs Bakshi syndrome'. Mrs Bakshi is a character in the Hollywood/Bollywood film *Bride and Prejudice*, which is based on Jane Austen's novel *Pride and Prejudice*. The character of Mrs Bakshi is based on Mrs Bennet, a woman who is preoccupied with finding suitable husbands for her five daughters. Sakina claimed that in such a social order the unwritten laws of *izzat* are not only dictated by the often-dishonourable and hypocritical masses but have become a vehicle by which the most vulnerable can be further oppressed. The oppressed need not be women or those experiencing domestic violence per se but are most likely to be those who fail to play the game.

To leave the abuser, or not to leave

Kouser's husband had married a second wife in Pakistan. He spent six months in the UK with Kouser and six months in Pakistan with his second wife. Kouser did not leave her husband, believing that her future would be very bleak if she left the marital home. The stigma of divorce and associated lack of male protection concerned her greatly. The symbolic significance of marriage was clearly apparent in Kouser's case, where being married was more important than having a 'live-in' husband. The Mirpuri women in this study were older, first generation immigrants, involved in long-term marital relationships. Their abusers had over decades to reinforce a culture of submissiveness, social isolation and dependency. Sakina commented on how leaving the marital relationship was akin to social 'suicide'. She explained she could not contemplate leaving and asked, '*Who would I be if I leave? What would I do? How would I act?*' – sentiments which echo Giddens (1991: 70), who presents these questions as ones we all contend with in postmodern society. For her, leaving the abusive relationship involved searching for a new identity.

Conclusion

European Orientalist ideologies have constructed South Asian women as 'passive' (Brah 1992) and oppressed by *barbaric* cultural practices (Chandler 2006). Such reductionist approaches to identity construction have served to undermine the complexity surrounding South Asian women's lives. South Asian female victims of domestic violence have been termed as 'afraid to leave' (CSPR 2004: 45) violent relationships. These stereotypes have served to undermine the complexity surrounding women's decisions to find appropriate solutions. For older, first generation immigrant Mirpuri women, the most appropriate solution may not always involve leaving the abusive relationship. The interdependency between victims and perpetrators (Chantler 2006) in the Mirpuri community has a serious impact upon women's decisions. Considering that not only are women in most danger of being killed by their abusers at the point of leaving (Walby and Allan 2004), and also combining this with the reality of facing social isolation, it may be in their interest to remain in the relationship at least until appropriate alternative solutions can be found.

Current social responses to domestic violence adopt an 'empowerment' approach to service provision. The approach has 'legitimately prioritised services to women and children' as a primary means of 'women gaining control of their lives' (Guru 2006: 153). However, the effectiveness of the approach for women who do not leave their abusers is less well understood. Furthermore, South Asian women experiencing domestic violence have their own set of challenges to overcome before reaching any decisions. Within the Pakistani Muslim Mirpuri community, key practices adopted by perpetrators and the community have the potential to create serious power imbalances between victims of domestic violence and their abusers. The manipulation of religious text to serve the interests of the perpetrator, communities' notions of honourable conduct and consanguineous marital relationships have a serious impact upon Mirpuri women's decisions to disclose violence. Power imbalances give perpetrators the opportunity to further coerce women into remaining in abusive relationships. The complexities are further compounded by Mirpuri social practices which are based on a strong clan-style structure. These structures have the potential to socially isolate women should they decide to leave violent relationships. Hence, the decision-making process for victims becomes far more complex than initially envisaged by Western discourses.

Notes

1 Subgroups include Indian, Pakistani, Bangladeshi and Sri Lankan.
2 Part of Kashmir that is administered by Pakistan.
3 This expression is sometimes used as a derogatory term, particularly amongst Pakistanis. The researcher does not intend it to be used in this way here.
4 Names have been changed to maintain anonymity; please note that ethnographic notes were written after the sessions, hence there are very few verbatim quotes.
5 The *Braelvi* school of thought has its origins in Sufism. For an in-depth discussion of *Braelvis* see Ballard (1994).
6 Though Islam does not advocate a caste system, there is still a caste system within South Asian Muslims in particular.
7 National language of Pakistan.
8 Teachings of the Prophet Mohammed (p.b.u.h).
9 It is prudent to remember that not all women have a subordinate role in the household (Ballard undated). Power relations in the family environment are complex and within these relations the role of some women may be more powerful than men.
10 The intention of this research was not to problematise cousin marriages per se. Instead the research highlights that in violent relationships such marriages can seriously change the dynamics of the relationship and reinforce power imbalances. They have the potential to influence women's decision not to disclose violence.
11 Such marriages are not exclusively a Mirpuri or a Pakistani phenomenon and exist in other South Asian communities.
12 Honourable.
13 Traditional Pakistani dress.
14 The researcher does not intend for this term to be perceived as manipulative but instead for readers to comprehend the dynamics of people's behaviour in an extremely competitive environment.

Bibliography

Adams, E. C. (1998) *Asian Survivors of Domestic Violence*, Norwich: Social Work Monographs.

Afshar, H. (1994) *Muslim Women in West Yorkshire*, in Afshar, H. and Maynard, M. (eds) *The Dynamic of 'Race' and Gender; Some Feminist Interventions*, Portsmouth: Taylor and Francis.

Anitha, S. and Gill, A. (2009) 'Coercion, Consent and the Forced Marriage Debate in the UK', *Feminist Legal Studies*, Vol. 17, No. 2, 165.

Ayyub, R. (2000) 'Domestic Violence in the South Asian Muslim Immigrant Population in the United States', *Journal of Social Distress and the Homeless*, Vol. 9, No. 3, 237.

Azam, N. A. (2006) 'How British Mirpuri Pakistani Women Identify Themselves and Form their Identity', unpublished thesis, University of Huddersfield.

Ballard, R. (1980) 'Introduction: The Emergence of Desh Pardesh' in Ballard, R. (ed.) *Desh Pardesh*, London: Hurst and Company.

——(1991) 'The Kashmir Crisis, A View From Mirpur', *Economic and Political Weekly*, Vol. 26, No. 9/10, 513.

——(undated) *Riste and Ristedari: The Significance of Marriage in the Dynamics of Transnational Kinship Networks*, Centre for Applied South Asian Studies, University of Manchester, Accessed 12 June 2006. Available at http://www.arts.manchester.ac.uk/casas/papers/networks.html.

Bano, S. (2010) *Shariah Councils and the Resolution of Matrimonial Disputes: Gender and Justice in the Shadow of the Law*, in Thiara, R. K and Gill, A. K. *Violence Against Women in South Asian Communities: Issues for Policy and Practice*, London: Jessica Kingsley.

Batsleer, J., Burman, E., Chantler, K., McIntosh, S., Pantling, K., Smailes, S. and Warner, S. (2002) *Domestic Violence and Minoritisation: Supporting Women towards Independence*, Women's Studies Research Centre, Manchester Metropolitan University.

Brah, A. (1992) *Women of South Asian Origin in Britain: Issues and Concerns,* in Braham, P. et al. (eds) *Racism and Anti-racism: Inequalities, Opportunities and Policies*, London: Sage.

Chantler, K., Burman, E., Batsleer, J. and Bashir, C. (2001) *Attempted Suicide and Self Harm (South Asian Women)*, Women's Studies Research Centre, Manchester Metropolitan University.

Chantler, K. (2006) 'Independence, Dependency and Interdependence: Struggles and Resistances of Minoritized Women within and on Leaving Violent Relationships', *Feminist Review*, Vol. 82, 217.

Choudry, S. (1996) *Pakistani Women's Experience of Domestic Violence in Great Britain*, Research Findings No. 43, Home Office Research and Statistics Directorate.

Cohen, D. (1997) 'Ifs and Thens in Cultural Psychology', in Wyer, R. (ed.) *Advances in Social Cognition,* Mahwah, NJ: Erlbaum.

CSPR (2004) *Identifying Gaps in Service for Black Minority Ethnic Women experiencing Domestic Violence in Middlesborough – A Case Study*, University of Teesside, Centre for Social and Policy Research.

Fernandez, M. (1997) 'Domestic Violence by Extended Family Members in India', *Journal of Interpersonal Violence*, Vol. 12, 433.

Giddens, A. (1991) *Modernity and Self-Identity. Self and Society in the Late Modern Age*, Cambridge: Polity.

Gill, A. (2003) 'Maintaining Izzat/Honour: Domestic Violence in the South Asian Community', *Community Care*, April 2003, 42.

——(2004) 'Voicing the Silent Fear: South Asian Women's Experiences of Domestic Violence', *Howard Journal of Criminal Justice*, Vol. 43, No. 5, 465.

Guru, S. (2003) *Transmission and Transformation of Asian Femininity in Everyday Life*, Everyday Cultures Working Papers, National Everyday Cultures Programme, Open University.

——(2006) 'Working with Asian Perpetrators of Domestic Violence – The British Experience', *Practice*, Vol. 18, No. 4, 153.

Hassan, Y. (1995) *The Haven Becomes Hell, A Study of Domestic Violence in Pakistan*, Lahore: Shirkat Gah / Women Living Under Muslim Law.

Hague, G. And Malos, E. (2005) *Domestic Violence, Action for Change*, Cheltenham: New Clarion Press

Heise, L. L. (1998) 'Violence Against Women: An Integrated Ecological Framework', *Violence Against Women*, Vol. 4, No. 3, 262.

Imkaan (2003) *Safety and Justice: Response from Imkaan*, London: Imkaan.

Johal, A. (2003) 'Struggle not Submission: Domestic Violence in the 1990s', in Gupta, R. (ed.) *From Homebreakers to Jailbreakers: Southall Black Sisters*, London: Zed Books.

Latif, Z. P. (forthcoming) *The Impact of Domestic Violence on the Housing Needs of Pakistani Muslim Mirpuri Women*, unpublished thesis, University of Birmingham.

Mama, A. (1989) *The Hidden Struggle: Statutory and Voluntary Responses to Violence Against Black Women in the Home*, London: Race and Housing Research Unit.

Minhas, N., Hollows, A., Kerr, Y. S. and Ibbotson, R. (2002) *South Asian Women's Experiences of Domestic Abuse: Pillar of Support*, Survey and Statistical Research Centre, Sheffield Hallam University.

Rai, D. K. and Thiara, R. K. (1997) *Redefining Spaces: The Needs of Black Women and Children in Refuge Support Services and Black Workers in Women's Aid*, Bristol: Women's Aid Federation of England.

Richards, L. (2004) *Getting Away with It: A Strategic Overview of Domestic Violence Sexual Assaults and 'Serious' Incident Analysis*, London Metropolitan Police.

Sahgal, G. (2000) 'Secular Spaces: The Experiences of Asian Women Organizing', in Sahgal, G. and Yuval-Davis, N. (eds) *Refusing Holy Orders: Women and Fundamentalism in Britain*, London: Virago Press.

Shakespeare, W. (2005) *Julius Caesar*, London: Penguin Classics, New Edition.

Shaw, A. (1988) *A Pakistani Community in Britain*, Oxford: Basil Blackwell.

——(2000) *Kinship and Continuity: Pakistani Families in Britain*, London: Routledge.

——(2001) 'Kinship, Cultural Preference and Immigration: Consanguineous Marriage among British Pakistanis', *The Journal of the Royal Anthropological Institute*, Vol. 7, No. 2, 315.

Singh, R. and Unnithan, N. P. (1999) 'Wife Burning: Cultural Cues for Lethal Violence Among Asian Indians in the United States', *Violence Against Women*, Vol. 5, No. 6, 641.

Takhar, S. (2005) *South Asian Women, the 'Community' and Multicultural (Mis) Understandings*, CRONEM Conference, Roehampton University, 14–15 June 2005.

Vandello, J. and Cohen, D. (2003) 'Male Honor and Female Fidelity: Implicit Cultural Scripts that Perpetuate Domestic Violence', *Journal of Personality and Social Psychology*, Vol. 84, No. 5, 997.

Walby, S. and Jonathan, A. (2004) *Domestic Violence, Sexual Assault and Stalking: Findings from the British Crime Survey, Home Office Research Study 276*, Home Office Research, Development and Statistics Directorate, March 2004.

Wilson, A. (2006) *Dreams, Questions, Struggles: South Asian Women in Britain*, London: Pluto Press.

Chapter 4

"There is nothing 'honourable' about honour killings"

Gender, violence and the limits of multiculturalism[1]

Veena Meetoo and Heidi Safia Mirza
Institute of Education, University of London

Introduction

Honour killings have been defined as ' ... the killing of women for suspected deviation from sexual norms imposed by society' (Faqir 2001: 66). Honour killings are extreme acts of violence perpetrated upon a woman when an honour code is believed to have been broken and perceived shame is brought upon the family. Women can also carry the burden for the shame of male violations of their sexual 'honour' and have been killed because they have fallen pregnant as victims of incest and rape. Being suspected of sexual deviancy such as pregnancy outside marriage or adulterous behaviour is also seen as enough to justify punishing a woman. What marks so-called honour killings is that it is not just the husband or partner that may carry out the act, but also the community and other family members such as mothers, brothers, uncles and cousins.

The UN estimates 5,000 women are being killed each year in the name of 'honour' (UNFPA 2000). Honour killings have been documented in Bangladesh, Brazil, Ecuador, Egypt, India, Israel, Italy, Jordan, Morocco, Pakistan, Sweden, Turkey, Uganda and the UK (Sajid 2003). While more than 100 women are killed by their partners in England and Wales every year, the Metropolitan Police estimates that in 2003 there were approximately 12 honour killings across Sikh, Muslim and Christian communities (see Gupta 2003a). Southall Black Sisters (SBS), a campaigning group for the rights of minority ethnic women, deals with over 2,500 cases of domestic violence a year and reports over 20 honour killings in the UK between 2001 and 2003 (RWA 2003). While many of these reported cases come from the Pakistani, South Asian and Kurdish communities, African and Caribbean women are also affected by crimes of 'honour' (RWA 2003).[2] In this sense the experiences of violence and of honour are not confined to women in Asian communities, or the preserve of Muslim communities.

However, in the UK honour killing as a specifc phenomenon is perceived by the media and government agencies as a crime that is practiced only among certain minority ethnic groups. Thus, honour killings as domestic violence have become 'ethnicised' within the British multicultural context. While the authors recognise that ethnic groups and communities do have specific religious and cultural traditions which they may themselves label as honour-based, why, in the context of ethnicity, is domestic violence treated as a culturally specific honour crime by wider organisations and institutions? In this chapter we argue that ethnicised women[3] are caught up in a collision of discourses. They are caught between the contradictions inherent within the cultural relativism of the British multicultural discourse and the private/public divide which characterises the domestic-violence discourse. On one hand, these women are at personal risk from patriarchal, cultural and religious belief systems of 'honour and shame' that can lead to what have been popularly termed as 'honour killings'. On the other hand, their personal risk is amplified as they are invisible to protective agencies and social services. Multiculturalism, which is underpinned by notions of 'respecting diversity and valuing cultural difference', unwittingly engenders non-intervention when dealing with domestic violence rooted in cultural and religious practices in the private sphere of the home. In this chapter we explore these contradictions and suggest that these women 'slip through the cracks' of both the domestic violence and the multicultural discourses. As Beckett and Macey argue,

> Multiculturalism does not cause domestic violence, but it does facilitate its continuation through its creed of respect for cultural differences, its emphasis on non-interference in minority lifestyles and its insistence on community consultation (with male self defined community leaders). This has resulted in women being invisibilised, their needs ignored and their voices silenced.
>
> (Beckett and Macey 2001: 311)

Critique of multiculturalism

While Beckett and Macey highlight the contradictions of gendered multiculturalism which invisibilises women, particularly in terms of service provision, we also question the concurrent growing concern for the hitherto marginalised ethnicised woman. Why has the issue of violence to young ethnicised women been selected for attention now, at this time? In this chapter we suggest that not only do young women 'slip through the cracks' of the shifting liberal democratic discourse on multiculturalism, but since September 11 young ethnicised women have become highly visible. However, they are now problematically contained and constructed in the public consciousness within a discourse of fear and risk posed by the presence of the Muslim alien 'Other'. Thus, ethnicised women are visible and yet pathologised as victims in relation to the negative media attention in the current discourse of Islamophobia. Ultimately, the need for a human-rights approach to domestic violence which transcends the cultural context may provide a way forward, as it highlights patterns of domestic violence across all cultures,[4] and gives gendered violence the status of a global risk through creating a collective awareness of the issues.

Is killing ever 'honourable'? The cultural context of domestic violence

Hannana Siddiqui of Southall Black Sisters argues that the term 'honour' is a misnomer. 'The crimes themselves are dishonourable: they are merely justified by the perpetrator, and wider community, in the name of honour' (RWA 2003: 6). In this sense, honour crimes are essentially a justification for male violence and essentially about domestic violence. However, only in relation to religious and ethnic communities is the concept of honour invoked as motivation for domestic violence, or a reason why women are unable to escape domestic violence.[5] What is important to note is that the concept of honour plays a part in perpetuating violence against women in two ways. On the one hand, it is used by the perpetrator as an excuse or a mitigating factor when they commit acts of violence against women. As Siddiqui argues: 'The state thinks that honour crimes are about cultural beliefs that they should not criticise. Implicitly this means the state accepts honour as a mitigating factor and condones crimes perpetuated in the name of it' (RWA 2003: 6). From the perspective of the women themselves, the concept works differently. What is particular about the concept of 'honour' and the fear of 'shame' is that it isolates women further, and this results in preventing them seeking outside help when affected by domestic violence. Women fear punishment for having brought shame on the family or community honour, and they can suffer anything from social ostracism, to acts of violence, or, as in the cases here, murder itself.

Focusing on culturally specific forms of domestic violence is often seen as very controversial. The Southall Black Sisters suggest that 25 per cent of all domestic homicides concern the killing of women, and in many of these cases men invoke a cultural defence (CIMEL/Interights 2001). Some UK cases of honour killings have shown that the defendant tried to push for a more lenient sentence by pleading a cultural defence (see the cases of Rukhsana Naz and Shaida Mohammed, for example). These cases have been unsuccessful. But cultural pleas have been made with the aim of reducing sentences to manslaughter. Shabir Hussain, who argued on appeal for manslaughter on the grounds of provocation, is evidence of this. He argued for loss of self-control which led to him running over his sister-in-law Tasleem Begum numerous times. When he was retried his original life sentence was cut to six and a half years (Phillips 2003). The case of Kiranjit Ahluwahlia, who was tried for the murder of her physically abusive husband, suggests that culture can become available to female defendants only when they conform to the model of the subservient non-Western wife (Phillips 2003). The judge asked the jury to consider that she was an Asian woman, married to an Asian man, but also an educated woman, suggesting that because she was an Asian woman she was more likely to be trapped in her marriage, but the fact that she had a university degree might cancel this out. She eventually had her conviction overturned through medical evidence that she was suffering from a major depressive disorder.

It is generally disputed that culture can explain how and why particular practices happen (Dobash and Dobash 1998). However, as the African-American writer Toni Morrison asserts, we must raise difficult issues of sexism and domestic violence within our own (black) communities (Morrison 1993). In vulnerable and racialised communities there are tensions between protecting men from the racism of state agencies and negative media representation on the one hand, and the need to raise the issue of gendered violence and protect women's rights in these communities on the other (Williams Crenshaw 1994).[6] As Salim explains in relation to the Kurdish community, there is a fear amongst some that putting honour crimes on the public agenda might cause a dangerous backlash in the immigration debate and heighten xenophobic sentiments against asylum seekers (Salim 2003).

As a counter to the racist assertion that black and Asian men are more barbaric, Gupta (2003a) argues we must take a global perspective on domestic violence and see honour killing as part of a wider global patriarchal phenomenon of violence. The problem of femicide is not particular to one culture or religious group or community. Women are beaten and murdered across the globe for similar reasons. She argues that domestic violence cuts across race, class, religion and age. Patriarchy uses violence extensively to subjugate women – it is not an issue of racial or ethnic differences. It is a question of the economic, political and social development of a society and the levels of democracy and devolution of power within communities. Gill (2003) suggests that research shows that low-violence cultures have female power and autonomy outside the home, strong sanctions against interpersonal violence, a definition of masculinity that is not linked to male dominance or honour, and equality in decision-making and resources within the family. These progressive qualities are absent from societies in which female sexual purity is still linked to familial and community dignity and social status, where the male is the custodian of that honour.

As there is often community and wider familial involvement in honour killings, this demonstrates that violence against women is not only about the relationship between male and female, but is also about systems of power (Walby 1990). In what Rubin (1975) has called Sex/gender systems, oppression is not always inevitable, but rather the product of the specific social relations which organise it. Black feminists argue, however, that gender oppression is not just about a natural division of the sexes, but about understanding the social organisation of differences and in particular the race and class dimensions that structure these economic and political systems of power (Williams Crenshaw 1994; Mohanty 2003). These raced and classed patriarchal systems are embedded in our social, political and economic systems, and are especially manifest in our legal frameworks and judicial systems. Women's agency within these systems requires further exploration for a more complex understanding of female participation in systems of patriarchal violence (Carby 1982). Such an exploration would include women who are implicated as perpetrators and abusers, as well as the young women who are bound into the values of the system itself. As Araji (2000) shows, dishonour can so totally undermine a family's economic status by ruining a husband's reputation or the marital prospects of sons that mothers sometimes do not interfere with the abuse or murder of their daughters. In some cases the women's family of origin, that is her male and female relatives, are expected to bear the responsibility for punishing her rather than her husband, as her actions have brought shame on them. Women's involvement in honour crimes is not just a phenomenon in relation to so-called 'ethnic' communities. As Stanko (1985: 53) shows, survivors of domestic violence in a Western context who have attempted to seek help from their own mothers do not always receive support, being told to put up with it because 'he's your husband'.

The 'gender trap': multiculturalism and the marginalisation of women

Multiculturalism in the UK is a contested term meaning different things to different people (Hall 2000). It is often used loosely in political discourse to affirm the distinctness, uniqueness and individual validity of different cultures, groups or communities, and also recognises the importance of acknowledging and accommodating this distinctness and difference (Fisher 2004). The Commission on the Future of Multi Ethnic Britain (Runnymede Trust 2000, MEB) highlighted a need to move towards a multicultural post-nation in which Britain would be a 'community of communities', in which we have shared values but also the autonomy of cultural expression to wear the Muslim Hijab headscarf or eat Halal meat. State intervention, policy and professional discourse in the UK are predicated upon a loose and historically haphazard notion of what Hall (2000) has called 'multicultural drift'. Here multicultural policies have been piecemeal and based on concessions, extensions and exemptions such as scheduling exams to avoid key festivals for various religious groups, Sikhs being exempt from wearing helmets, and slaughterhouses for Jews and Muslims (Harris 2001). These concessions have been won or lost through the struggles of post-war migrant communities living in Britain.

However, multiculturalism as it has evolved in the British context is also deeply racialised (Hesse 2000). While liberal multiculturalism is popularly and politically conceived as celebrating diversity and 'tolerating' different cultural and religious values between groups, the notion of mutual tolerance is fragile. Multiculturalism in this sense is 'skin deep', and it works only if the demands of visible and distinct ethnic groups are not too 'different' and not too rejecting of the welcoming embrace of the 'host' society (Ahmed 2004). This fragility was tested when the MEB report suggested that Britishness had unspoken racial connotations linked to empire. This was met with a hostile media backlash against multiculturalism as it was seen to challenge the homogeneity of an exclusive imaginary 'white' Britishness (McLaughlin and Neal 2003).

In the face of growing racist political rhetoric and anti-asylum and anti-immigration policies in the UK, we are witnessing a retreat from multiculturalism and a move towards 'civic integration'. As part of the civic-integration agenda, newcomers have to swear an oath at ceremonies; there has been a toughening of the English language requirement for acquiring British citizenship; and mandatory citizenship and democracy education has been introduced at English schools (Joppke 2004). In the context of racial unrest and ethnic segregation in the Northern towns of Britain in 2001, 'social cohesion' and 'civic integration' has become the new discourse on multiculturalism (Bhavnani et al. 2005). Social cohesion emphasises 'building bridges' between segregated communities through interfaith and cultural understanding, legitimating the link between citizenship and nationhood as essential for multicultural coexistence. Integration and active citizenship are now seen as the solutions to economic inequality, political representation and structural segregation in housing and education, which are the core issues of racial unrest.

However, liberal multiculturalism in its many and shifting manifestations has consistently functioned to privilege 'race' and ethnicity over gender (Samantrai 2002; Mirza 2003). Multiculturalism deals with problems *between* communities, but not problems *within* communities, as it fails to recognise the gendered power divisions within ethnic groups. Gender differences within the multicultural discourse now and in the past have yet to be recognised (Okin 1999). In the Commission on the Future of Multi Ethnic Britain's 314-page report women get a three-page mention (Mirza 2003). The Government's Community Cohesion reports fail to look at the specificity of gendered social action (Bhavnani et al. 2005). A gender-blind multicultural discourse means women remain invisible, locked into the private sphere where gender-oppressive cultural and religious practices are still played out. As Beckett and Macey argue: 'The "honour killing" of women who are viewed as having disgraced their community highlights the problems inherent in both multiculturalism and the public: private' (2001: 313).

To understand the invisibility of gender and violence in multicultural discourse we need to look at the way in which ethnicity has become reified and essentialised in the Western construction of difference (Fisher 2004). Yuval Davis (1997) calls this process of reification 'ethnic fundamentalism'. Here ethnic group identity is defensive, constructed in fixed 'immutable collectivity boundaries'. The inherent cultural reductionism in the multiculturalist discourse not only assumes cultural homogeneity among local communities, with each one spatially segregated, but it also means we cannot talk about racial difference and hierarchies of cultures, as this is politically incorrect (Stolcke 1995). As a consequence of this culturalist tendency in political discourse, the exclusion of ethnic minorities, and especially of women, is legitimated through insensitive multicultural policies that locate them in marginal spaces, on the periphery of decision-making both politically and in terms of policy (Bhavnani et al. 2005).

Such reductionism fails to see the intersectionality of structural inequalities that affect all women, including an understanding of the interrelationship between global patriarchy, racism and domestic violence (Williams Crenshaw 1994). Domestic violence cuts across class, race and different societies where violence is used as a way of maintaining control over female behaviour. There is thus a need to do something about the patterned use of violence, both physical and mental coercion to control and dominate women across cultures (Merchant 2000). Women who stray from their 'owners', whether their husband, partner, wider family or in-laws, often suffer the consequences, experiencing regulation through violence:

> To understand the experience of gender based violence, we need to ask questions about the ownership of different kinds, including with regard to ownership and access to women's bodies within and outside marriage, to public and private space.
>
> (Astbury 2003: 163)

Such bodily regulation can be explained, in part, by looking beyond individual 'ownership' to the wider discourses that frame such regulation. As Cockburn (1998) argues, the brutal ethnic wars in Northern Ireland, Bosnia, Israel and Palestine, fuelled by religious nationalist discourses are in effect gender wars. She argues primordial gendered forms of violence evoked in nationalist struggles, such as rape, sexual humiliation, murder of husbands, sons and babies, and expulsion from homes,

> ... seek to install (among other things) gender regimes. As well as defining a relation between peoples and land, they shape a certain relation between women and men. It is a relation of male dominance, in some cases frankly patriarchal. It is constituted at best in a refusal to challenge the existing balance of power enforced by male violence, at worst in an essentialist discourse that reasserts a supposedly natural order and legitimates violence.
>
> (Cockburn 1998: 13)

It has been argued that the multicultural discourse contains connotations of nationalism which have negative consequences for women (Abbas 2004). Some parallels with nationalism are the belief in the necessity of each culture, the loyalty demanded to it, and the duty to transfer it to the next generation. Anthias and Yuval Davis (1992) argue for the need to understand the symbolic role attributed to women as carriers and bearers of ethnic group identity. In the experience of migration, identity of new arrivals and indeed established communities may be contested, often leading to communities feeling the need to uphold their identity from their homeland. While identity and culture are not static, the woman's body is the site over which identity is asserted and culture is maintained. She, as the carrier and bearer of her ethnic group, has the obligation not to stray and disrupt the group's identity by mixing with 'others'.

Furthermore, there is a link between migration experience and violence (Akpinar 2003). If communities feel discriminated against in host societies, there is the risk that those who hold conservative and patriarchal values will turn inwards and will 'continue exerting pressure on females by holding on to patriarchal values which are remnants of a rural/feudal culture' (2003: 428). For migrant women patriarchal practices can be amplified in Western countries. Fadime Sahindal, a 22-year-old Kurdish–Swedish woman, and her Swedish boyfriend were killed by her father in 2002. Before her death, Fadime was a celebrity. She went public and spoke about problems of immigrant women and maintaining family honour. This arose out of the problems she faced from her own family, where she had been threatened with her life if she were to continue her relationship with her Swedish boyfriend (Kurkiala 2003). What this case demonstrates is that Fadime's family's honour was disrupted by her having a relationship with a Swedish man. It is within a migratory context that these problems are more likely to arise. Families fear loss of identity and feel the need to continue culture and practices from their homeland. The need to uphold values and identity from the homeland have to be maintained through regulating female behaviour, by ensuring that women maintain the group's ethnic identity through mixing with their 'own'. If a woman somehow strays from this code of behaviour, she may no longer be desirable and risks ostracising herself and her family from further networks being built within the community.

Dealing with difference: domestic violence and multicultural services

The focus on racialised positions rather than gender has paradoxically given rise to some acute cases of women's exclusion from services (Burman and Chantler 2004). Women from ethnic-minority communities can lack protection because organisations are fearful of being seen as racist when taking a positive stance in relation to culturally specific problems such as honour crimes. Elders and patriarchal leaders of many ethnic communities have used the liberal discourse of multiculturalism as a means of localised empowerment though claiming to be the vanguards of women's traditional 'honour' codes. They often act as gatekeepers between minority and majority communities. As Johal argues, if the state colludes with community leaders, what kind of protection can we expect from the state? She points out that gendered violence is seen as a community issue:

> The issue of preserving family honour remains central to the community attitude to domestic violence. If a woman brings dishonour to her family, then any violence committed against her can be justified on this basis.
>
> (Johal 2003: 37)

But despite the struggles of black and Asian women's groups to empower women, male community leaders are still influential within the communities. Ali Jan Haider, a Muslim social worker, explains the complex interrelationship and confusion between Islam and Pakistani culture on one hand and the practice of the social services and his white and non-Muslim colleagues on the other. The latter often see such practices as 'part of the culture'. This confusion often leads to inaction and resistance, preventing Muslim women from seeking out help when they most need it. He relates how male family and community elders personally threatened him and his family when he helped a 21-year-old woman and her five children to escape domestic violence and placed her in a refuge. The young woman had come to the UK aged 16 from the rural Mirpur district of Pakistan and had been subjected to persistent physical and mental abuse at the hands of her husband and her in-laws for several years. He explains the consequences of his actions:

> ... the community interference began in earnest. I had a phone call from a local Asian Councillor asking me if I could explain why I had taken mum and children away and broken up this respectable family. I then had phone calls and visits from countless community elders including a local religious leader. He did not waste any time castigating my actions and telling me what I had done was sinful. He told me how I should be personally held responsible for the family's loss of face, and the distress I had caused them.
>
> (Haider 2003: 4)

An overly sensitive multicultural approach, which Haider suggests is engendered by uninformed assumptions, can often lead to negative action or inaction and can replicate structures of oppression within communities. Based on primary research with healthcare physicians, Puri (2005) cites cases where GPs breached confidentiality, telling the family of the woman of her injuries, claiming that they did not know how to handle the patient's 'cultural baggage', or even allowing the patient's husband to stay for his wife's physical examination. As Burman et al. (2004) argue, community networks are usually seen as a support mechanism in minority ethnic communities, but some women in violent and life-threatening situations can be followed and caught through their community networks, which may make them reluctant to approach community organisations.

A multicultural approach to service provision has meant more involvement of different communities, and this has taken the form of multi-agency work (Gill and Rehman 2004). In a climate of increasing personal responsibility for professionals, services have had to relate to young women at risk of violence, abuse and death in the context of the discourse of multiculturalism in Britain. This emphasis on risk has consequences for how sensitive social problems such as domestic violence are dealt with. Radford and Tsutsumi (2004) argue that feminist activism against violence has taken place within a policy context of crime control, where risk assessment and risk management have become an increasingly important part of how agencies such as the police and probation handle their workloads, meet their targets and manage resources. They argue that while feminists have seen the risk discourse as an opportunity for opening up a dialogue with key agencies, uncovering violence and getting it taken seriously by the police and courts, it has also meant rationing strategies limited to women who are deemed 'most at risk', thus denying protection to the majority and subsuming the broader issue of gendered violence and human rights.

In the case of domestic violence, honour killings and the risk faced by young ethnicised women, the tendency to individualisation and accountability in the discourse on risk, along with a laissez-faire multicultural approach to dealing with violent gendered cultural practices within the private domestic sphere of the ethnicised family, can exacerbate a state of reluctant interventionism. The state's response to domestic violence in ethnic communities has been slow. The police until recently have lacked interest or even been hostile to cases of honour killings. Women's organisations such as the Southall Black Sisters have successfully campaigned to highlight the specific ways in which immigration law, welfare policy and protective practice impinge on the rights of black and Asian women. When there is a case of forced marriage which is on the continuum of domestic violence abuses, social services in the past have first tried to mediate, with safety and protection for these young women coming second. Mediation is not endorsed for women in the wider community. Siddiqui (2003) called for an end to mediation policies as women often lack power in mediation and after the honeymoon period, families often resort back to abuse and forced marriage. Mediation is a less threatening option than girls leaving their families and taking out injunctions against them. She goes on to argue that the solution lies in giving women alternatives from agencies where agencies can support and advise them in breaking away from abusive relationships. The input from women's groups such as the Southall Black Sisters has to some extent been successful in informing the revised Forced Marriage Unit's approach to dealing with these situations. In their recent guidelines to police, social workers and education professionals they recommend that community representatives and family members should not be approached as a means of reconciling differences and state that this method could be potentially dangerous (FCO 2004, 2005).

In their evidence to the Working Party on Forced Marriage, Southall Black Sisters were concerned about the failure of service providers to address the needs of women and girls at risk of forced marriages, which in some cases have led to honour killings (CIMEL/Interights 2001). Such service providers may cite cultural grounds for this failure, on the assumption that minority communities are self-policing, and they therefore do not have to intervene on behalf of these women. According to Siddiqui (2003) many community leaders who were consulted on the Working Group on Forced Marriages denied that there is a problem with forced marriage and are hostile to women who refuse these marriage and women's organisations that work with them. Some have argued that issues raised around forced marriage are a form of racism and an attack on the community, and on their cultural and religious heritage. In many cases of abduction and forced marriage of dual nationals, the Foreign and Commonwealth Office has refused to intervene formally as the young women are overseas, and it is argued it is not within their jurisdiction (CIMEL/Interights 2001).

Women's campaigning organisations have highlighted how immigration law continues to sideline women who may be fleeing a violent domestic situation, as gendered risk is not recognised as grounds for asylum (RWA 2003; Crawley 2001). Asylum is granted on the basis of proven political affiliation. This criteria is inherently male-biased as women are less likely to be officially involved as dissidents (Kofman 2004). The burden of proof is so onerous on women who have been raped, sexually threatened or forced to marry that they often face death or incarceration rather than be publicly shamed (FCO 2000). Eligibility for service support is denied to many women by virtue of their immigration status and can be excluded from service and welfare support (Burman et al. 2004). Women have been turned away from refuges because they did not have proper immigration status (Burman and Chantler 2004). In response to black and Asian women's activism, in 1999 the government introduced a concession to the One Year Rule (which stated that women would have to stay with their husbands for one year, or otherwise would face deportation) for women experiencing domestic violence (Back et al. 2002). The women have to prove that they have been victims of domestic violence if they are within the first year of marriage. But proof levels consist of legal evidence: a court injunction, a police caution against the perpetrator and medical evidence alone will not be accepted. Many young women, regardless of ethnic background, would find it difficult to report a domestic violence situation to the police for fear of further violent action from their partner.

The 'new risk': Islamophobia and the ethnicised woman

Post 9/ 11, risks associated with gender-related violence are on the public and political agenda. For example, increased media attention has been accompanied by steps taken by the Metropolitan Police Diversity Directorate looking into honour crimes. UNIFEM has given money to NGOs to work on honour killings. In January 2005, the Foreign and Commonwealth Office and the Home Office jointly launched the Forced Marriage Unit, which works to prevent forced marriages taking place, proves assistance to potential victims, develops policy and undertakes project work. It views forced marriage as an abuse of human rights (FCO 2005). A recent project funded by the European Union's DAPHNE programme, 'Shehrazad', aims to create a European knowledge base about honour-related violence, and to facilitate an exchange of experiences and good practice between partner countries. Recently the Crown Prosecution Service held a one-day conference in London on addressing honour crimes specifically, and to raise awareness of such crimes in Europe (CPS 2004). We have also witnessed pronouncements by David Blunkett as Home Secretary on criminal measures to deal with the issue of forced marriage as it affects young Asian women living in Britain.[7] Similarly, when war was declared on Afghanistan in response to September 11, Cherie Blair and Laura Bush, the wives of the UK prime minister and the US president, took up the issue of 'Taliban oppression of women and children in Afghanistan' (*The Telegraph*, 17 November 2001). Holding special meetings at 10 Downing Street to 'give back a voice' to Afghani women, Cherie Blair chose to spotlight the 'shocking and inspiring stories' of the women and raise charitable funds for the cause (*The Guardian*, 20 November 2001).

However this raises the question: What is behind this growing concern for the hitherto invisible and marginalised 'ethnic woman'? It is argued we are living in a 'risk society'. Mary Douglas (1992) suggests some risks are selected for concern at particular times, and constructed and legitimated for public attention. She argues that risks are chosen for their usefulness to the social system. Beck (1992) also argues that risk is malleable and open to social definition and construction. He was aware that the elite, such as the media, scientists, politicians and legal professionals, can define and legitimate risk. The mass media have a big part to play in public perceptions of risk. It is a filter in the way lay people and experts receive news and interpret events (Gabe 1995). Questions should repeatedly be asked, such as whose definition of risk is being used, and how has the perception of risk been constructed? How are some risks selected for concern and how are they legitimated for public attention? In the case of violence to young, ethnicised, and in particular Muslim women, the question arises as to why their risks are selected for attention over others right now?

While the increased attention given to honour killings in the media has opened up the issue of individual human rights for these women, it has also had the effect of exacerbating Islamophobia and 'fear of the Other'. Honour killings have become associated with Islam and the risk of terrorism in our midst (Majid and Hanif 2003). Sara Ahmed (2003) argues that discourses of fear and anxiety which have circulated since September 11 work by securing what is the 'truth' about 'the Other'. She states:

> fear operates as an effective economy of truth: fear slides between signs and sticks to some bodies and not others. For example the judgment that someone 'could be' a terrorist draws on past and affective associations that stick various signs (such as Muslim, fundamentalist, terrorist) together. At the same time, fear is reproduced precisely by the threat that such bodies 'may pass (us) by.' Such bodies become constructed as fearsome and as a threat to the very truths that are reified as 'life itself.'
>
> (Ahmed 2003: 377)

Thus, the increased focus on 'honour'-based crimes needs to be seen within the current climate of Islamophobia. Fekete (2004) has written of the climate of claimed global threat to security from Islamic extremism. We are living in a time when it is not just a case of fear from 'outsiders' but also those within. Resident Muslim and Asian citizens within Western countries are now under the spotlight. The current discourse on 'Others' is about the threat that multicultural policies pose to core values, cultural homogeneity and social cohesion. To minimise the risk of threat we now have increased citizenship laws and security legislation, the introduction of compulsory language and civic tests for citizenship applicants, and codes of conduct for trustees of mosques. As Fekete explains:

> The stereotyping of all aspects of Muslim culture as backward creates a climate in which politicians and the media can attack multiculturalism as the cover behind which reactionary cultural practices can flourish.
>
> (Fekete 2004: 19)

Honour killings, when reported in the British press, are often sensationalist, and coverage tends to engage in cultural stereotyping which puts the gaze on the 'Other' (Majid and Hanif 2003). These reports are often sensationalised with a negative spin, and they can engage in a 'pornography of violence' focusing on the individual family and their barbarity and senselessness (CIMEL/Interights 2001). They also suggest it is often younger women in their late teens and early twenties who are victims of this crime. At this age, young women's emerging sexuality comes under increasing regulation and control by the family and wider community. It is the young woman's sexual purity and 'honour' that is seen to define the status and regard with which the family is held in the community. One such case in the press is that of the 16-year-old Heshu Yones, who was murdered in West London in 2002 by her Kurdish father as he feared she was becoming too Westernised. Rukhsana Naz, 19, was murdered by her brother and mother in 1998 because she was expecting an illegitimate child. To the mother, Rukhsana was guilty of insult to the honour or *izzat* of her family. She was held down by her mother and strangled by her brother. There is the well-known case of Zena Briggs. Zena declined to marry a cousin in Pakistan and ran away with her English boyfriend. Her family hired professional 'bounty hunters' and hitmen from within their community to track down both her and her boyfriend. A TV documentary was made and the couple are still in hiding after several years. In an interview, Sawsan Salim (2003) of the Kurdistan Refugee Women's Organisation in London (KRWO) suggests that although there are widely reported cases, such as the murder of Sobhiea Abdullah Nadar and Heshow Abdullah, there are also many cases which are not reported, as well as situations of women being driven to suicide because they are afraid of familial and community retribution.

In these media narratives the young women are constructed as either romantic heroines, struggling for the benefits of the 'West' against their cruel and inhuman fathers and families, or victims, succumbing to their backward and traditional 'Eastern' culture (Puwar 2003; Ahmad 2003). Parallels can be drawn to colonial times, when women's bodies were part of the debate over the civilising mission. The British abolition of *sati*, the practice of widow-burning in India, was a case of the heroic white male colonists 'saving brown women from brown men' (Spivak 1988). In the current discourse, the gaze, as ever, is on the woman. As heated public debate, triggered by Labour Minister Jack Straw on the matter of Muslim women wearing the face veil, demonstrates (Bunting 2006), her vulnerable yet overdetermined body has become symbolic in the battle against Islam and the barbaric 'Other' (Dwyer 1999). But unlike in colonial times, the woman is not 'saved' within the current climate of Islamophobia and multiculturalism. The laissez-faire discourse of liberal multiculturalism ensures community and group cultural practices are not to be interfered with. It contributes to further construction of the Other's barbaric customs and cultures (Said 1985), which are left alone but condemned.

While honour killings are real in *effect*, in that women are brutally murdered, they are also constructed as ethnicised phenomena within the racialised multicultural discourse, and are as such also an *affect* of this discourse. In this regard the media reports have real consequences. They contribute to putting women at risk through sensationalising these crimes in their style and content of reporting, which results in voyeuristic spectacle (cries of 'how dreadful!') followed by multicultural paralysis and inaction ('nothing to do with us! It is part of their culture'):

> The combination of sex and violence involved in honour crimes lends itself readily to lurid images and, in the case of the western media, cultural stereotyping, which can result in a backlash on the issue at a national level.
>
> (CIMEL Interights 2001: 31)

Sensationalist images and analysis are in frequent use in the media, as are generalised and simplified explanations of honour crimes (CIMEL Interights 2001). By not acting in conjunction with human-rights activists, women's groups and academics the mainstream media collude in undermining the subjectivity and agency of the marginal ethnicised woman. In what Mohanty (1988) has called the 'latent ethnocentrism' of the West, these women are presented as voiceless, stereotyped, racialised victims, rather than as active agents working to determine and engage their rights as individuals. Such sexualised objectification of ethnicised women disavows the relationship of gender, power and patriarchy within the negative social construction of Islamophobia.

Feminism, diversity and human rights: challenging the multicultural state

Black and minority ethnic women's groups have been central in raising awareness and tackling problems related to domestic violence, sexuality and cultural and religious conservatism within specific communities and groups.[8] Since the 1980s, the Organisation of Women of African and Asian Descent (OWAAD), SBS, Newham Asian Women's Project (NAWP), RWO (Refugee Women's Organisation), WLUML (Women Living Under Muslim Laws) and WAF (Women Against Fundamentalism), to name a few, have contributed to placing minority ethnic women's issues on the agenda. Black feminists have long argued that race and gender matter in their differential effects (Williams Crenshaw 2000; Mirza 1997; Brah 1996; Collins 1998; Mama 1989).

However Samantrai (2002) argues that black British feminist activism has been more than just about accessing rights and services. Black women's activist groups such as SBS are a contingent and politically destabilizing force, in a constant state of flux, where neither allies nor enemies are readily identifiable and where even their own subjects may become obsolete. Samantrai argues that black British feminists are 'a privileged interlocutor of the similitudes and differences that constitute postimperial Englishness' (Samatrai 2002: 2). In their interrogation of the racial subtext of English majority and minority identities, she argues they are engaged in refining the 'we' of the nation. Samatrai explains,

As the experiences of women move from the margin to the centre in a community's self definition, women no longer have to choose between belonging or exile in a collective that itself remains fixed. They become central actors in the regeneration, through translation of their communities and histories of belonging.

(2002: 164)

SBS has effectively mobilised around the insistence that domestic violence does not signify cultural difference, but also demonstrates a refusal to abandon their claims on their community of difference. However, the strategic actions, values and beliefs of feminists in achieving their goals are determined in part by both domestic sociocultural and international conditions (Savery 2005). Walby (2002) notes that a reframing of feminism in terms of globalisation and the human-rights discourse constitutes a major challenge to feminist treatments of difference and diversity, especially in terms of ethnic, national, religious and racialised divisions between women. She suggests that in the UK, rather than relying on women's own resources in civil society, feminists have tended to draw on the wider political resources of the transnational movement against male violence in their engagement with the British State. At a CIMEL and Interights round table held to address the issue of honour crimes (2001), a discussion of human rights as protection for women came under the spotlight. It was recommended that it is important to raise honour crimes as a human-rights violation before as many UN human-rights bodies as possible. It is also important to work with community leaders and submit shadow reports to UN treaty bodies such as the Human Rights Committee, the Committee on the Elimination of Racial Discrimination, the Committee on Economic, Social and Cultural Rights, the Committee Against Torture, and the Committee on the Rights of the Child. The conference concluded that a human-rights approach would need to take into account a country's civil societal role in addressing honour crimes and include their own national concerns about sexuality, patriarchy and sexual autonomy. Such an approach calls for a redefinition of community, citizenship and the individual and challenges the false dichotomy between community and women, where women are placed outside of the community.

While the human-rights approach offers a way forward to protecting women from violence and abuse, mainstreaming women's concerns and experiences into the human-rights framework does raise many issues. Kelly (2005) poses several questions in this regard: Does the mainstreaming of rights-based claims by 'insider' transnational feminist coalitions into UN and international law undermine the foundations and transformative effects of 'outsider' grass-roots feminist activism? Has the vocabulary and machinery of human rights the ability to transcend differences and create a common language and agreed goals that can really tackle deeper causes of oppression and domination which are at the root of violence in gender relations? Clearly a human-rights approach is not without its problems when considering intersectional engagement with rights issues and for creating a positive legal and political culture for equality-seeking initiatives. As Conaghan and Millns explain, the Human Rights Act 2000 in the UK should be approached with caution as regards its capacity to improve women's lives and contribute more generally to a just and equal society. However, they argue that while it is imbued with the deficiencies inherent within national and human-rights instruments, it also provides the opportunity to open up a 'new constitutional space', not only in terms of new litigation strategies, but it can also provide 'the potential audibility of previously unheard dialogue about the rights of women and others whose concerns have been traditionally eclipsed by the legal perpetuation of dominant (hetero) sexist norms and practises' (Conaghan and Millns 2005: 12).

The 1995 Beijing Platform for Action resulted in the declaration that culture, tradition and religion could not be used by the state to avoid their obligation to protect women (Kelly 2005). Radhika Coomaraswamy, the special Rapporteur to the UN Commission on Human Rights on Violence against Women, highlights the importance of the state's willingness to be active and interventionist in promoting these new norms of international law if they are to permeate down to the realm of the everyday. She suggests the creativity and innovation of Asian women's activist groups in India demonstrate how a bridge can be made between the discourse of international human rights and the private sphere of personal lives. Indian women have adapted tradition to support women's rights within the family by arguing for their individual right to choose between the competing human-rights law at the national level or personal law as it affects their daily lives (Coomaraswamy 1997, in Kelly 2005: 488–9).

Ultimately, as Savery (2005) argues, we need to explain why some international norms of sexual non-discrimination have been incorporated into domestic state practices and not others. In developing a critical realist approach she suggests we need to understand the dynamic interplay of international and domestic structures, various agents, discourse and power. In particular, she points to tension between the gender-biased corporate identity of many states, which resist diffusion of gender-based human-rights norms, with the articulation of international and domestic pressure from a variety of actors. For many women's groups, such as SBS, KWRO (Kurdish Women's Refugee Organisation) and WLUML (Women Living Under Muslim Laws), that are campaigning against honour killings in the British multicultural context, Savery has a strategic message:

> … advocates struggling for change at the domestic level need to be aware that discursively challenging political elites' ideas of proper and

appropriate gender roles and relations in society contributes to generating State behavioural change.

(Savery 2005: 111 [sic])

Conclusion: from multiculturalism to Islamophobia: contextualising the collision of discourses

By highlighting domestic-violence issues in specific cultural and religious ethnic communities in the UK are we at risk of stereotyping these communities as backward and barbaric? Does this place a disproportionate 'gaze' on the 'Other' woman – racialise her, separating out this form of domestic violence as a special cultural phenomenon needing special cultural sensitivity? These questions lie at the heart of understanding the tensions between recognising gender oppression in the cultural context and preserving multicultural difference. This debate has been raised in relationship to other practices, such as female genital mutilation and forced marriages, where the sanctity of (male) community rights is privileged over the bodily rights of individual (female) victims when the cultural context is brought to bear (Beckett and Macey 2001).

Phoenix (1996) suggests that there is a normative absence/pathological presence response with regard to women from black and minority ethnic communities. Indeed, ethnicised women are caught up in a collision of discourses. They are visible and yet pathologised as victims in relation to the negative media attention in the current discourse of Islamophobia. However, these women are at the same time largely absent in the normative discourse on domestic violence in the West (Mama 1989; Carby 1982). Many young women from minority ethnic communities are at risk of not being fully protected by the state as equal citizens, as they are invisible. Within the discourse of multiculturalism, women 'fall between the cracks'. In this discourse 'race' and ethnicity are prioritised, and gender differences and inequalities are rendered invisible.

However, the killing of women must never been seen as cultural matter, but always as a human-rights issue (Salim 2003). The power struggle between community leaders and women's groups within a multicultural policy framework needs to be reassessed in terms of who should agencies be working and consulting with. Questions should be repeatedly asked, such as who is getting marginalized and why, and who is speaking on whose behalf and why? For example while issues of 'intimate femicide' have been raised and highlighted by radical feminist scholarship over the last 30 years, the particular situation of the ethnicised woman has been marginalised within the domestic-violence discourse. The cultural specificity of honour and shame, and community and familial violence as opposed to intimate male violence, means that often the ethnocentricity of gendered violence is not addressed (Carby 1982). However, if honour killings and forced marriage as forms of domestic abuse and violence are constructed as ethnicised problems by politicians and the media, as witnessed in the current preoccupation with 'the Muslim woman', it can create not only more multicultural marginalisation but also a racist backlash at a local and national level.

While the intersectionality of race, class and gender power dynamics produce culturally specific manifestations of domestic violence, which are important to acknowledge and address in local service delivery, the responses and funding should be mainstreamed into informing domestic violence interventions more generally. Policies such as not putting non-English-speaking women into white-run refuges because of a perceived lack of 'cultural fit' can leave desperate women without care or shelter (Williams Crenshaw 1994). At the same time it is important for Asian women's sense of empowerment to be in domestic violence projects that enable their equal participation and value their decision-making (Gill and Rehman 2004). The climate that multiculturalism has produced in relation to racism is one of 'walking on eggshells', where cultural differences are respected, often without question, for fear of not offending communities and ethnic groups. In these situations, young ethnic-minority women can suffer from a lack of protection because they 'slip through the cracks' of not only conflicting discourses but also services. Organisations that deal with their protection are fearful of being seen as racist, feel they lack the cultural expertise or cannot access ring-fenced specialist funding.

With the appropriate enforcement of the Human Rights Act 1998 (enforced on 1 October 2000) in the UK, it is possible to move away from the 'gender trap' of cultural relativism inherent within liberal democratic discourse on multiculturalism, where gender is rendered at best marginal, or at worst invisible. In the absence of global social and political reform of violent patriarchal cultures where masculinity and honour is linked to female control, we can use challenges based in human-rights law to develop a more equitable and culturally neutral perspective where women's rights are ensured and privileged over patriarchal cultural practices. By adopting a realist human-rights approach (Savery 2005) which is predicated upon challenging the gender-biased corporate identity of the British multicultural state, black and Asian feminist activists who are in the process of redefining the 'we', not only in their own communities but in the multicultural nation (Samantrai 2002), have already begun to challenge the injustice of culturally endorsed domestic violence at its heart.

Notes

1 This chapter is reproduced by kind permission of Elsevier: Meetoo, V. and Mirza, H. S. (2007) '"There is Nothing Honourable About Honour Killings": Gender, Violence and the Limits of Multiculturalism', *Women's Studies International Forum*, Vol. 30, No. 3, 187.

2 There are the well-known cases of the two Nigerian women, Safiya Hussaini and Amina Lawal, who both faced being stoned to death but were then spared following an international campaign (*The Guardian*, 10 September 2002; *The Guardian*, 26 September 2003). There are many cases in the Caribbean; for example, see Coomaraswamy (1999).

3 We use the term 'ethnicised women' in preference to the official and much contested collective term 'Black and minority ethnic women' (Bhavnani, Mirza, & Meetoo 2005). While the latter term denotes the social construction of difference through visible racial (Black) and cultural (ethnic) markers, it does not emphasise the *process* of racial objectification implied by the former term. Thus *being or becoming* 'ethnicised' brings into play the power relations that inform and structure the gaze of the 'other' which, we suggest, frames the women's experience. Despite women's agency and activism, women deemed as 'the other' are often 'ethnicised' or typified by the media and state agencies in terms of their perceived (backward) cultural and religious practices.

4 For a discussiron of the globalization of domestic-violence issues in different cultural contexts see Nair 2001; Walby 2002; Radford and Tsutsumi 2004; Kelly 2005.

5 It is most often in relation to religious and black and minority ethnic communities that the concept of honour is invoked. Various forms of political and religious violence against women are culturally specific practices but are more likely to be seen as the consequence of systems of patriarchy (Araji 2000) and less likely to be perceived as honour crimes. For example, in the 1970s women in Northern Ireland were tarred and feathered for dating British soldiers (The HistoryNet.com 2005). Similarly, in the 1900s unmarried mothers in Ireland were cruelly incarcerated with their babies, often for life, in state-funded homes (Smith 2004).

6 There are also further issues of conflicting interest between white and black women evident in feminist movements. The Reclaim the Night marches in the 1970s attempted to make the streets safer for women. These marches are still in operation today. The areas that were under the spotlight were often black areas, and demands were made for better policing. However, it was argued that police protection is not the same for black women, highlighting the different relations women have to power structures (see Bhavnani and Coulson 2005).

7 Clearly government intervention is a controversial matter that raises the issue of community rights and women's rights. Blunkett, in calling for an end to arranged marriages outside the UK, was criticized by Mr. Siddiqui, Head of the Muslim Parliament, for 'using racist language' and Labour Peer Baroness Uddin for being 'deeply offensive'. A female Muslim human-rights lawyer, Virendar Sood, stated that Blunkett was contravening human rights by imposing his views on the Asian community, and failed to see the difference between forced and arranged marriage. A Sikh Community Action Network spokesperson said it was a serious issue hidden behind a barrier of cultural diversity, and Ann Cryer, MP for Keighley, West Yorkshire, welcomed the debate and the extra protection for young women (8 February 2002). Available at http://news.bbc.co.uk/1/hi/uk_politics/1807885.stm.

8 See Gill and Rehman 2004; Thiara 2003; Gupta 2003b; Takhar 2003; Samantrai 2002; Sudbury 2001.

Bibliography

Abbas, T. (2004) 'The Rise and Fall of Multiculturalism: Philosophical Considerations' Conference Paper presented to the Federal Centre for Research on Nationalism, Ethnicity and Multiculturalism, 15 March, Roehampton University.

Ahmad, F. (2003) 'Still in Progress? Methodological Dilemmas, Tensions and Contradicitions in Theorizing South Asian Muslim Women', in N. Puwar and P Raghuram (eds) *South Asian Women in the Diaspora*, Oxford: Berg.

Ahmed, S. (2003) 'The Politics of Fear in the Making of Worlds,' *International Journal of Qualitative Studies in Education*, Vol. 16, No. 3, 377, May-June.

——(2004) *The Cultural Politics of Emotions*, Edinburgh: Edinburgh University Press.

Akpinar, A. (2003) 'The Honour/Shame Complex Revisited: Violence Against Women in the Migration Context', *Women's Studies International Forum*, Vol. 26, No. 5, 425.

Alexander, J. and Mohanty, C. T. (eds) (1997) *Feminist Genealogies, Colonial Legacies, Democratic Futures*, London: Routledge.

Anthias, F. and Yuval Davis, N, (1992) *Racialised Boundaries: Race, Nation, Gender, Colour and Class and the Anti-Racist Struggle*, London: Routledge

Araji, S.K. (2000) 'Crimes of Honour and Shame: Violence Against Women in Non-Western and Western Societies', *The Red Feather Journal of Postmodern Criminology*. Available at http://www.rf-institute.com/journal-pomocrim/vol-8-shaming/araji.html.

Arin, C. (2001) 'Femicide in the Name of Honour in Turkey', *Violence Against Women*, Vol. 7, No. 7, 821.

Astbury, J. (2003) 'Whose Honour, Whose Shame? Gender Based Violence, Rights and Health', in Manderson, L. and Bennett, L. R. *Violence Against Women in Asian Societies,* London: Routledge Curzon.

Back, L., Keith, M., Khan, A., Shukra, K., and Solomos, J. (2002) 'The Return of Assimilation: Race, Multiculturalism and New Labour', *Sociological Research Online* Vol. 7, No. 2. Available at http://www.socresonline.org.uk.

Beck, U. (1992) *Risk Society: Towards a New Modernity*, London: Sage.

Beckett, C. and Macey, M. (2001) 'Race, Gender and Sexuality: The Oppression of Multiculturalism', *Women's Studies International Forum*, Vol. 24, No. 3/4, 309.

Bhavnani, K. K. and Coulson, M. (2005) 'Transforming Socialist Feminism: The Challenge of Racism', *Feminist Review,* Vol. 80, No. 1, 87.

Bhavnani, R., Mirza H. S. and Meetoo, V. (2005) *Tackling the Roots of Racism: Lessons for Success*, Bristol: Policy Press.

Brah, A. (1996) *Cartographies of Diaspora: Contesting Identities*, London: Routledge.

Bunting, M. (2006) 'Straw's Storm of Prejudice', *The Guardian*, 13 October.

Burman, E. and Chantler, K. (2004) 'There's No Place Like Home: Emotional Geographies of Researching "Race" and Refuge Provision in Britain', *Gender, Place and Culture*, Vol. 11, No. 3, 375.

Burman, E., Smailes, S. L. and Chantler, K. (2004) '"Culture" as a Barrier to Service Provision and Delivery: Domestic Violence Services for Minoritized Women', *Critical Social Policy*, Vol. 24, No. 3, 332.

Carby, H. (1982) 'White Women Listen! Black Feminism and the Boundaries of Sisterhood', in Centre for Contemporary Cultural Studies (ed.) *The Empire Strikes Back: Race and Racism in 70s Britain*, London: Hutchinson.

CIMEL/Interights (2001) *Roundtable on Strategies to Address 'Crimes of Honour': Summary Report*, Women Living Under Muslim Laws Occasional Paper, No. 12. November. Available at http://www.wluml.org/english/pubs/pdf/occpaper/OCP-12.pdf.

Cockburn, C. (1998)   *The Space Between Us: Negotiating Gender and National Identities in Conflict*, London: Zed Books.

Collins, P. H. (1998) *Fighting Words: Black Women and the Search For Justice*, Minneapolis: University of Minnesota Press.

Conaghan, J. and Millns, S. (2005) 'Special Issue: Gender, Sexuality and Human Rights', *Feminist Legal Studies*, Vol. 13, 1.

Coomaraswamy, R. (1997) 'Reinventing International Law: Women's Rights as Human Rights in the International Community', Edward Smith Lecture, Harvard University Law School. Available at http://.law.harvard.edu/programms/hrp/Publications/radhika.html.

——(1999) Oral Statement of the Special Rapporteur on Violence Against Women, United Nations Human Rights Commission, 13 April. Available at http://www.unhchr.ch/huricane/huricane.nsf/0/4071D15A148B4F0EC125697D005560D4 (accessed 27 February 2006).

CPS, (2004) Crown Prosecution Service 'London Honour killings "Running at Six a Year"'. Available at http://www.cps.gov.uk/london/cps_london_news/honour_crimes_conference.

Crawley, H. (2001) *Refugees and Gender: Law and Process*, Bristol: Jordan Publishing.

Dobash, R. E. and Dobash, R. P. (1998) *Rethinking Violence Against Women*, London: Sage.

Douglas, M. (1992) *Risk and Blame: Essays in Cultural Theory*, London: Routledge.

Dwyer, C. (1999) 'Veiled Meanings: Young British Muslims Women and the Negotiation of Difference', *Gender, Place and Culture,* Vol. 6, No. 1, 5.

Faqir, F. (2001) 'Intrafamily Femicide in Defence of Honour: The Case of Jordan', *Third World Quarterly,* Vol. 22, No. 1, 65.

Fekete, L. (2004) 'Anti-Muslim Racism and the European Security State', *Race and Class,* Vol. 46, No. 1, 3.

FCO (Foreign and Commonwealth Office) (2000) '*A Choice by Right: Working Group on Forced Marriage*'. Available at http://www.fco.gov.uk.

——(2004) *Young People and Vulnerable Adults Facing Forced Marriage: Practice Guidance for Social Workers* London: FCO. Available at http://www.fco.gov.uk.

——(2005) *Dealing with Cases of Forced Marriage: Guidance for Education Professionals* 1st Edition, January, London: FCO. Available at http://www.fco.gov.uk.

Fisher, L. (2004) 'State of the Art: Multiculturalism, Gender and Cultural Identities', *European Journal of Women's Studies,* Vol. 11, No. 1, 111.

Gabe, J. (1995) *Medicine, Health and Risk: Sociological approaches*, Oxford: Blackwell.

Gill, A. (2003) 'A Question of Honour', *Community Care*, 27 March. Available at http://www.communitycare.co.uk/articles.

Gill, A. and Rehman, G. (2004) 'Empowerment Through Activism: Responding to Domestic Violence in the South Asian Community in London', *Gender and Development*, Vol. 12, No. 1, 75.

The Guardian (2001) 'Cherie Blair pleads for Afghan Women', 20 November.

——(2002) 'Rome Honours Woman Saved from Stoning', 10 September.

——(2003) 'Nigerian Woman Escapes Death by Stoning,' 26 September.

Gupta, R (2003a) 'A Veil Drawn over Brutal Crimes', *The Guardian*, 3 October.

——(2003b) 'Some Recurring Themes: Southall Black Sisters 1979–2003 – and Still Going Strong', in Gupta, R. (ed) *From Homemakers to Jailbreakers; Southall Black Sisters*, London: Zed Books.

Haider, A. J. (2003) 'Domestic Violence: An Islamic Perspective', Paper delivered at the Conference, Tackling Domestic Violence in the Asian Community, Cardiff, September.

Hall, S. (1992) 'New Ethncities', in J. Donald and A. Rattansi (eds) *'Race', Culture and Difference*, London Sage.

——(2000) 'The Multicultural Question' in B. Hesse (ed.) *Un/Settled Multiculturalisms: Diasporas, Entanglements, Transruptions*, London: Zed Books.

Harris, C. (2001) 'Beyond Multiculturalism: Difference, Recognition and Social Justice', *Patterns of Prejudice*, Vol. 35, No. 1, 13.

Hesse, B. (ed.) (2000) *Un/Settled Multiculturalisms: Diasporas, Entanglements, Transruptions*, London: Zed Books.

TheHistoryNet.com (2005), 'Today in History'. Available at http://www.thehistorynet.com/tih/tih1110 (accessed 14 June 2005).

Inam, M. (2003) 'Taking or Giving Refuge? The Asian Women's Refuge Movement', in Gupta, R. (ed.) *From Homebreakers to Jailbreakers*, London: Zed Books.

Johal, A. (2003) 'Struggle not Submission: Domestic Violence in the 1990s', in Gupta, R. (ed.) *From Homebreakers to Jailbreakers*, London: Zed Books.

Joppke, C. (2004) 'The Retreat of Multiculturalism in the Liberal State: Theory and Policy', *The British Journal of Sociology*, Vol. 55, No. 2, 237.

Kelly, L. (2005) 'Inside Outsiders: Mainstreaming Violence Against Women into Human Rights Discourse and Practice', *International Feminist Journal of Politics*, Vol. 7, No. 4, 471.

Kevorkian, N. S. (2003) 'Re-Examining Femicide: Breaking the Silence and Crossing 'Scientific Boarders', *Signs: Journal of Women in Culture and Society*, Vol. 28, No 2, 581.

Kofman, E. (2004) 'Family Related Migration: A Critical Review of European Studies', *Journal of Ethnic and Migration Studies*, March, Vol. 30, No. 2, 243.

Kurkiala, M. (2003) 'Interpreting Honour Killings', *Anthropology Today*, Vol. 19, No. 1, 6.

Majid, R. and Hanif, S. (2003) *Language, Power and Honour: Using Murder to Demonise Muslims*, October, Islamic Human Rights Commission. Available at http://www.ihrc.org.

Mama, A. (1989) 'Violence Against Black Women: Gender, Race, and State Responses', *Feminist Review*, No. 32, Summer, 30.

Merchant, M. (2000) 'A Comparative Study of Agencies Assisting Domestic Violence Victims: Does the South Asian Community Have Special Needs?', *Journal of Social Distress and the Homeless*, Vol. 9, No. 3, 249.

Mirza, H. S. (1997) *Black British Feminism: A Reader*, London: Routledge.

——(2003) '"All the Women are White, All the Blacks are Men – But Some of Us Are Brave": Mapping the Consequences of the Invisibility for Black and Minority Ethnic Women in Britain', in Mason, D. (ed.) *Explaining Ethnic Differences: Changing Patterns of Disadvantage in Britain*, Bristol: Policy Press.

Mohanty, C. T. (1988) 'Under Western Eyes: Feminist Scholarship and Colonial Discourses', *Feminist Review*, No. 30, Autumn, 65.

——(2003) *Feminism Without Borders: Decolonising Theory, Practicing Solidarity*, Durham and London: Duke University Press.

Morrison, T. (1993) 'Friday on the Potomac', in Morrison, T. (ed.) *Race-ing, Justice – Engendering Power*, London: Chatto & Windus.

McLaughlin, E. and Neal, S. (2004) 'Misrepresenting the Multicultural Nation: The Policy Making Process, News Media Management and the Parekh Report', *Policy Studies*, Vol. 25, No. 3, 155–174.

Nair, S. (2001) 'Violence Against Women: Initiatives in 1990s', *Development*, Vol. 44, No. 3, 82–84.

Okin, S. M. (1999) *Is Multiculturalism Bad for Women?* (with respondents) Cohen, J., Howard, M. and Nussbaum, M.C. (eds), Princeton, NJ: Princeton University Press.

Phoenix, A. (1996) 'Social Constructions of Lone Motherhood: A Case of Competing Discourses', in Bortolia Silva, E. (ed.) *Good Enough Mothering?* London: Routledge.

Phillips, A. (2003) 'When Culture Means Gender: Issues of Cultural Defence in English Courts', *The Modern Law Review*, Vol. 66, No. 4, 510–531.

Puri, S. (2005) 'Rhetoric v. Reality: The Effect of "Multiculturalism" on Doctors' Responses to Battered South Asian Women in the United States and Britain', *Patterns of Prejudice*, Vol. 39, No. 4, 416–430.

Puwar, N. (2003) 'Melodramatic Postures and Constructions', in Puwar, N. and Raghuram, P. (eds) *South Asian Women in the Diaspora,* Oxford: Berg.

Radford, L. and Tsutumi, K. (2004) 'Globalization and Violence Against Women: Inequalities in Risks, Responsibilities and Blame in the UK and Japan', *Women's Studies International Forum*, Vol. 27, 1–12.

Rubin, G. (1975) 'The Traffic in Women: Notes on the Political Economy of Sex', in Reiter, R. (ed.) *Toward an Anthropology of Women,* New York: Monthly Review Press.

Runnymede Trust (2000) *The Parekh Report: Commission on the Future of Multi-ethnic Britain,* London: Profile.

RWA (2003) *Refugee Women's Association: Refugee Women's News* June and July, Issue 23.

Said, E. W. (1985) *Orientalism: Western Concepts of the Orient,* Harmondsworth: Penguin.

Salim, S. (2003) 'It's About Women's Rights and Women's Rights are Human Rights', interview with Sawsan Salim, Coordinator of Kurdistan Refugee Women's Organisation (KRWO) London: KRWO, received at Stop Violence Against Women Honour Killing Conference, 28 October 2005: London.

Sajid, I. J. (2003) 'Honour Killing: A Crime Against Islam', October, Muslim Council of Britain. Available at http://www.mcb.org.uk/jalil-sajid.html (accessed 8 March 2004).

Samantrai, R. (2002) *AlterNatives: Black Feminism in the Post Imperial Nation,* Stanford: Stanford University Press.

Savery, L. (2005) 'Women's Human Rights and Changing State Practices: A Critical Realist Approach', *Journal of Critical Realism*, Vol. 4, No. 1, 89.

Siddiqui, H. (2003) 'It was Written in her Kismet: Forced Marriage', in Gupta, R. (ed.) *From Homebreakers to Jailbreakers,* London: Zed Books.

Smith, J.M. (2004) 'The Politics of Sexual Knowledge: The Origins of Ireland's Containment Culture and the Carrigan Report (1931)', *Journal of the History of Sexuality*, Vol. 13, No. 2, 208.

Southall Black Sisters (2001) *Forced Marriage: An Abuse of Human Rights One Year After 'A Choice by Right',* London: SBS.

Spivak, C. G. (1988) 'Can the Subaltern Speak?' in Nelson, C. and Grossberg, L. (eds) *Marxism and the Interpretation of Culture,* London: Macmillan Education.

Stanko, E. A. (1985) *Intimate Intrusions: Women's Experience of Male Violence*, London: Routledge and Kegan Paul.

Stolcke, V. (1995) 'Talking Culture: New Boundaries, New Rhetorics of Exclusion in Europe', *Current Anthroplogy*, No. 36, 1.

Sudbury, J. (2001) '(Re)Constructing Multiracial Blackness: Women's Activism, Difference and Collective Identity in Britian', *Ethnic and Racial Studies*, Vol. 2, No. 1, 29.

Takhar, S. (2003) 'South Asian Women and the Question of Political Organisation', in Uwar, N. and Raghuram, P. (eds) *South Asian Women in the Diaspora*, Oxford: Berg.

The Telegraph (2001) 'Cherie Blair in Campaign to Liberate Afghan Women', 17 November.

Thiara, R. (2003) 'South Asian Women and Collective Action in Britain', in Andall, J. (ed.) *Gender and Ethnicity in Contemporary Europe*, Oxford: Berg.

UNFPA (United Nations Population Fund) (2000) *The State of the World Population: Chapter 3 Ending Violence Against Women and Girls*. Available at http://www.unfpa.org/swp/2000/english/press_kit/summary.html.

Walby, S. (1990) *Theorising Patriarchy*, Oxford, Blackwell.

——(2002) 'Feminism in a Global Era', *Economy and Society*, Vol. 31, No. 4, 533–57.

Williams Crenshaw, K. (1994) 'Mapping the Margins: Intersectionality, Identity Politics and Violence Against Women of Color', in Fineman, M.A. and Mykitiuk, R. (eds) *The Public Nature of Private Violence*, New York: Routledge.

——(2000) Background Paper for the UN Expert Meeting on the Gender-Related Aspects of Race Discrimination, Zagreb. Available at http://www.wicej.addr.com/wcar_docs/crensaw.tlr (accessed 25 May 2005).

Yuval-Davis, N. (1997) *Gender and Nation*, London, Sage.

Chapter 5

Collective crimes, collective victims

A case study of the murder of Banaz Mahmod

Joanne Payton
Information and Research Officer, Iranian and Kurdish Women's Rights Organisation (IKWRO)

The Iranian and Kurdish Women's Rights Organisation (IKWRO) works to prevent 'honour' crimes and other forms of violence against women in the UK and to campaign for women's rights in the Middle East. IKWRO advocates for women and girls (and occasionally men) who speak Kurdish, Turkish, Farsi, Dari and Arabic. In 2008–9, IKWRO intervened in 85 cases of potential 'honour'-based violence or forced marriage. The majority of clients in these cases are young Kurdish women. The murder of Banaz Mahmod, a 20-year-old divorcee of Iraqi Kurdish origin, who was killed by order of her uncle (Ari Mahmod) and father (Mahmod Mahmod) because she had a romantic relationship with an Iranian Kurd called Rehmat Suleimani, thus relates very closely to our work and the experiences of our client base.

The republic of men and the bride economy

In the spring of 2007, the Mahmod brothers stood in the dock attempting to portray themselves as progressive men with a respect for women's rights, making a bold statement that 'honour' killings had not happened in Iraqi Kurdistan for 'fifty years'. Meanwhile, the practice of 'honour' killing reached its nadir in the public stoning to death of 17-year-old Du'a Khalil Aswad in Bashiqa, Iraqi Kurdistan, in front of an audience of hundreds of men and boys cheering her killers. While this murder was particularly prominent, as the spectators filmed and distributed the grisly footage via their mobile phones, it was just one of many 'honour' killings in a country with a severe and increasing problem of femicide and female suicide. Over the first three months of 2007, UNAMI (the United Nations Assistance Mission for Iraq) was aware of 40 'honour' killings in Iraqi Kurdistan, necessarily a tiny proportion of the real figure; Kurdish hospitals every day receive women and young girls who have been killed or committed suicide via the painful method of immolation with petrol or kerosene.

The Mahmod family originated in Kaladiza in Pshdar, a mountainous region which borders Iran. Austrian charity WADI e.V. (*Verband für*

Krisenhilfe und solidarische Entwicklungszusammenarbeit)[1] report that forced marriage, 'honour' killing, female genital mutilation, illiteracy, child marriage, compensation and exchange marriages are endemic in this area,[2] classing Pshdar as the worst region of Iraqi Kurdistan in which to be a woman. As in many predominantly agrarian economies, women's value is located in their fertility. Children are valued for the economic value of their labour, and as a form of social security for old age. With a very high prevalence of exchange marriages (*jin be jin*), the trade in women's bodies forms a parallel ' bride economy'. In 2006 women's rights groups in Pshdar held a survey where people could come forward and register their marriages as having been conducted by exchange. Over five percent of the population of Pshdar came forward within just a few weeks, despite the attendant stigma and familial pressure (Mohammed 2007). According to WADI e.V., some men in the area also exchange their infant daughters in order to gain more wives for themselves. Exchanging women for money is also common through bride price. Jasvinder Sanghera identifies a strong correlation between societies that practice forced and non-consensual marriage and those which practice 'honour' killings (Sanghera 2006). According to the UK police, more than half of the cases of 'honour'-based violence in the UK relate to forced marriage, which echoes IKWRO's experiences. The Lévi-Straussian relationship of exchange which constitutes traditional marriage is more than an extension of kinship under such circumstances; it becomes a transaction. In these circumstances, 'honour' is the convention that underwrites patriarchal marital transactions. Bourdieu explains how 'honour' in this sense represents a form of self-interest:

> When ... the acquisition of symbolic capital and social capital is more or less the only possible form of accumulation, women are assets which must be protected from offence and suspicion and which, when invested in exchanges, can produce alliances, in other words social capital, and prestigious allies, in other words symbolic capital. To the extent that the value of these alliances, and therefore the symbolic profit they can yield, partly depends on the symbolic value of the women available for exchange, that is their reputation and especially their chastity – constituted as a fetishised measure of masculine reputation, and therefore of the symbolic capital of the whole lineage – the honour of the brothers and fathers, which induces a vigilance as attentive, and even paranoid, as that of the husbands, is a form of enlightened self-interest.
> (Bourdieu 2001).

The use of marriage to gain power and influence can be illustrated by the cases of women coming forward to IKWRO who have been threatened with death by relatives for refusing to divorce husbands that they loved, and who had been chosen for them by their families in the first place, but who had lost political influence through the changing balance of power in Iraq and were therefore judged no longer suitable alliances for the family.

The ideology of 'honour,' as expressed in Kurdistan, as in much of the Middle East, is a dichotomous concept. 'Honour' translates two words, '*namus*' and '*sharaf*', denoting a polarisation of characteristics which maps onto binary stereotypes of gender. 'Honour' in its more feminine aspect is located in negative, passive characteristics: stoicism, endurance, obedience, chastity, domesticity, servitude. In its more masculine form it features active and positive qualities: dynamism, generosity, confidence, dominance and violence. Female 'honour' is static: it can neither be increased nor regained, and once lost is lost forever. Male 'honour', by contrast, is dynamic, and maintained and increased through active participation and competition in the life of the community, and as such is in a constant state of flux. The positive, autonomous male 'honour' of any man, family or tribe is built upon the foundation of the negative, dependent female 'honour' of female relatives and tribeswomen, just as a trader's reputation is based on his merchandise. In its most repressive form, this means that women are not entitled to make any decisions about their own lives, with sexual and reproductive decisions being particularly circumscribed. Even in a lesser form, women's decisions will be ratified by male relatives who may do so with regard to how the woman's actions will reflect upon and benefit the family, and affect their ability to carry out further beneficial marital transactions. Guardianship in one sense denotes the protection and support of women, itself a source of inequality and patronage, but it also has another purpose in protecting a woman's market value and maintaining the reputation of the family brand. Women who are deemed to be deficient in this sense, in particular those who fail to meet a fetishized measure of chastity, become liabilities to the reputation of that family. Thus murders are carried out as much in a spirit of damage limitation as revenge or punishment.

Within the family context, Banaz's elder sister Bekhal had already depressed the market value of the family brand by absconding the parental home after Ari Mahmod threatened her for talking to an unrelated male prior to Banaz's marriage, divorce and murder. Her flight led her father to be harassed and rejected by others in the community, who sent faxes and made calls in Kurdish, English and Arabic, holding that a father who does not dominate his daughters is derelict in his duty as a man. Mahmod Mahmod attempted to reassert his control by ordering, and paying, his son to carry out a murderous attack on his daughter.

The self-interested vigilance of brothers and fathers to maintain the family reputation creates a level of surveillance of women which any totalitarian state would envy (Boudjak 2008). The council meeting that decided Banaz's death was based on a cousin's report of a stolen kiss at Mitcham Underground Station; Bekhal was threatened with immolation because she was seen by a cousin in conversation with an unrelated man; Banaz was referred to a psychiatrist during her marriage because she claimed she was afraid to leave the house since she was being followed by associates of her husband. The psychiatrist found that this was no paranoid delusion, but the reality of her life. Bekhal Mahmod is still unable to visit her remaining relatives and wears a niqab (a form of Islamic dress which includes a full-face veil) to avoid being seen by men of the extended family and so to protect herself from further violence.

Banaz had met her husband just three times on the family allotment before the wedding. It is likely that Mahmod Mahmod pushed early marriages upon his other daughters in order to restore his image as a patriarch after Bekhal's flight, and to enforce control over daughters he feared would rebel. Where a family's reputation for surveillance and control over its women is called into question, marriage becomes an effective tool to further suppress female autonomy. Placing a woman under the control of a husband extends the responsibility for her behaviour beyond her father and her extended family to her husband and *his* extended family, doubling the control over her. Banaz's husband Ali Abbas proved to be a violent and brutal man, and Banaz sought to end the marriage after just a few years of beatings and sexual violence. Just as her marriage was not her decision, neither was she permitted to make a divorce without the imprimatur of male approval. Banaz was called before her family to justify herself in a humiliating assembly. In response to her charge of marital rape, Abbas retorted that it could not be called rape when she always said no (in which case it was *always* rape) to which she replied that she only refused sex when she was menstruating. The appeal to religious taboos suggests that she felt unable to justify refusing sex for any other reason. She, like her sisters, had been subjected to clitidorectomy in order to reduce sexual sensation. Within this expectation of sexuality as a wife's duty, her post-divorce romance with Rehmat was as poignant as it was transgressive: the regular text messages she sent him were effusive and ardent, displaying the passion of a young woman experiencing love for the first time.

Banaz's murder was brutal and prolonged. In covert recordings one of her murderers gleefully recounted 'slapping' and 'fucking' her, stamping on her throat and strangling her, laughing about the grotesque details of her hair and elbow protruding from the suitcase which Ari Mahmod used to carry her corpse across a busy London road in daylight. Kurdish sources reported that the fugitives in Iraqi Kurdistan also boasted of having taken part in gang-rape. Bourdieu's observations on gang-rape are relevant here:

> Practices such as some gang rapes ... are designed to challenge those under test to prove before others their virility in its violent reality, in other words stripped of all the devirilizing tenderness and gentleness of

love and they dramatically demonstrate the heteronomy of all affirmations of virility, their dependence on the judgements of the male group.

(Bourdieu 2001)

While the press focused on the father's part in the murder, in court the uncle was identified as the dominant force and accordingly given a longer sentence. Ari Mahmod, who had a wide range of business activities and contacts in the community, and daughters of his own, had more status to lose through the perceived loss of family 'honour'; *The Times'* investigation reveals a hypermasculine and dominant man who relished his wealth and status. Ari Mahmod also had connections with the family of Ali Abbas – at the time of the marriage, the Mahmod brothers were estranged (possibly due to the situation with Bekhal), and Ari Mahmod attended the wedding at the invitation of the Abbas family, rather than at his brother's request. A United Nations survey (focusing mainly on the Kurdish regions of Turkey) suggests that women's relationships after divorce are particularly problematic under the 'honour' code; the former husband is still authorised to control the sexual behaviour of his former wife. Field-workers uncovered four murders justified by this perception, in a village in Adana where the Muhtar forbade divorced women to remarry (Kardam 2005). Divorced and married women both share a similar heightened level of risk of 'honour' violence through their dual connections, and through the tensions created between families when a woman is perceived as having obviated a negotiated marital transaction.

Failure to protect

Nadera Shalhoub-Kevorkian coined the phrase 'death zone' (Shalhoub-Kevorkian 2002) to describe the period which begins when a woman sentenced to an 'honour' killing realises her family has made the decision to kill her and which ends with her murder. In Banaz's case, the 'death zone' was between the family council meeting of 2 December 2005 and 24 January 2006, over which period Banaz made contact with police five times. Mahmod Mahmod had first attempted to murder Banaz himself on New Year's Eve. Presumably assuming that it would be easier to kill an intoxicated woman and to disguise the murder as an alcohol-related death on the busiest binge-drinking night of the year, he forced her to drink a bottle of brandy before the attack. Although unaccustomed to the effects of alcohol, Banaz escaped, trying to draw attention to herself by breaking the window of the house next door and then running into the street, in fear of her life, and her boyfriend Rehmat's safety.

PC Angela Corne, the attending officer, characterized Banaz as 'melodramatic and manipulative' from the outset. Corne's response, gleaned from her own testimony in court, displayed a lack of knowledge of 'honour' crime: when

Banaz claimed that her father had been trying to kill her, and that she was facing threats from four men, this was taken by PC Corne as evidence of inconsistency and exaggeration. A greater knowledge of 'honour'-based violence would have informed her that 'honour' killings in the Kurdish community are often planned by a conspiracy of males. When discussing Banaz's drunken state, Rehmat described Mahmod Mahmod as a 'strict Muslim'. Corne did not take this opportunity to ask whether he was also a strict parent or to establish her home situation. For Corne, Banaz's drunken state was another reason to disbelieve her; yet, the fact that Banaz had never drunk alcohol in her life before was confirmed by Rehmat and should have raised an alert.

Procedurally, Corne failed to follow up on a serious allegation: she failed to make a referral to the Domestic Violence Unit; she did not look for any background information (such as the recorded attack on Bekhal); she contacted the family directly to resolve the broken-window issue without considering whether this was appropriate in the light of Banaz's serious allegation; and worse, and most dangerously, she shared Banaz's allegation with her family members. She made a perfunctory follow-up visit at a time when she was unable to speak to Banaz in privacy and without interruption, which she did not attempt to do.

The last person to see Banaz alive was PC Wray at Wimbledon Police Station on the day when Banaz and Rehmat agreed to report the threats against them. The officer taking Banaz's statement offered her a safe house – which Banaz refused. Victims of 'honour' crime frequently underestimate the level of risk. Banaz was murdered on the following day, when her family became aware that she had contacted the police. Banaz died not just through the actions of her family, but due to the multiple failures of those who were there to protect her. Although many officers received disciplinary action, Angela Corne was in fact promoted, receiving only 'words of advice', the lowest sanction available, for her failures. IKWRO repeatedly asked the Independent Police Complaints Commission (IPCC) to answer a number of questions relating to the case, by letter and in a public meeting; the IPCC have not as yet replied to these questions.

As with forced marriages, with 'honour' violence there is a pressing need for awareness from all sectors of public servants, including housing officers, social workers, teachers, medical professionals and any other public servants that may have contact with women, girls and couples at risk. Policies must be put in place *before* they are required. 'Honour' crime, as a serious, collective and organised form of crime, may require an immediate response. Awareness must form part of every public official's training, not just to avoid cases like Banaz's, but also to dispel common misperceptions of a crime which is coming into the public eye with increasing frequency. Police involvement is key; whether a potential victim is identified by a teacher or doctor, risk assessments and protection measures need to be implemented rapidly by a police officer with knowledge of the issues and sensitivity towards the individual. Women in the 'death zone' should never again be ignored.

Collective, premeditated, public crime

Violence against women knows no boundaries. Some societies and circumstances are more conducive to male violence than others: the rate of domestic abuse, for example, is extremely high in Nigeria, and extremely low in Japan (Garcia-Moreno et al. 2005). These rates do not necessarily correlate to the situation of women within society. Sweden has the lowest 'gender gap', yet just as in Syria and the United Kingdom, statistics suggest that one woman in four will experience domestic violence over her lifetime. The similar rate of intimate partner violence in the latter two countries does not correlate with the rate of crimes justified in the name of 'honour'. The UK has a rate of spousal murder half the size of Syria's estimated 'honour' killing figures, despite a population over three times greater.[3] 'Honour' killing is not just an outgrowth of private violence; it is a distinct phenomenon existing within its own parameters.

'Honour' killing differs from spousal violence in three respects: it is collectively decided and planned, it is premeditated and it is an act committed for the benefit of a presumed audience. In the case of Banaz one can see the classical structure of a family council meeting, where her death was ordained, and the painstaking arrangement of both murder attempts. According to the prosecution case (based on covert recordings and mobile phone records), many of the Mahmods' relatives and associates, including uncles, cousins, children and their spouses and Ari's business associates, appeared to have knowledge of the murder. Ari Mahmod was even reproached by one man who felt slighted at not being invited to take part in the murder, resenting missing out on an opportunity to prove his masculinity.

Mahmod Mahmod arranged no funeral for the recovered body of his daughter, in a final public act of rejection, intended to be understood as such by the community. 'Honour' and 'shame', unlike pride and guilt, are social phenomena. 'Honour' killing is typically described as taking place behind a veil of secrecy. This only reflects the view from the outside: 'honour'-based communities are regulated by gossip, and many community members may be aware of a murder. 'Shame', which can be concealed from the community (through abortion or hymenoplasty, for example), may not necessarily be punished violently (Ermers 2009). It is in the family interest to reduce community awareness of the supposed 'shaming' incident, as well as the retribution, hence the common practice of destroying the personal effects of a victim of 'honour' killing, essentially erasing her existence from the family history. However, where there is widespread public knowledge of 'dishonour', the restoration of reputation needs to be enacted for a double audience: community members who are aware of the 'shaming' incident must be reassured of the worthiness of the family, and women in the community must be 'terrorised' against committing similar transgressions. The extent of the community's knowledge of the violent restoration of 'honour' will mirror the community's knowledge of the supposed loss of 'honour'. Hence a well-known transgression like the elopement of Du'a Khalil, which had been politicised by local youth groups due to the cross-religious nature of her relationship, received a public and violent retribution – violence as theatre – whereas most crimes remain more discreet, in direct proportion to the public knowledge of the supposed offence.

Women and 'honour' killing

Women may collude tacitly or explicitly in an 'honour' killing, often out of their own individual self-interest – out of personal fear, or a desire to maintain the social standing of the male-dominated family within the male-dominated community. 'Honour' killing is a form of violence against women which may be committed by women as well as men (Sen 2005). Patriarchal societies cannot function without ideologies and structures designed to network individual men into an oppressor class; nor can they permit corresponding attempts to foster women's solidarity against them. Each individual woman has a number of different and intersecting identities and loyalties (such as religious, ethnic and tribal identification) which may take precedence over her identity as a woman. Where women are lacking in political influence, a decision to identify with the least empowering aspect of their identity is almost an act of heroic perversity. The actions of the Israeli Arab women of the Abu Ghanem family, who united to prosecute their male relatives for multiple murders (Ha'aretz 2007), are remarkable no less for their rarity than for the egregious actions of the males: eight women of the family had been murdered in just seven years, demonstrating how much insult can be taken before women recognise the value in identifying their collective self-interest as women before their other respective identities.

In Banaz's case, an Instant Messenger chat between female cousins demonstrated a brief flicker of solidarity, when Banaz's cousin Ala Mahmod stated, 'If I find out anyone will kill her I will go to the police', to be warned by another cousin, 'They'll kill you next', a warning which, according to the prosecution case, became a real threat later in the same day. Rehmat claims that Banaz's mother Behya personally warned him that they were both in danger shortly after the family council meeting of 2 December. It is clear that Banaz trusted her mother and counted on her support: in her last visit to the police the day before her disappearance, she declined the offer of a safe house, saying that as long as her mother was present she would be safe at home. Ari Mahmod's prison recordings indicate that Behya had herself been threatened by her husband to comply with the murder, and in the end she, along with her husband, left Banaz in the family house on the day of the murder, from where the killers came and collected her.

Women are made complicit with the ideology of 'honour' through conditioning and coercion; dissent is suppressed by threats and violence. Patriarchal structures do not just unite men against women, but the older generation against the younger. Older women may be included in family councils and take a role in conspiracies, provided they have internalised the gender roles of the 'honour' system and play a masculine role in enforcing them on the younger generation.

Heshu Yones: chronicle of a death foretold

Heshu Yones, who was murdered in 2002 by her father Abdallah, marked perhaps the first time the phrase 'honour' killing entered the lexicon of the popular press. Heshu was attacked with extreme violence, with 11 stab wounds – to the extent that the knife point broke off in the attack. Initially, Abdallah Yones concocted an improbable explanation that his daughter had been killed by Al-Qaeda (or that she had committed suicide), but he subsequently changed his plea to guilty. According to DCI Hyatt, he did so at the point when it appeared that the police investigation would implicate other family members in the crime. Due to Yones' guilty plea, much of the evidence gathered by Hyatt's team was not heard. Yones had received information through a letter that his daughter was bringing shame on the family, and a school teacher had inadvertently informed the family that Heshu had a romantic relationship. In response, he took her to Iraqi Kurdistan to marry her to her cousin. Upon subjecting her to a virginity test he found that her hymen was ruptured and that an 'honourable' marriage would be impossible, so they returned to the UK. From this point Heshu was in the 'death zone': like Banaz, she made attempts to contact various agencies, and as with Banaz, they all failed to adequately apprehend the risk to her life. So while the evidence for premeditation, historic abuse and the possibility of a collective will to murder was not considered, Yones was able to argue that he was 'provoked' by Heshu's Western dress, her Lebanese boyfriend[4] and a letter he received at the offices of the Patriotic Union of Kurdistan (a political party), where he volunteered, which labelled Heshu a 'prostitute'. The defence argued that Yones had been 'forced to kill', that the stain on his 'honour' had put him in an 'untenable position' (Smartt 2006). Judge Neil Denison accepted the grounds of provocation as mitigation and accordingly reduced the tariff from 20 years to 13, citing the 'irreconcilable cultural difficulties between traditional Kurdish values and the values of Western society' [unreported].

Kurdish women's groups reacted with horror to this decision and to the implications of the language of 'cultural difference'. If culture is defined as being the qualities that make a society distinctive, male violence is too near universal to form part of any society's culture. Collective violence against those who transgress traditional sexual morality exists in societies as diverse as Papua New Guinea[5] and Calvin's Geneva (Naphy 2004) – or even in the mob attacks on supposed paedophiles in the wake of the Sarah Payne murder (Eden 2000). 'Honour' plays a significant part in Kurdish history and social and familial structures, but to define it as part of Kurdish 'culture' is to collude with those Kurds who defend 'honour' killing as a national tradition and opposition to it being due to corrupting 'Western' influences.

In an open letter to Judge Denison, Kurdish Women's Action Against Honour Killing argued:

> We acknowledge that honour killing is often culturally and historically defined. However, this statement should not invite the idea that all Kurds accept this practice. The Kurds, both here and elsewhere, contain within their number both hidden and visible dissenters, different voices that defy the idea that 'the community' is a homogeneous entity, static and incapable of reflection.
>
> (Dr Nazand Begikhani, KWAHK) [unreferenced]

Judge Denison, by taking Yones's own definition of his culture, effectively privileged the conservatism of patriarchal Kurds over the progressive voices calling for a more egalitarian future and reproduced in the United Kingdom the notion of reduced sentences for those who claim a defence of 'honour', which had been abolished as part of the Kurdish legal code since 2002.

Intimate crimes

In Britain and Europe, 'honour' crime is still often seen as a form of domestic violence. Rahila Gupta argues that creating a distinct category for 'honour'-related violence risks increasing racial tension (Gupta 2003). Creating divisions and hostility between communities is self-evidently deeply counterproductive. However, the assumption that domestic and honour-related violence require similar approaches because they occur at the hands of the family fails to take account of some of the particular characteristics of 'honour' crimes. Gupta compares the Yones murder with a case of spousal murder, correctly pointing to both as examples of males responding to female autonomy and the threat to male privilege with deadly violence. However, evidence against Yones also revealed the existence of a large conspiracy and community support. Investigating officer DCI Brent Hyatt reveals that Yones, who lived on state benefits, was able to raise an enormous surety in order to be released on bail, during which time a fake 'abduction' was plotted to return him to Iraqi Kurdistan with the intention of placing him beyond the reach of British justice. Many Kurdish men attended the trial in support of Yones; witnesses were threatened by community members.

Such conspiracies and communal support would be extremely rare in the realm of spousal murder, as would be the use of hired killers, as seen in Banaz's case, and, according to police, in one in eight other UK 'honour' killings.

While it may sometimes be appropriate to find protection for potential victims of 'honour'-related violence within the existing systems set up to protect victims of domestic violence, this must be decided in the context of the level of risk to the individual. Shelters predicated on the paradigm of intimate partner violence enacted by a single aggressor against a single victim may be unable to protect women facing not just a single abusive man, but a large, organised conspiracy, with varying levels of support from the extended family and other members of the community. Tight-knit communities can form a veritable network of spies, where it has been known for photographs to be circulated to shopkeepers and taxi-drivers, and where professional agencies exist to find, and sometimes kill, those women who have been deemed to have stained 'family honour' (Hill 2004). In one case known to IKWRO, a father with no previous record of violence against his daughter raised a bounty of £100,000 to be paid upon her death. This creates enormous challenges not just for agencies which exist to protect women, but also for the police in their investigations. The case of Ghazala Khan (in which nine of her relatives were successfully prosecuted for their part in her murder in Norway) demonstrates a great leap forward in European understanding of 'honour'-related violence, echoed in the innovative police work used to gain a conviction in Banaz's case in the absence of information from the community. The failures to protect Banaz demonstrate that this understanding is dangerously fragmentary. It is clearly irresponsible, particularly within a xenophobic environment, to classify each and every act of violence within minority communities as being related to the ideology of 'honour', coloured by the otherness of minority culture. The existence of 'honour' killings is very frequently, and inaccurately, used within racist discourses hostile to minorities in general, and Muslims in particular, creating animosity and exacerbating racism in the majority community and leading to defensiveness and denial in the affected minority communities. While this is a serious concern that requires delicate treatment, it is also misguided to elide differences when this may erase the specific protection needs of potential victims.

The names of the dead

The existence of 'honour' killings within a community affects all women who belong to that community. For every crime committed in the name of 'honour', there is also a resultant check upon the individual liberties of behaviour and thought of women who live constrained by the constant threat of male violence held to be legitimate within their milieu. As the trial judge in the Banaz case, Brian Barker remarked in sentencing, 'This offence was designed to carry out a wider message to the community and designed to discourage the legal behaviour of girls and women in this country.'[6] In 2004, the *Evening Standard* carried an interview with a young woman from Iraqi Kurdistan who was being pursued by her cousin, who had been commissioned to kill her. He threatened to stab her a hundred times, 'worse than what Abdallah did to Heshu'. Just a few days after the Mahmods were pronounced guilty, a young woman from North London was taken into police protection after receiving a letter from her family saying she would be 'the next Banaz' (Bird 2007). One of IKWRO's clients reports that her father held a gathering to celebrate news reports of Banaz's murder, where the guests applauded the 'honour' killing, and where her father announced, to the cheers of those present, that he would similarly kill her if she jeopardised family 'honour', a sentiment seconded by her mother (Anon. 2007). The young woman was terrified, as she was intended to be. The names of the dead are used as weapons against the living.

The most fitting analogy for 'honour' killing is not to be found in the private sphere, but within the history of collective violence: 'honour' killing, like lynching, is a collective, theatrical act, building solidarity within the oppressor class, combining a punishment for any rebel who transgresses systemic oppression, a public restoration of the oppressors' norms in the face of challenge, and a form of terrorism against any others who may be chafing against the circumscription of their lives.

Notes

1 From private email correspondence.
2 Another native of Kaladiza, Kazim Mahmud Raschid, stabbed and set fire to his former wife Sazan Bajez-Abdullah on the day she had been granted a divorce by the German courts. While on trial, Raschid explained that he was obliged to kill her by his 'culture and religion', and that Sazan's father had approved the murder. Raschid held that the German state was ultimately responsible for the murder because they 'gave women too many rights' (Doinet 2007).
3 Syrian Women's Observatory estimate 200–300 'honour' killings per year in Syria (Elass 2007); there are over 100 femicides per year through domestic violence in the UK, and police estimate 12 'honour' killings. (Gupta 2003). Syria has reduced sentences for 'honour' killings (with a two-year minimum) as part of its penal code.
4 Contrary to most media reports, the court records and other articles, Nizam al-Khouri, Heshu's boyfriend, is a Muslim (Smith 2003). I suspect that Yones claimed that Nizam was a Christian so that he could rule out the possibility of accepting a legitimate relationship between the youngsters on Islamic grounds.
5 Islands Business reported in 2007 that 'a young woman in Mt Hagen ... was burnt to death by villagers on such purported charges as having extra marital affairs, engaging in sorcery and spreading the HIV/AIDS virus to one of the men. The woman, probably still in her late teens, had logs strapped to her abdomen and back, her hands tied and mouth gagged with rags before she was set alight.'
6 Times online, 20 July 2007, available at: http://www.timesonline.co.uk/tol/news/uk/crime/article2110457.ece?token=null&print=yes&randnum=1151003209000.

Bibliography

Anonymous (2007) IKWRO Client Interview. (J. Payton, Interviewer).

Bird, S. (2007). ' "Honour" Killing Used to Threaten Others'. *The Times*. 13 June 2007.

Boudjak, C. (2008) *Un totalitarisme contre les femmes: Répercussions des crimes et du système de l'honneur familial sur les conditions de vie des femmes*. London: International Campaign Against Honour Killings.

Bourdieu, P. (2001) *Masculine Domination*. Cambridge: Polity Press.

Doinet, R. (2007) 'Ein gespenstisches Bekenntnis'. *Stern*. 4 October 2007.

Eden, R. (2000) 'Paediatrician Attack: "People Don't Want No Paedophiles Here"'. *The Telegraph*. 3 September 2000.

Elass, R. (2007) '"Honor" Killing Spurs Outcry in Syria'. *Christian Science Monitor*. 14 February 2007.

Ermers, R. (2009) *Honour Related Violence*. 7 June 2009. Retrieved September 1, 2009, from WUNRN: http://www.wunrn.com.

Evening Standard (2004) 'How I Escaped from a Brutal Honour Killing', *The Evening Standard*. Available at http://docs.newsbank.com/s/InfoWeb/aggdocs/WLSNB/103862E6A209F7E7/0ECC8117B7A430B7?p_multi=ESTC&s_lang=en-US.

Garcia-Moreno, C., Jansen, H. A., Ellsburg, M., Helse, L. and Watts, C. (2005). *WHO Multi-country Study on Women's Health and Domestic Violence: Intial Reports on Prevalence, Health Outcomes and Women's Responses*. Geneva: World Health Organisation.

Gupta, R. (2003) 'A Veil Drawn over Brutal Crimes', *The Guardian*. 3 October 2003.

Ha'aretz. (2007) 'Abu-Ghanem Women Speak Out Against Serial Honor Killings', *Ha'aretz*. 23 February 2007.

Hill, A. (2004) 'Runaways Stalked by Bounty Thugs', *The Observer*. 18 April 2004.

Islands Business (2007) *WE SAY: Women Have Suffered in Silence*. Retrieved August 6, 2009, from Islands Business: http://www.islandsbusiness.com.

James, D. (2007) 'Sins of the Father', *The Sunday Times Colour Supplement*. 11 Novembr 2007.

Kardam, F. (2005) *The Dynamics of Honor Killings in Turkey: Prospects for Action*. Ankara: United Nations Development Programme.

Mohammed, N. (2007) '"Exchange" Marriages a Bad Deal for Iraqi Brides', *Middle East Times*. 7 March 2007.

Naphy, W. (2004) *Sex Crimes: From Renaissance to Enlightenment*. Stroud: Tempus.

Sanghera, J. (2006) Violence in the Name of 'Honour' – A Victim's Story. *Honour Killing: How Many More? Conference*. London: IKWRO.

Sen, P. (2005) 'Crimes of Honour, Value and Meaning', in Welchman, L. and Hossain, S. (eds) *'Honour:' Crimes, Paradigms and Violence Against Women*, London: Zed Books.

Shalhoub-Kevorkian, N. (2002) 'Growing from Within: The De-Colonization of the Mind', in Abdo-Zudi, N. and Lentin, R. (eds) *Women and the Politics of Military Confrontation: Palestinian and Israeli Gendered Narratives of Dislocation*. New York: Berghahn Books.

Smartt, U. (2006) 'Honour Killings', *Justice of the Peace Journal*, 4–7.

Smith, R. (2003) 'Heshu's Boyfriend Tells of Loss', *Evening Standard*. 30 September 2003.

Times (2007) '"Honor Killing" Father Jailed for Life', *Times Online*. Available at http://www.timesonline.co.uk/tol/news/uk/crime/article2110457.ece?token=null&print=yes&randnum=1151003209000.

Chapter 6

Honour and shame in domestic homicide

A critical analysis of the provocation defence

Dr Anna Carline
Lecturer in Law, Liverpool John Moores University

This chapter will contribute to the debate on honour and violence via a critical examination of the provocation defence and will argue that the law has, for many years, tolerated and mitigated 'honour killings' committed by the dominant group in Western society. The aim of the chapter is to problematise the manner in which notions of honour, shame and 'honour killings' have recently been constructed as specific to certain cultural, ethnic and religious groups and as being 'other' to the norms and standards of Western society[1] (see, for example, Bennetto 2004; Bird 2007; Jones 2003; Marshall 2007; Merge 2006). This self/other construction enables the law and society to condemn killings by ethnic-minority groups, or more specifically Asian (and frequently Muslim) men, whilst potentially rendering invisible the relevance of honour and shame to those homicides committed by Western men. It will be argued that the partial defence of provocation has long been used successfully by men who kill their partners, and while the current law of provocation focuses on a loss of self-control, the roots of the doctrine are premised upon a white Western notion of male honour. However, the less emotive term 'domestic homicide' is generally used to refer to 'Western honour killings'. In addition to illustrating how the defence of provocation mitigates 'Western honour killings', this chapter will also critically examine the requirements of the provocation defence as it has operated to date and query whether the law could and indeed should mitigate 'ethnic honour killings'.

The chapter will commence with an overview of the historical development of the provocation defence and its links to male honour and then proceed to examine how the modern-day defence still protects a form of male honour and problematically shames women. In addition to examining the requirements of the modern defence of provocation and the problematic of 'ethnic honour killings', the latter part of the chapter will also comment upon the issues relating to the admissibility and relevance of cultural evidence. The chapter will conclude by arguing that the law should not be allowed to mitigate any homicides which are premised upon patriarchal and oppressive attitudes towards women.

Male honour and the provocation defence

Provocation is a partial defence to murder which operates to reduce the conviction to one of manslaughter and restores the judge's discretion in sentencing, thus enabling the accused to avoid a mandatory life sentence. The defence, at present, is contained in the Homicide Act 1957.[2] Section 3 states:

> Where on a charge of murder there is evidence on which the jury can find that the person was provoked (whether by things done or by things said or by both together) to lose his self control, the question whether the provocation was enough to make a reasonable man do as he did shall be left to be determined by the jury; and in determining that question the jury shall take into account everything both done and said according to the effect which, in their opinion, it would have on the reasonable man.

Provocation developed as a common-law defence and is frequently cited as representing a concession to human infirmity.[3] The defence amounts to a legal recognition that in certain situations an individual's actions may be brought about by extenuating circumstances, circumstances which provoke the individual to be so overcome with anger that a conviction for murder and the corresponding life (or historically, death) sentence is considered to be unduly harsh. Significantly, the defence developed in response to the provocative circumstances in which men historically found themselves, and thus embodies a male construction of, and a male response to, provocative acts. More emphatically, it has been argued that the foundations of the doctrine are premised upon a concern to protect and promote 'male honour' (Horder 1993: 22–42).

A successful plea of provocation requires the accused to satisfy two tests, one subjective and the other objective. Established during the seventeenth century, these two tests, Horder has argued, are concerned with the protection and promotion of a distinct form of 'natural' male honour (Horder 1993: 26). While Horder notes that the 'superstructure of the law' has undergone transformation since this time, and therefore one should not overemphasise continuities (Horder 1993: 23), it is important to note that the law of provocation initially developed as a defence for 'honour killings': killings that were committed in order to protect or restore a man's honour. Although the legal landscape has changed significantly since the seventeenth century, and the requirements of the defence likewise, the initial theoretical and moral underpinnings of the doctrine have shaped and informed what is legally and socially considered to a be homicide worthy of mitigation.

With regard to the subjective test, the law would only mitigate those killings which were committed in hot blood. Similar to the defence today, cold-blooded, premeditated killings would fall outside of the defence. The provocation defence has always been limited to those defendants whose actions were caused by an emotional reaction and, historically, that emotion was anger (Horder 1993). Legally and socially it was (and still is) recognised that a person who kills because they have been provoked into an angry reaction should not necessarily be treated as harshly as one who kills in cold blood. However, the law would not mitigate all forms of hot-blooded killing. The second restriction placed upon the defence was that the provocation must be sufficiently grave so to warrant leniency. The accused's actions were judged against an evaluative standard, or an objective test. Historically, the law only recognised four circumstances as being sufficiently provocative to trigger the defence: (1) a grossly insulting assault; (2) witnessing the attack of one's friend, relative or 'kinsman'; (3) witnessing an Englishman being unlawfully deprived of his liberty; and (4) witnessing a man in the act of adultery with his wife.[4] In such situations, Horder argues: ' ... the law recognized the gravity of the provocation ... as a significant threat to natural honour, and mitigated the offence' (Horder 1993: 29).

However, to simply acknowledge that the law mitigated a killing which was committed in one of the four scenarios fails to adequately capture the true extent to which male honour informed the defence. While the law recognised that a man may feel anger and retaliation may result, there was also a societal expectation that a man of honour would retaliate in anger, in order to restore the honour he had lost. Hence, Horder argues that the 'hot-blooded' response did not represent a complete loss of self-control, but rather related to 'anger as outrage' (Horder 1993: 42). It was considered virtuous for a man to feel a certain amount of anger and retaliate in a manner which would accordingly restore his honour.

Although the requirements of the defence have evolved over the years, it can be argued that the emergence of distinct circumstances amounting to provocation and the corresponding legal recognition of killings in hot blood construct these four scenarios as representative of justifiable and acceptable anger. Clearly, what is relevant to this chapter is the fact that, historically, the law considered that a wife's adultery was sufficiently provocative to provide the husband with a defence. More emphatically, in *R v. Mawgridge*[5] Holt CJ stated: ' ... when a man is taken in adultery, with another man's wife, if the husband shall stab the adulterer, or knock out his brains, this is bare manslaughter: for jealousy is the rage of the man, and adultery the highest invasion of property'.[6] Furthermore, it was also argued that the law could not provide a sufficient remedy for the man whose wife or daughter was the subject of seduction. Only his own death or the death of the 'despoiler of peace and honour' would provide the necessary relief (Horder 1993: 39). Hence the development of the provocation defence was informed by patriarchal attitudes which constructed women as male property and also recognised that a man may be led to commit homicide due to the sexual behaviour of his wife or daughter. Indeed this was deemed necessary if he was to retain his status as a man of honour.

Although the law is no longer explicitly connected to notions of male honour and female shame, the modern-day defence is informed by a societal and legal expectation that a man of honour will respond with homicidal anger if his wife commits adultery. Hence the law has for many years mitigated certain forms of 'honour killings.'

Provocation in the twentieth and twenty-first centuries

The provocation defence, along with the law relating to homicide generally, has been subject to significant scrutiny over the past couple of years and is undergoing a process of reform (see, for example, the Coroners and Justice Act 2009). The aim of this chapter, however, is to emphasise how the defence has over the years continued to mitigate homicides which arguably amount to a Western cultural form of 'honour killing'. This requires analysis of the law as it has operated to date, as opposed to focusing on the reforms. This section of the chapter will provide a general discussion of the provocation defence and the issue of 'honour killings' prior to moving on to a more detailed examination of the current requirements of the defence.

As discussed above, during the seventeenth century the defence was available to a man who killed the seducer of his wife or daughter. Mariticide and/ or filicide, arguably, were not mitigated. Horder, however, suggests that this was probably due to the fact that women were considered to be incapable of rational thought and therefore not responsible for their actions (Horder 1993: 24). Over the years, however, the defence has been successful in cases involving men who kill their partners. This chapter argues that these cases represent an evolution of the provocation defence as it developed during the seventeenth century, in that they are concerned with a certain cultural form of male honour.

However, while a certain Western cultural form of male honour remains protected by the provocation defence, Western law and society distances itself from the concept of 'honour killing', and this term is reserved for cases involving ethnic minorities, specifically Asian and frequently Muslim men (see, for example, Bennetto 2004; Bird 2007; Jones 2003; Marshall 2007; Merge 2006). Significantly, the provocation defence has overwhelmingly not been used successfully in the 'honour killing' cases committed by Asian men (in this jurisdiction).[7] The issue of concern is that the intense focus which has been placed on 'honour killings' committed by minority groups may permit the dominant society to render invisible the true extent of domestic violence and domestic homicide which exists within Western culture. Asian Muslim culture, in particular, is 'othered' and the spectre of the 'dangerous Muslim male' (Meetoo and Mirza 2007) is used in order to construct the Western man and Western society as non-sexist, non-violent and protective of vulnerable groups. Unfortunately the reality is far removed from this picture. Western men frequently get away with murder when they kill their female partners.

Honour, shame and domestic homicide

The argument that the provocation defence continues to be linked to notions of male honour can be derived from the research conducted over the past 20 years or so which amply illustrates that the provocation defence is frequently successful in cases involving men who kill their unfaithful, departing or nagging partners (see, for example, Bandalli 1995; Burton 2003; Edwards 1987; Horder 1993; McGolgan 2000). It was not until 2002 that Lord Hoffman, in the House of Lords case of *R v. Smith*, stated: ' ... male possessiveness and jealousy should not today be an acceptable reason for loss of self-control leading to homicide, whether inflicted upon the woman herself or her new lover'.[8] Such a statement is clearly far removed from the 'male honour' premises of the defence, especially as portrayed by Holt CJ in *R v. Mawgridge*.[9] Ostensibly the law no longer constructs male anger and jealousy as appropriate reactions to infidelity or otherwise non-conformist sexual behaviour. Unfortunately, however, other cases do not seem to have followed this approach.

In 2002 the Court of Appeal heard three appeals against sentencing in manslaughter cases.[10] In two of the cases the male defendants, Leslie Humes and Mark Paul Wilkinson, had been convicted for manslaughter on the grounds of provocation after killing their partners (wife and girlfriend respectively). The victims in both cases had children with the defendants, and the fatal incidents occurred some time after the women had left the relationships. Moreover, in both instances the women were killed after they admitted to the defendants that they were involved with other men. Leslie Humes stabbed his wife Madeleine 11 times when she admitted to him that she had feelings for another man and further implied that she would sleep with him in the near future. Nicole Lewis died from asphyxiation when Mark Paul Wilkinson placed a plastic bag in her mouth after she informed him that she was considering moving in with another man, who would be a 'surrogate father' to their children.

As provocation was successful, not only was it accepted that the defendants suffered a loss of self-control, but also that a 'reasonable person' would respond in a similar manner. Akin to the seventeenth-century model, female adultery was considered sufficiently grave provocation; indeed these cases illustrate that a mere admission of adultery or likely adultery amounts to adequate provocation. Furthermore, the Court of Appeal rejected the Attorney General's argument in relation to Leslie Humes that the provocation was slight, noting:

> In accepting the offender's plea, the prosecutor did not dispute that the offender's loss of self control was reasonable in all the circumstances and was sufficiently excusable to reduce the gravity of the offence. We find it difficult to understand how consistently with that the degree of provocation can be said to be slight.[11]

This was despite the fact that the attack continued after Madeleine tried to escape and was also witnessed by one of their children. Similarly, in relation to Wilkinson, it is recognised that the trial judge was ' ... as merciful as his public duty allowed him to be',[12] despite the fact that Mark had told Nicole to 'do [him] a favour and die'.[13]

Although the Court of Appeal judgement does not explicitly refer to notions of male honour, the reactions of Leslie Humes and Mark Wilkinson are expressions of male possessiveness, jealousy and anger; emotions which are historically linked to male honour (see also Burton 2003). As noted by Holt CJ in *R v. Mawgridge*[14] jealousy is considered to be a natural reaction of a man of honour, and possessiveness is a product of the patriarchal view of women as the property of men. The women in these two cases were killed because they chose to leave a relationship and become involved with other men, and the law constructs such circumstances as sufficiently provocative to warrant mitigation.

Furthermore, the manner in which the law constructs the behaviour of Madeleine and Nicole as blameworthy, it can be argued, invokes notions of shame. In relation to Madeleine, the judgement explicitly mentions how Leslie Humes was provoked after he blamed himself for the breakdown of the relationship, only to subsequently discover this was not the case:

> During the police interviews he said that over the days before the attack he had built himself up to believe that his marriage had failed because he had been a bad father and husband, to discover on the morning ... that his wife had someone else.[15]

Madeleine's deception of not only having feelings for another man, but also allowing the defendant to blame himself became the main focus and was constructed as the cause of Leslie's loss of self-control.[16] Little reflection is given as to why Madeleine developed feelings for another man, or why she thought it might be prudent not to disclose this information sooner. The behaviour of Nicole Lewis is also judged as being far from appropriate, indeed the judgement states that she ' ... took more than she gave, going out frequently, spending more than they could afford and consequently causing financial problems'.[17] Mark is stated as being very angry and upset and that ' ... he had found it very difficult to cope with Ms Lewis going ... '.[18]

As with the notion of 'male honour', although the judgement does not refer explicitly to the concept of shame, it can be argued that the law's focus on the behaviour of the victims, and the blame which is attached to them for their own demise, is linked to notions of shame. Law implicitly shames women when they are judged and condemned for failing to live up to societal expectations of appropriate scripts of femininity (Carline 2003; Nicolson 1995). Moreover, the notion of shame has played a significant role in cases involving women who kill their partners, and unfortunately this has tended to be emphasised more strongly in those cases in which the defendant was an Asian woman. The oft-cited examples are the cases of Zoora Shah[19] and Kiranjit Ahluwalia.[20] Both women were convicted for murder when they killed their partners after enduring years of abuse. On appeal against their convictions it can be seen that their ability, or otherwise, to act with the appropriate shame was fundamental to the success of their appeals. Zoora's appeal was rejected, and she was considered to be insufficiently shamed. Indeed she was interpellated as an 'unusual woman' whose way of life, in the opinion of the court, was such that ' … there might not have been much left of her honour to salvage'.[21] In contrast, Kiranjit's appeal was upheld. The facts of the case clearly illustrate that she experienced a high level of shame, not only for the abuse she had suffered but also for her actions in killing her husband (Carline 2005b; Philips 2003).

Hence, it is argued that the notions of honour and shame are instrumental in domestic homicide cases. Although the discourse of the modern-day defence may not explicitly state that a woman who engages in an affair or leaves her partner for another man acts in a shameful way that affronts male honour, this can be seen to be implicit due to the manner in which the law appropriates blame, scrutinises the woman's behaviour and acknowledges male anger and retaliatory action.

The next section of this chapter will examine the specific requirements of the current provocation defence in order to examine why the defence has remained limited to 'Western honour killings' and consider whether the defence could and/or should be extended in order to mitigate 'ethnic honour killings'. In conclusion it will be argued that the law should not mitigate any cultural form of 'honour killing'.

The subjective test – time lapses and revenge

As noted above, the modern-day defence of provocation is contained within Section 3 of the Homicide Act 1957 and involves a subjective and an objective test. The main legal authority for the modern day subjective test is *R v. Duffy*,[22] in which Lord Diplock emphasised that the accused must suffer a 'sudden and temporary loss of self control, rendering the accused so subject to passion as to make him or her for the moment not master of his mind'.[23] The subjective test has been interpreted as requiring the homicide to be committed in timely connection with the provocative act. Any significant time lapse between the provocation and the homicide will be used as evidence that the accused actually regained their self-control and acted in revenge as opposed to anger.[24] This requirement has, however, been subjected to substantial criticism, especially from those analysing the law from the perspective of a battered woman who kills. In particular, it has been argued that the requirement of a sudden and temporary loss of self-control has emerged and responded to the predicaments in which Western men generally find themselves, and hence embodies a particular masculine reaction to provocation (Horder 1993; O'Donovan 1991).

The requirement of a sudden and temporary loss of self-control does, prima facie, appear to exclude 'honour killings' from its purview. Indeed one of the reasons behind the decision to retain the notion of a 'loss of self control' in the reformed defence, as contained in sections 54–55 of the Coroners and Justice Act 2009, is to ensure that 'honour killings' are not mitigated (Ministry of Justice 2008: 12). Any time lapse which exists between the last 'provocative' act and the homicide indicates that the killing was an act of revenge, as opposed to an angry response. The honour killing cases which have been extensively detailed within the media seem to have involved planning and premeditation and thus fall within the category of revenge killings (Siddiqui 2005).[25] However, it would be a mistake to assume therefore that there is little point in further considering the defence of provocation when looking at honour killings, due to a number of factors.

First, the predicament of abused women who kill their partners has led to a loosening of the time constraints. A time lapse between the last provocative act and the homicide will not by law prevent a plea of provocation, although it does amount to evidence which suggests revenge as opposed to loss of self-control.[26] Second, the notion of slow-burn anger, which has developed in relation to abused women who kill, seems to have been accepted within the law, and this could potentially be used in 'honour killing cases', with cultural evidence being used in order to substantiate such an argument.[27] Third, the fact of planning itself does not necessarily preclude the defence if it can be shown that when the homicide eventually occurred the accused was suffering from a loss of self-control; this may particularly be the case if an argument erupted immediately prior to the fatal act. This strategy may succeed due to the 'last straw' analogy, which is now accepted within the criminal law.[28] Fourth, it would be a mistake to assume that honour killings are always conducted in a premeditated manner. Such homicides may be committed without a time lapse. For example, in the case of *R v. Mohammed*[29] the applicant stabbed and killed his daughter upon finding her boyfriend in her bedroom, although his provocation plea was unsuccessful on the basis that his behaviour failed to satisfy the objective test. Arguably, planning and premeditation are not the defining features of an honour killing; the reasons behind the killing are more significant. One example which emphasises the last two points is the case of *R v. Shabir Hussain*.[30] On appeal the accused was found guilty of manslaughter on the grounds of provocation after he repeatedly ran over his sister-in-law, Tasleem Begum, in his car. Tasleem, whose husband from an arranged marriage was in Pakistan, was killed while she was waiting for her lover, a married man. The judge recognised that Hussain had suffered a loss of self-control on seeing her, stating 'something blew up in your head that caused you a complete and sudden loss of self control'.[31] Fifth, as already discussed, historically it has been understandable for a man to become angry and kill a woman due to her infidelity or contravention of the perceived approved scripts of female sexuality. Constructing the honour-killing scenario as necessarily outside the defence of provocation not only problematically fails to acknowledge how honour and shame continue to inform the provocation defence, but also does not recognise that the law does mitigate 'Western honour killings'.

The objective test – would a reasonable person react in a similar manner?

In contrast to the seventeenth-century defence, the evaluative aspect of provocation questions whether a 'reasonable person' would have reacted in a similar manner to the defendant. This test has caused the judiciary no end of difficulties as the courts have endeavoured to decide how this reasonable person is constructed. The main legal authority is that of *DPP v. Camplin*,[32] in which Lord Diplock stated that the ' ... reasonable man ... is a person having the power and control to be expected of an ordinary person, but in all other respects sharing such of the accused's characteristics as they think would affect the gravity of the provocation'.[33] Ostensibly, Lord Diplock's statement draws a distinction between the level of self-control a person is expected to maintain and the gravity of the provocation. Whilst age and sex may alter the level of self-control, any other characteristics, for example ethnicity, sexuality, disability, will only be relevant to the gravity of the provocation; they will not be permitted to alter the level of self-control he/she is expected to maintain. The logic of the 'Camplin distinction' was criticised by the House of Lords case of *R v. Smith*,[34] and it was held that Lord Diplock did not intend to differentiate between the standard of self-control and the gravity of the provocation. According to *R v. Smith*, when the jury apply the objective test they should be able to take into account any of the characteristics of the accused they consider to be relevant when considering whether or not his loss of self-control was 'reasonable', or to be more precise, 'excusable'.[35] The *Smith* approach, however, was rejected by the Privy Council in the case of *Attorney General for Jersey v. Holley*,[36] and hence an individual's ethnicity and culture will only be relevant to the gravity of the provocation; they are not relevant when assessing the level of self-control the defendant is expected to maintain.

The question of the accused's characteristics, or more specifically their culture, becomes particularly relevant when dealing with honour-killing cases. The next section of this chapter will address two interrelated points: first, the composition of the law's reasonable person, and second, the relevancy and admissibility of cultural evidence.

The standard of self-control – sex, age and constructing the reasonable person

The reasonable-person test is presumed to invoke a universal standard, a standard of behaviour which is common to all within society. However, analysis from feminists amply illustrates that the 'reasonable person' actually embodies the characteristics of the white, middle-class, Western, heterosexual man (McGolgan 2000; O'Donovan 1991). From a feminist perspective, the recognition in *Camplin* that sex is relevant to the standard of self-control potentially improves the situation, as a woman who is provoked will be evaluated against the standard of the 'reasonable woman' as opposed to the 'reasonable man'. Nevertheless, in our modern-day multicultural society it is difficult to maintain that sex or gender is a more important aspect of identity than, for example, ethnicity or culture. Moreover, the courts' analyses of provocation's reasonable person have tended to focus on the more unusual elements of human identity such as glue sniffing,[37] brain damage,[38] attention-seeking disorder,[39] depression[40] and chronic alcoholism.[41] Although it is not disputed that such afflictions have a dramatic impact on a person's identity and can duly alter how they interpret and react to provocative situations, the courts tend to presume the existence of a 'reasonable person' that is affected by these conditions, as opposed to presenting a critical reflection upon the construction of the reasonable person itself.

Despite their differences in opinions, the Law Lords in both *Smith* and *Holley,* recognised difficulties caused by the concept of the 'reasonable man' and favoured the phrase 'ordinary person' or a 'person of ordinary self control',[42] and this shift in terminology is reflected in the reforms (Ministry of Justice 2008: 43). Furthermore, the courts have also recognised that powers of self-control are not universal and static, but may alter over time, as the law refers to ' … such powers of self control as everyone is entitled to expect that his fellow citizens will exercise in society as it is today.'[43] Nevertheless, it can be questioned whether a semantic shift from 'reasonable' to 'ordinary' will avoid the criticisms that haunt the notion of the reasonable man. The 'ordinary standard' test is just as likely to allow the experiences and perspectives of the Western man to remain at the heart of the provocation defence. As provocation developed primarily as a defence used by men, it is difficult to see how simply shifting from the term 'reasonable' to 'ordinary' will automatically result in a move away from contemplating the standard of self-control possessed by Western men.

The admission of cultural evidence

Although culture is not relevant when contemplating the 'ordinary standard of self control', it is, however, relevant when discussing the gravity of the provocation. In relation to 'honour killings', if such evidence is permitted, there is little reason to assume, provided the subjective element of the defence is satisfied, that the defence would not be successful. Although it has been argued the 'standard of self-control' reflects the standard possessed by the Western man, the gravity of the provocation is judged by the cultural perspective of the defendant. Hence a defendant could argue that his cultural background rendered the actions of the female family member so gravely provocative that any person with 'ordinary' levels of self-control would also lose their self-control. Thus, in the case of *Shabir Hussain* the judge commented that the illicit affair of the victim ' … would be deeply offensive to someone with your background and your religious beliefs',[44] and in *R v. Mohammed* the trial judge directed the jury to take into account the applicant's strongly held cultural and religious beliefs when assessing the gravity of the provocation.[45] Moreover, given that the law of provocation has historically recognised, and continues to recognise, that 'ordinary men' often lose their self-control due to the behaviour of women, it is difficult to see why the argument would fail in such 'honour killing' cases. Indeed, when one takes into account how provocation has frequently been successful in cases involving adulterous women, it can be questioned whether cultural evidence with regard to the gravity of the provocation is strictly necessary.

Nevertheless, it is important to acknowledge that the provocation defence has been more concerned with male honour in relation to partners and/or wives, whilst 'ethnic honour killings' tend to be much wider in scope, in terms of the victim and the perpetrators. More specifically, many cases have involved a daughter whose way of life was considered to have 'shamed' the family, and many family members have been involved in her death, including women.[46] Clearly, in cases where the death of the woman has been ordered by the family, the defence of provocation will not succeed as there is ample evidence of planning, hence there would not have been a sudden and temporary loss of self-control.

However, it needs to be recognised that the law and the provocation defence is a cultural phenomenon which has continually mitigated Western forms of honour killing. If the law recognises certain cultural forms of honour killing, than why should it not be extended to cover other cultural forms? Hence, in addition to considering the relevance of cultural evidence with regard to the objective test, one also needs to question whether cultural evidence should be permitted to significantly alter the scope of the defence.

The relevance of cultural evidence has become a rather vexed issue (see, for example, Philips 2003; Renteln 2004), and the debate has tended to become side-tracked by the rather unfortunate multiculturalism/feminism binary (Maguigan 1995). On a very general level, some feminist commentators have adopted the stance that 'multiculturalism is bad for feminism' (Okin 1999). The main argument from the anti-multicultural feminists is that allowing cultural evidence into the courts is detrimental to women as such evidence tends to reinforce patriarchal attitudes towards women and allows abusive behaviour towards women and children. Considering that cultural evidence in relation 'honour killings' would maintain that, in certain cultures, it is acceptable to punish a woman's 'shameful' behaviour in order to restore the family's honour, it is not difficult to see why feminists (amongst many others) are opposed to the introduction of such evidence. From a slightly different perspective, admission of cultural evidence is objected to on the basis that it tends to have a detrimental impact upon ethnic-minority groups in general, as they are constructed in a rather essentialised manner, as being unable to escape the constraints of their cultural backgrounds. Minority culture is problematically portrayed as static and traditional, a culture that is not as advanced or as civilized as the white Western world (Volpp 2001, 1994).

Nevertheless, advocates of women who kill their abusive partners have drawn significant attention to the specifics of a particular woman's situation, a move which has required the law to be cognisant of not only the differences between men and women, but also the differences that exist amongst women (Carline 2005a; McColgan 2000; Nicolson 1995). Although feminist approaches are critical of those aspects of a culture which reinforce patriarchal attitudes and violence towards women, it would be a mistake to assume, as the multiculturalism/feminism binary does, that feminists are opposed to the introduction of evidence which illustrates that the specific situation of the accused needs to be recognised in order for justice to be achieved. Use of the battered woman syndrome is just one example of this (Walker 1979). It is undoubtedly important for the law and society to recognise that women are not a homogenous group (Crenshaw 1991). Although abuse against women is a cross-cultural phenomenon, one should not assume that the causes, forms and responses to abuse are universal (Volpp 2003); indeed the problem of 'honour killings' is a very good example of this. While there are some commonalities, such as patriarchal views with regard to women and the desire to control female sexuality (Araji 2000), there are significant differences between the 'Western honour killings' that are currently mitigated by the provocation defence and some of the 'ethnic honour killings' (see Sen 2005).

From a multiculturalist and postmodern perspective, one cannot ignore the importance and significance of culture. Not only does culture inform and construct law, it also informs and constructs our identities and our experiences (see Benhabib 2002). One cannot simply abandon one's culture. But this does not mean that we are completely determined by our culture (Butler 1993), nor should we uncritically embrace the more oppressive elements of our own culture, nor indeed of the cultures of others. To emphasise the importance of culture does not therefore mean that cultural evidence of honour and shame should necessarily be admissible when deciding the subjective test or analysing the gravity of provocation; neither does it call for a more radical reform of the defence. What is necessary is a critical reflection upon those cultural practices which are oppressive towards women. This author argues that cultural evidence which promotes and perpetuates violence towards women should not be admitted to support a claim of provocation, and therefore supports the approach adopted by Lord Hoffman in *Smith*:[47] male jealousy and possessiveness should no longer be considered appropriate 'characteristics' when considering a claim of provocation. The law should no longer support claims that insist that a man with ordinary standards of self-control would respond violently upon discovering that their partner has had/is having an affair and/or leaving them for another person. Indeed the Home Office proposed that sexual infidelity be excluded from the 'loss of self control' defence which will replace the partial defence of provocation, as contained in the Coroners and Justice Act 2009 (Ministry of Justice 2008: 11–12).

Not only should one be critical of 'cultural evidence' which perpetuates violence against women, but one also needs to recognise the extent to which women suffer violence in Western cultures, and in particular those forms of 'honour killing' which are mitigated due to the provocation defence. A critical analysis of 'honour killings' needs to avoid the self/other binary which problematically renders violence against women in Western cultures invisible, and constructs Asian culture as inherently violent towards women.

Conclusion

This chapter has argued that the defence of provocation has, for many years, mitigated a form of 'Western honour killing.' Western men who kill their partners on the grounds of adultery or threats to leave have frequently avoided a murder conviction and been convicted for the lesser offence of manslaughter, and the law of provocation has historically protected and promoted male honour. Without disputing the horror and traumatic experiences minority ethnic women suffer due to a culture of 'honour' and 'shame', it has been argued that violence against women is prevalent within Western society and care needs to be taken not to construct minority ethnic culture as violent towards women in a manner which does not also recognise the problems that exist in Western culture. Although culture is a constitutive element of an individual's identity, and different cultures need to be respected, it is argued that one needs to remain critical in relation to those elements of a culture which promote violence against women and perpetuate patriarchal attitudes. The law should not mitigate a homicide which is committed in order to restore male honour.

Notes

1 'Honour killings' committed by the dominant group in society will be termed 'Western honour killings' and those committed by ethnic-minority groups will be termed 'ethnic honour killings'. The author uses the terms 'Western', 'ethnic' and

'honour killings' with caution, acknowledging that such generalisations are very problematic.

2 See sections 54–5 of the Coroners and Justice Act 2009. This Act was passed on 12 November 2009.

3 *R v. Hayward* (1908) 21 Cox C.C. 692 per Lord Tindal CJ at p. 694; *R v. Smith* [2001] 1 AC 146 as per Lord Hoffman, 159.

4 *R v. Mawgridge* (1707) Kel 119.

5 (1707) Kil. 119, 137.

6 Ibid.

7 Provocation was used successfully by Shabir Hussain, who killed his sister-in-law, Tasleem Begum, by running her over in his car when she was waiting to meet her partner. On appeal the judge acknowledged that her affair 'would be deeply offensive to someone with your background and beliefs'. *R v. Shabir Hussain* [1997] EWCA 2876. (Phillips 2003: 526).

8 *R v. Smith* [2001] 1 AC 416, 196G.

9 (1707) Kel 119.

10 *R v. Suratan; R v. Humes; R v. Wilkinson* [2003] 2. Cr App R (S) 42 EWCA Crim 2982.

11 Ibid.: para 62.

12 Ibid.: para 76.

13 Ibid.: para 69.

14 (1707) Kil. 119, 137.

15 *R v. Suratan; R v Humes; R v Wilkinson* [2003] 2 Cr App R (S) 42 EWCA, para 58.

16 Ibid.: para 58.

17 Ibid.: para 71.

18 Ibid.: para 70.

19 *R v. Shah* [1998] EWCA Crim 1441.

20 *R v. Ahluwalia* [1993] 96 Cr App R 133. See also the case of *R v Bakhshish Kaur Sangha* [1997] 1 Cr App R (S) 202.

21 *R v. Shah* [1998] EWCA Crim 1441, 67.

22 (1949) 1 All ER 932.

23 Ibid.

24 See for example: *R v. Ibrams* Gregory (1982) 74 Cr. App. R 154; *R v. Ahluwalia* [1993] 96 Cr App R 133; *R v. Thornton* [1992] 1 All ER 306; *R v. Thornton* (No. 2) [1996] 2 Cr App R 108.

25 Recent cases include Banaz Mahmod, who was killed by her father and uncle (Marshall 2007) and also the case of Surjit Athwal, who was murdered by her grandmother and uncle (Verkaik 2007).

26 *R v. Ahluwalia* [1993] 96 Cr App R 133.

27 See *R v. Smith (Josephine)* [2002] EWCA 2671.

28 *R v. Humphreys* [1995] 4 All ER 1008.

29 [2005] EWCA Crim 1880.

30 [1997] EWCA Crim 2876.

31 *R v. Shabir Hussain*, Newcastle Crown Court, 28 July 1998 (cited by Phillips 2003: 527).

32 [1978] 2 All ER 168.

33 Ibid.: 175.

34 [2001] 1 AC 146.

35 Ibid.: 173.

36 [2005] 2 AC 580.

37 *R v. Morhall* [1995] 2 Cr App R 502.

38 *Luc Thiet-Thuan v. R* [1996] 2 Cr App R 178.

39 *R v. Humphreys* [1995] 4 All ER 1008.

40 *R v. Smith* [2001] 1 AC 146.
41 *Attorney General for Jersey v. Holley* [2005] 2 AC 580.
42 *R v. Smith* [2001] 1 AC 146 at 173; *Attorney General for Jersey v. Holley* [2005] 2 AC 580 Lord Nicholls, para 7.
43 *DPP v. Camplin* [1978] AC 705, 717.
44 *R v. Shabir Hussain* [1997] EWCA Crim 2876.
45 *R v. Mohammed* [2005] EWCA Crim 1880.
46 See *R v. Abdul Haq* [2005] EWHC 304 (Edwards and Welstead 1999).
47 [2001] 1 AC 146.

Bibliography

Araji, S. (2000) 'Crimes of Honour and Shame: Violence Against Women in Non-Western and Western Societies', *The Red Feather Journal of Postmodern Criminology*. Online. Available HTTP: <http://critcrim.org/redfeather/journal-pomocrim/vol-8-shaming/araji.html> (accessed 30 September 2009).

Bandalli, S. (1995) 'Provocation – A Cautionary Note', *Journal of Law and Society*, Vol. 22, 398.

Bennetto, J. (2004) 'Suspicious Deaths of Young Asian Women to be Re-examined for Honour Killing Link', *The Independent*, 7 December, 8.

Benhabib, S. (2002) *The Claims of Culture: Equality and Diversity in the Global Era*, Princeton, NJ: Princeton University Press.

Bird, S. (2007) '"Honour" Killings Used to Threaten Others', *The Times*, 13 June, 15.

Burton, M. (2003) 'Sentencing Domestic Homicide Upon Provocation: Still Getting Away With Murder', *Feminist Legal Studies*, Vol. 11, 279.

Butler, J. (1993) *Bodies that Matter: On the Discursive Limits of Sex*, London: Routledge.

Carline, A. (2003) 'Women Who Kill Their Abusive Partners: An Analysis of Queer Theory, Social Justice and the Criminal Law', unpublished thesis, University of Hull.

——(2005a) 'Women Who Kill Their Abusive Partners: From Sameness to Gender Construction', *Liverpool Law Review*, Vol. 26, No. 1, 13.

——(2005b) 'Zoora Shah: An "Unusual Woman"', *Social and Legal* Studies, Vol. 14, No. 2, 215.

Crenshaw, K. (1991) 'Mapping the Margins: Intersectionality, Identity Politics and Violence against Women of Color', *Stanford Law Review*, Vol. 43, 1241.

Edwards, S. and Welstead, M. (1999) 'Death before Familial Dishonour', *New Law Journal*, June 4, 867.

Edwards, S. (1987) '"Provoking Her Own Demise:" From Common Assault to Homicide', in Hanmer, J. and Maynard, J. (eds) (1987) *Women, Violence and Social Control*, London: MacMillan Press, 152.

Horder, J. (1993) *Provocation and Responsibility*, Oxford: Clarendon.

Jones, D. (2003) 'As Yet Another Father is Jailed for an Honour Killing, a Special Investigation Reveals Haunting Stories of the Asian Girls Whose Desire for Love and Freedom Lost Them Their Lives', *Daily Mail*, 9 October, 48.

Maguigan, H. (1995) 'Cultural Evidence and Male Violence: Are Feminist and Multiculturalist Reformers on a Collision Course in the Criminal Courts?', *New York University Law Review*, Vol. 70, 36.

Marshall, C. (2007) 'Killed for Loving the Wrong Man', BBC Online. Available HTTP: <http://news.bbc.co.uk/1/hi/uk/6733653.stm> (accessed 1 July 2009).

McColgan, A. (2000) 'General Defences''' in Bibbings, L. and Nicolson, D. (ed.) *Feminist Perspectives on Criminal Law*, London: Cavendish, 137.

Meetoo, V. and Mirza, H. S. (2007) 'There is Nothing "Honourable" About "Honour Killings": Gender, Violence and the Limits of Multiculturalism', *International Forum*, Vol. 30, No. 3, 187.

Merge, A. (2006) 'One in 10 Young Asians Says Some Honour Killing Justified', *The Evening Standard*, 4 September, 10.

Ministry of Justice, (2008) *Murder, Manslaughter and Infanticide: Proposals for Reform of the Law* CP19/09, London: HMSO.

Nicolson, D. (1995) 'Telling Tales: Gender Discrimination, Gender Construction and Battered Women Who Kill', *Feminist Legal Studies*, Vol. 3, 185.

O'Donovan, K. (1991) 'Defences for Battered Women Who Kill', *Journal of Law and Society*, Vol. 18, 219.

Okin, S. M. (1999) *Is Multiculturalism Bad for Women?* Princeton, NJ: Princeton University Press.

Phillips, A. (2003) 'When Culture Means Gender: Issues of Cultural Defence in the English Courts', *Modern Law Review*, Vol. 66, No. 4, 510.

Renteln, A. D. (2004) *The Cultural Defense*, Oxford: Oxford University Press.

Sen, P. (2005) '"Crimes of Honour", Value and Meaning', in Welchman, L. and Hossain, S. (eds) (2005) *'Honour': Crimes, Paradigms, and Violence Against Women*, London: Zed Books, 42.

Siddiqui, H. (2005) '"There is No 'Honour' in Domestic Violence, Only Shame!" Women's Struggles Against "Honour" Crimes in the UK', in Welchman, L. and Hossain, S. (eds) (2005) *'Honour': Crimes, Paradigms, and Violence Against Women*, London: Zed Books, 263.

Verkaik, E. (2007) 'Grandmother Gets Life for Honour Killing', *The Independent*. Online. Available HTTP: <http://news.independent.co.uk/uk/crime/article2979899.ece> (accessed 1 December 2008).

Volpp, L. (1994) '(Mis)Identifying Culture: Asian Women and the "Cultural Defense"', *Harvard Women's Law Journal*, Vol. 17, 57.

——(2001) 'Feminism versus Multiculturalism', *Columbia Law Review*, Vol. 101, 1181.

——(2003) 'Symposium: On Culture, Difference and Domestic Violence', *American University Journal of Gender, Social Policy and Law*, Vol. 11, No. 2, 393.

Walker, L. (1979) *The Battered Woman*, New York: Harper and Row.

Welchman, L. and Hossain, S. (eds) (2005) *'Honour': Crimes, Paradigms, and Violence Against Women*, London: Zed Books.

Chapter 7

Does the Qur'an condone domestic violence?

Sadia Kausar and Sjaad Hussain
Faizan al-Rasool Educational Institute, Birmingham, UK

Mohammad Mazher Idriss
Senior Lecturer in Law

Introduction

Since the atrocities and acts of violence of 9/11 and 7/7 questions concerning the teachings of the Qur'an and the *Sunnah* (the traditional teachings of Islam through the Prophet Muhammad, peace be upon him, hereafter p.b.u.h.) have come under intense scrutiny in the arena of legal, sociological and religious studies.[1] In this chapter, the authors examine verse 4:34 of the Qur'an, entitled *The Women*, which contains important clauses regarding the social interaction between husband and wife. This chapter encompasses the dimension of interpersonal relations between the genders in Islam, where the authors argue that it is not enough to qualify the use of the word *Idribu-hunna* in the text of the verse, generally interpreted as permission for the use of physical force in order to establish notions of obedience upon women, with words like 'lightly' or 'gently', as is done in most Qur'anic translations.[2] The authors believe that there is a need to go much further if domestic violence is to be desacrilised and treated as an excess (and a crime), as opposed to a fundamental right of a husband to exercise over his wife. A traditional exegesis of the Qur'an and the *Ahadith* is undertaken, providing an explanation of the relevant verses and passages within Islamic scriptures. The authors are of the opinion that traditional (cultural) interpretations and perspectives of the thirty-fourth Qur'anic verse, amongst others, perpetuate an oppressive patriarchal system not intended by Islamic law viewed in its genesis, and serve as incorrect justifications for the oppression of women in Muslim societies, whether in the East or West. This chapter will contain some Islamic views that will not be seen positively by others, but they are nevertheless dominant views and need to be understood as such (if not entirely accepted). As a chapter in this current collection, it provides yet another view on how violence is read and experienced by Muslim women. It should also be noted that this chapter is not concerned with discussing the role of 'honour' in Islam per se – rather it intends to explore the issue of whether violence in a domestic context is permitted with reference to the primary sources of Islamic law. There are other chapters in this collection that usefully explore notions of honour, violence and how it is experienced in relation to Muslim *and* non-Muslim communities. From the outset, and as we draw towards a conclusion, the authors argue that we do not condone the view that *any* violence towards women is legitimate.

Islam and domestic violence

The issue of domestic violence within Islam is a controversial subject, with media and newspaper depictions of Muslims (and, in particular, Muslim men) as extremist and violent. These depictions also portray the image that Islam is irrational and oppressive towards women.[3] Whenever there are media accounts of South Asian (Muslim) women murdered in apparent 'honour killings', those accounts appear to support the proposition that Islam condones honour killings and honour-related violence (HRV). The issues surrounding the permissibility of violence, force and chastisement within a Muslim household prompted the authors to pose the following questions: Does Islam condone domestic violence? Do Islamic scriptures permit the use of violence upon women who, it is alleged, have transgressed religious injunctions? Such important questions, the authors feel, require addressing in the current political climate. There is some deliberation about whether there are instances where a Muslim husband is lawfully permitted to use physical force against his wife in the matrimonial home. In some Islamised texts there is evidence that some *Ulama* (Islamic scholars) believe that a husband is permitted to use force, referring to the Qur'an in relation to passages on the social interaction between husbands and wives. One of the most often cited verses in this context is verse 4:34 entitled *Surah An-Nisa*. In fact, this is the only Qur'anic verse that appears to deal with 'disciplining' Muslim women. Verse 4:34 in its English translation from Arabic, permits a form of marital 'discipline' by the husband[4] and is translated as follows:[5]

> Men are the protectors, guardians and maintainers of women, because Allah has made the one of them to excel the other, and because they spend (to support them) from their means. Therefore the righteous women are devoutly obedient (to Allah and their husbands), and guard in the husband's absence what Allah orders them to guard (e.g. their chastity, their husband's property etc). As to those women on whose part you see ill-conduct (i.e. disobedience, rebellion, *nashuz* in Arabic) admonish them (first), (next), refuse to share their beds, (and last) *beat them (lightly, if it is useful)*, but if they return to obedience, seek not against them means (of annoyance). Surely, Allah is Ever Most High, Most Great (emphasis added).

Abdel Haleem has translated verse 4:34 as follows:

> Husbands should take full care of their wives, with [the bounties] God has given to some more than others and with what they spend out of their own money. Righteous wives are devout and guard what God would have them guard in the husbands' absence. If you fear high-handedness from your wives, remind them [of the teaching of God], then ignore them when you go to bed, *then hit them.* If they obey you, you have no right to act against them. God is most High and Great (emphasis added).[6]

Abdullah Yusuf Ali has translated the relevant part of verse 4:34 as:

> … As to those women on whose part ye fear disloyalty and ill-conduct, admonish them (first), (next), refuse to share their beds, (and last) *beat them* (lightly) … (emphasis added).[7]

Finally, Ahmed Ali has translated verse 4:34 very differently from other authors above. His translation is:

> … As for women you feel are averse, talk to them cursively; then leave them alone in bed (without molesting them), and *go to bed with them* (when they are willing) (emphasis added).[8]

An explanation of verse 4:34 according to the various interpretations is necessary as all of the above-cited interpretations are potentially misleading. First, men, by their very physical nature, are enshrined with the task of providing material support to their wives. Women are not burdened with the duty of nursing or directly caring for children *and* supporting the family financially, therefore this injunction is prescribed to men. Second, the verse ordains women to be virtuous and to act obediently in relation to what Allah (*subhanahu wa t'ala*, hereafter s.w.t., translated into English as "may he be glorified") prescribes in the Qur'an. It requires Muslim women to guard their modesty, chastity and property while their husbands are, for example, at work. However, obedience is only required in relation to the dictates of Islam. There is a well-known Islamic maxim on this issue in that 'there is no obedience in creation in the disobedience in the Creator'.[9] Third, if a Muslim wife appears to have transgressed religious injunctions (on, for example, chastity), verse 4:34 ordains that the husband first admonish (i.e. talk, lecture, educate) the wife in order to reveal to her those transgressions in accordance with Prophetic injunctions. It is recommended by some Islamic scholars that the husband reason with his wife, bringing to her attention some of the relevant teachings from the Qur'an and the *Ahadith*. If that fails, and the Muslim wife fails to appreciate her actions, the second step is for the husband to separate from his wife (i.e. literally sleep in another bedroom or location, or on a more contextual interpretation, avoid having a sexual relationship with his wife until their dispute is resolved). This can include avoiding physical contact or conversation of any kind. This separation may help both parties to consider their actions. For the separation to work, the husband should have sufficient control over his own sexual desires, otherwise he may be driven to end the separation before it has any meaningful spiritual effect on their relationship. Importantly, if the wife returns to obedience, a duty is placed upon the husband not to constantly remind his wife of her failings if their marriage and relationship is to remain stable and successful.[10]

Further interpretation, however, is required of certain concepts used in verse 4:34. They are: 'disobedience', 'guarded' and, importantly in relation to the question of HRV that this book addresses, the controversial 'beat (lightly)'. In the context of domestic violence,[11] the use of physical force against Muslim women has created huge controversy surrounding the role and safety of women in Muslim societies, which apply verse 4:34 as a method to control and dominate women.

What is meant by 'disobedience'?

When discussing the word 'disobedience' or *nashuz* in Arabic some Muslim commentators have clearly outlined its meaning and application relating to the thirty-fourth verse.[12] A famous Baghdadi theologian named 'Ala ad-Din 'Ali once wrote: 'The disobedience of a woman relates to (1) her becoming abhorrent towards her husband; (2) when she absolves herself from her responsibility/obedience towards him; and (3) when she displays extreme arrogance against him.'[13] An exegesis of verse 4:34 therefore appears to demonstrate a level of control and/or minimises the autonomy of Muslim women because the injunctions contained within that verse imply that the movements of women appear to be in the control of men. However, it is imperative to understand that this level of 'control' or 'authority' bestowed upon a Muslim husband should not be likened to that of an unjust dictator or ruler. The relationship between a husband and wife in Islam should demonstrate a great level of intimacy, love and affection which must characterise that relationship, as translated in the following verse in the Qur'an by Taqi-ud-Din Al-Hilali and Muhsin Khan (2007):

> (30:21) And among His Signs is this, that He created for you wives from among yourselves, that you may find repose in them, and He has put between you affection and mercy. Verily, in that are indeed signs for a people who reflect.

Love and affection within a Muslim marriage should therefore be replicated in the way that a husband performs his authority in relation to any Islamic injunction. In particular, a husband should always take into account the feelings of his wife; he should instil love and confidence in his wife and make clear that the only reason he exercises any authority rendered permissible in the Qur'an is to seek the pleasure of Allah (s.w.t.) and purify their relationship as one that adheres to the teachings of Islam, something that both parties voluntarily entered into at the time of marriage. It is incumbent upon a Muslim husband to take account of the views of those in his charge, including his wife, and this is all the more necessary in the context of Muslim marriages. The word 'obedience' referred to in verse 4:34 should not be construed as 'forced obedience'. It should be 'natural obedience' out of love and affection for a husband. If this cannot be achieved then Allah (s.w.t.) has stated in the following verse 4:35 that both parties should appoint judges, one from each of their own families, to help resolve any marital difficulties. If both parties are still in disagreement, some Islamic scholars are of the opinion that the best course of action should be that of divorce; in no way does a wife's non-compliance in any matter give licence to a Muslim husband to cause her any physical harm. 'Obedience' is necessary only in those matters which Islamic law has allowed for a husband. It is *not* something that a husband can enforce from his own whims or desires. 'Obedience' in personal matters is required only if it concerns a reasonable request on the part of a husband; it is *halal* (i.e. lawful in Islam); and does not violate any of the rights of one's wife. Therefore, if a husband commands a wife to act contrary to the teachings of the Qur'an and *Sunnah*, the wife has full rights to rebel against his wishes. As will be explained in more detail below, according to the Qur'an and the *Ahadith*, a woman's defiance should never provide a husband with *any* justification to retaliate violently. The term *nashuz* is also further explored within the next section.

What is meant by being 'guarded'?

In Islamic terms, 'guarding' may be understood as meaning guarding the husband's 'honour' and property, as well as protecting a woman's own loyalty and 'honour'. In return for his affection and material support, Muslim and non-Muslim wives are expected to love their husbands, remain loyal and look after their husband's interests – a natural relationship between a husband and a wife in any religion.[14] While many Muslim marriages demonstrate successful compromise between husbands and wives, in some cases compromise within the relationship sometimes proves difficult. When some Muslim women appear to transgress certain boundaries, some Muslim men react by 'punishing' their wives for their rebellion. Unfortunately, patriarchal communities not fully conversant with Qur'anic injunctions concerning the relationship between a husband and wife often omit to disclose that the term *nashuz* is something that can be committed by a *husband* as well as a wife.[15] For example, verse 4:128 states:

And if a woman fears cruelty, desertion or rebellion (*nashuz* in Arabic) on her husband's part, there is no sin on them both if they make terms of peace between themselves [i.e. divorce lawfully and peacefully]; and making peace is better. And human inner-selves are swayed by greed. But if you do good and keep away from evil, verily, Allah is Ever Well-Acquainted with what you do.

This suggests that it is permissible for a Muslim wife to divorce a Muslim husband on account of his cruelty, violence and *nashuz*. In both verses 4:34 and 4:128, reference to *nashuz* or rebellion relates to both men and women in the context of marriages. This would then suggest that *nashuz* means the type of behaviour on the part of a husband or wife that is so detrimental to the marriage that the husband and the wife's residing together becomes difficult or impossible, and it is the only occasion when any of the advice contained within verses 4:34 and 4:128 may be followed. Imam Abu Mansur al-Lughawi has confirmed this when he explained that *nashuz* is abhorrent behaviour or ill-will from one of the spouses to the other.[16] Within the context of both verses 4:34 and 4:128, husbands can be equally considered rebellious, not just wives. A wife must demonstrate *true* and *real* signs of 'rebellion' against her husband in order for the guidance in verse 4:34 to apply. If the wife does not demonstrate true rebellion, the recommended guidance is inapplicable. What is also clear is that the injunction requires husbands to act as the 'maintainers' and 'guardians' of their wives. If those responsibilities are not met by the husband, the verse does not apply, and the husband must not enact any of the guidance recommended within that verse. This means the husband is not in an Islamic position to admonish his wife or sleep in separate beds, let alone chastise his wife, as he has failed in *his* duties expected of him in the Qur'an. However, what is witnessed today is the unfair application of these verses in a context where Muslim men abuse their positions of responsibility and supposed Qur'anic authority, when women have neither acted rebelliously, nor acted in a manner that justifies any of the recommended actions stated in verse 4:34. Muslim men who beat their spouses culturally manipulate these verses to control their wives in a manner that oppresses them, not intended by those Islamic verses. In the context of today's social world and in the light of progressive human values, liberties and human rights, this erroneous and biased interpretation is a gross misapplication of the Qur'anic verses, even when viewed in its classical exegesis context.

What is meant by 'beat them (lightly)?'

Perhaps the most controversial aspect of verse 4:34 relates to the physical chastisement of a woman if she is 'disobedient' or 'rebellious'. If admonishment and separation fail to have any effect in the dispute between husband

and wife, according to verse 4:34, Muslim husbands are permitted to undertake what is known in Arabic as *Idribuhunna*, which in English can be translated (or qualified by the majority of Islamic scholars) as the use of 'light force', in order to chastise a woman.[17] The equivalent in English to the use of 'light force' may be summarised as a 'gentle smack', similar to what a parent might use to warn a child that persistently goes towards an open fire. There are, however, a number of interpretations of the word *Idribuhunna*, and it is often within these interpretations that misunderstandings arise.[18] This is because these interpretations appear to permit violence upon Muslim women, which the authors are very uncomfortable with.

The word *Idribu* is generally translated by Islamic scholars to mean to 'strike', 'hit', 'chastise', or 'beat'. It has also been translated by Ahmed Ali to mean 'to forsake, to avoid, or to leave.'[19] As far as the English language is concerned, the above words are different and have different shades of emphasis, all of which appear negative in the context of women. How does one therefore define the word *Idribu* when the word is understood to have several meanings? It is important to note that linguistics is a central science in Qur'anic hermeneutics. Allah (s.w.t.) revealed the Qur'an in the clear Arabic tongue over 1,400 years ago, and the *Ulama* have emphasised the importance of understanding words in their context. It is important to understand the challenges faced in Arabic linguistics and the various shades of meaning that an Arabic word possesses, not only during the time of the Prophet Muhammad (p.b.u.h.), but also in a particular context. Arabic linguistics is thus very different to English linguistics and is more complex to construct.

It is common understanding that the terms hit/strike/beat in English denote the impression of a physical act taking place, undertaken by an individual intending to cause harm to another. It is this aspect that is of most concern to the authors, women's rights organisations and feminist groups. It would appear that the verse permits the infliction of force against women, something that can be manipulated and used to strike fear and intimidation into women, confirming a barbaric and violent view of Islam. However, one needs to first examine carefully the individual elements of verse 4:34: admonishment; separation; and then hit/strike/beat, as the translations provide. If one visualises these elements, the conduct used by the male gradually becomes stronger. The first involves admonishment: the verbal action of lecturing. The second element involves the physical act of separation, which can be considered as more than 'merely talking to', which the first element prescribes (alternatively, it could be viewed as an omission – omitting to share the same bed or home as the wife, albeit temporarily). The third element is, likewise, more powerful in its impact than the second element. It is accepted that under its traditional and classical interpretation, the third element means where there is a conflict between husband and wife a husband could chastise his wife, but only as a last resort.[20] However, another interpretation of the verse could mean: (a) the raising of the hand does not cause *any* physical harm to the wife (i.e. akin to the smacking of a child); or more preferably (b) it does not have to involve *any physical action at all*. The term could be interpreted through various meanings (referring to note 18), and it could therefore be interpreted as symbolically meaning 'striking out', 'showing one's displeasure', 'condemning' or to 'display one's serious concern' at a transgression or rebellious action. The authors, as do some others, prefer this latter interpretation: that the application of verse 4:34 does not involve any form of physical action,[21] although the authors do accept that the verse is generally understood by Islamic scholars to involve physical action. The first two elements of verse 4:34 (i.e. admonishment, separation) incorporate calm and peaceful resolutions to a marital dispute and which *must* be undertaken first. If these two options fail, only then is it permissible to 'condemn' and 'show one's displeasure', but in a manner that does not permit the infliction of force since the first two options themselves employ peaceful means. This may be the opinion of the classical jurist Imam Shafi'I (see Asad, 1980) who stated: 'Striking (gently) is lawful [according to the Qur'an], however it is better not to hit a woman at all.'[22] Unfortunately, this alternative interpretation is often overlooked. Muslim women have basic human rights that the authors acknowledge, and these rights are also secured by Islamic law, including the right to life, bodily integrity and security.

It is accepted by the authors that the translation of the word to 'beat (lightly)' conjures images of acts of violence and aggression against women. It is also the accepted opinion of many scholars of language that to 'beat (lightly)' or *Darb Shadid* has been interpreted to mean a comprehensive 'series of hits'.[23] Ahmed Ali has stated that the word *Daraba* means 'and go to bed with them (if they are willing, i.e. to have sexual intercourse with them, which contextually involves a 'series of hits') instead of the more accepted interpretation to 'beat (lightly)'.[24] However, Ali's translation is confused by appearing to supply a false addition to the parenthesis of the verse '(if they are willing)'. The confusion breaks the sequence and internal logic of the thirty-fourth verse, namely admonishment, separation from sex, to 'beat (lightly)'. In Ali's sequence, a husband goes from admonishment, to separating himself from his wife in the one instance, to having a sexual relationship (without remorse) in the other. This eccentric translation also serves as the background to many other misinterpretations, including leading some Muslim men to believe that they can request sex from their wives and that their wives must comply with this request; this request, in modern times, may be equated to marital rape if forced upon a Muslim woman without her consent. In relation to verse 4:34, a sexual relationship should only occur after the successful three-step process: *admonition*, *separation* (i.e. no sex) and then *striking out* (i.e. displaying one's condemnation) and a wife's subsequent remorse. Many of the translators cited above therefore disagree with Ali, whose translation appears to mix up the order.

While the Qur'an renders such light chastisement lawful, even the classic scholars of Islam recommend that one should refrain from acting upon the verse because it could lead to other undesirable consequences. Imam Fakhr Razi has commented that Muslim men should: 'Know that those who strike are not better than those who refrain.'[25] Although the third limb of verse 4:34 and 'striking' is viewed as a last resort, the authors are firmly of the opinion that it should be completely abandoned in favour of the first two limbs of the same verse (i.e. admonition or separation), as well as other steps involving relatives of the husband and wife mentioned in verse 4:35:

> If you fear a breach between them twain (the man and his wife), appoint (two) arbitrators, one from his family and the other from hers; if they both wish for peace, Allah will cause their reconciliation. Indeed, Allah is Ever All-Knowing, Well-Acquainted with all things.

There is no authority in the Qur'an for the type of regular and frequent acts of violence that some Muslim women experience within their homes at the hands of abusive husbands. The actions of many Muslim husbands are also contradictory. Such men do not exercise the level of control that is expected of them, as demonstrated in verse 4:34. The first element, it will be recalled, is admonishment; the second is separation. This not only involves physical separation, it also means abstaining from marital sex. Yet, in their injustice and oppression, Muslim husbands fail to exercise control over their own sexual desires, which is required in order to remain separate. Instead, some Muslim husbands sleep with their wives (violating the second element in verse 4:34) but then exact violence upon their wives. This type of conduct has been specifically condemned by the Prophet Muhammad (p.b.u.h.) when he said: 'How loathsome (*Ajeeb*) it is that one of you should hit his wife as a slave is hit, and then sleep with her at the end of the day.'[26] Ibn Kathir, a highly respected classical Islamic commentator, refers to another passage from another *Hadith* editor, named Muslim. It is reported that the Prophet Muhammad (p.b.u.h.) said at his farewell Hajj pilgrimage:

> Fear Allah regarding women, for they are your assistants. You have the right on them that they do not allow any person whom you dislike to step on your mat.[27] However, if they do that, you are allowed to *discipline them lightly* ... (emphasis added).[28]

Note that the word here has been translated as 'discipline'. The Prophet Muhammad (p.b.u.h.) himself strongly disliked and condemned any form of violence. While it is correct that the Qur'an in its classical exegesis mentions 'gently' chastising the wife, Islamic scholars are of the opinion that one cannot go beyond the 'gentle' nature that the chastisement should adopt. It is important to understand that any chastisement must be done within the limits defined by the Qur'an. According to some traditions, the Prophet Muhammad (p.b.u.h.) once said in his famous speech that 'striking' should be interpreted as *Ghayr Mubarrih*, which means done in such a way that should not cause injury or bruising:

> Lo! My last recommendation to you is that you should treat women well. Truly they are your help-mates, and you have no right over them beyond that – except if they commit a manifest indecency (e.g. adultery). If they do, then refuse to share their beds and *hit them* (as a last resort and only if benefit can be derived from it) without indecent violence (*fadribu hunna darban ghayra mubarrih*). Then, if they obey you, do not show them hostility any longer. Lo! You have a right over your women and they have a right over you. Your right over your women is that they not allow whom you hate to enter your bed, nor your house. While their right over you is that you treat them *excellently* in their garb and provision (emphasis added).[29]

On this basis, Islamic scholars such as Tabari and Fakhr Razi mention that the 'striking' should be extremely 'minimal' and should be administered according to what some Islamic jurists describe 'with a folded scarf'[30] or tapping 'with a miswak'[31] (i.e. in a modern day context, tapping with a toothbrush).[32] However, at the same time the discipline should be effective in its purpose. According to Islamic scholars, it is crucial that any discipline should be a means for the energetic demonstration of the concern, frustration and love that a husband has for his wife.[33] Therefore, any discipline should neither hurt the wife, nor become a meaningless motion devoid of any emotion or significance. Specifically, on the treatment of one's wife, the Prophet Muhammad (p.b.u.h.) was asked about the obligations of a husband, to which he replied: 'Feed her when you eat, and provide her clothing when you provide yourself. Neither hit her on the face, nor use impolite language when addressing her.'[34]

It is an accepted opinion of many scholars of Islam that verse 4:34 was actually revealed after a woman herself complained to the Prophet Muhammad (p.b.u.h.) that her husband had slapped her on the face,[35] and her cheek was still marked by the slap.[36] At first, the Prophet Muhammad (p.b.u.h.) informed the woman to 'Get even with him' as a form of retaliation,[37] however, upon reflection, he said: 'Wait until I think about it.' At that time, Allah revealed verse 4:34 of the fourth Qur'anic chapter as guidance for Muslims and humanity (i.e. that a husband should first talk to his wife, or separate, and not hit her), after which the Prophet explained: 'We wanted one thing, but Allah wanted another, and what Allah wanted is best.'[38] The wisdom mentioned by the *Ulama* on this point is that if the wife were to retaliate in kind, the dispute may escalate into a fight which may entail one or both parties suffering serious physical injury.

From a Muslim woman's perspective, in Islam the wife has no religious obligation to endure any form of violence from her husband, and it is permissible for her to seek a divorce on account of her husband's domestic abuse. And in Islamic jurisdictions, if a husband exacts violence upon his wife, she is permitted to take her complaint to an Islamic court for its determination.[39] The final commandment of verse 4:34 also makes reference to the fundamental Islamic belief that ' ... Allah is Ever Most High, Most Great.' This statement serves as a reminder to the husband and wife that it is Allah (s.w.t.) in whose name they were enjoined in holy matrimony. The end verse serves as a reminder that the husband should not take advantage of his position nor exceed justified limits. Allah (s.w.t.) further warns husbands and men in general that if they choose to keep hold of their wives in marriage, it should not be done to gain anything (i.e. control, authority) over them. Allah (s.w.t.) has stated in the Qur'an:

> (2:231) And when you have divorced women and they have fulfilled the term of their prescribed period, either take them back on reasonable basis or set them free on reasonable basis. *But do not take them back to hurt them, and whoever does that, then he has wronged himself.* And treat not the Verses [i.e. Laws] of Allah as a jest, but remember Allah's Favours on you [i.e. Islam], and that which He has sent down to you of the Book [i.e. the Qur'an] and *Al-Hikmah* [i.e. the Prophet's *Sunnah*, legal ways, Islamic jurisprudence etc] whereby He instructs you. And fear Allah, and know that Allah is All-Aware of everything (emphasis added).

Domestic violence occurs in many societies both in the East and the West, and Muslim societies are no exception. While the (classical) Qur'anic view of verse 4:34 appears to allow a 'gentle' form of chastisement on Muslim women, the authors are of the opinion that Muslim men should refrain from physically disciplining their wives, though this may be seen to be lawful in verse 4:34 of the Qur'an. This is also the position of Ibn Ashur, a Maliki Tafsir Scholar. It involves Sadd ad-Dhara'i's principle of 'blocking the means to harm'. This secondary legal principle of interpretation necessitates the prohibition of something permissible if it would inevitably lead to something else impermissible. Thus, while 'striking (lightly)' is permissible according to verse 4:34 of the Qur'an, Islamic scholars discourage its use because of the inability of man to obey its strict requirements. The Prophet Muhammad (p.b.u.h.) has stated that Muslim men are obliged to treat their wives with the greatest respect and courtesy and that this is linked to *Imaan* (faith in religion). The Prophet has also compared the perfect 'believer' to the one who treats his wife the best:

The most perfect believer is one who is the best in courtesy and amiable manners, and the best among you people is one who is most kind and courteous to his wife … the best among you is the one who treats his family best.[40]

While verse 4:34 is a commandment from Allah (s.w.t.), the Prophet was authentically reported to have never hit any of his wives at all, nor anyone else, save in the heat of battle. He never resorted to domestic violence and treated his wives with the greatest respect. Prophet Muhammad (p.b.u.h.) is reported to have said:

'Do not beat the female servants of Allah.' He further stated: 'Some (women) visited my family complaining about their husbands (beating them). These (husbands) are not the best of you.' He re-emphasised this position by stating: '[Is it not a shame that] one of you beats his wife like [an unscrupulous person] beats a slave and maybe he sleeps with her at the end of the day.'[41]

In another *Hadith* the Prophet Muhammad (p.b.u.h.) is reported to have said:

How does any one of you beat his wife as he beats the stallion camel and then he may embrace (sleep with) her?[42]

Domestic violence thus contradicts the *Ahadith* of the Prophet who repeatedly advised the believers 'not to beat women'. Physical assaults also contradict the Prophet Muhammad's (p.b.u.h.) instructions in relation to controlling one's anger, which is a central component of the inner (spiritual) duties of a believer. The Prophet Muhammad (p.b.u.h.) is reported to have explained that anger originates from Satan, describing it as 'a living coal in one's heart'. Islamic law expects believers never to act upon anger as this can lead to other forms of sinning. Muslims are also expected to follow the *Sunnah* of the Prophet Muhammad (p.b.u.h.) if they wish to be considered as true believers of the faith. Spiritually, the best of the believers is one who treats a woman the best. In this respect any devout Muslim man who wishes to follow the *Sunnah* of the Prophet should not exact *any* physical force upon his wife, whatever the transgression and however one may wish to qualify it.

Conclusion

What we have presented in this chapter is a summary of the main issues involved when examining domestic violence in Muslim households and the apparent justification for the infliction of force upon a wife for acting rebelliously, based on an exegesis of verse 4:34. It is clear that when one examines verse 4:34, for some Muslims it seemingly permits as lawful the 'gentle' chastisement of a woman by the husband. However, the reality is that the Qur'an and the *Sunnah*, rather than permitting violence against women, actually condemns it. Verse 4:34 of the Qur'an is a verse that is often cited to show the apparent legality and justification in using force against women, but the verse is largely misunderstood and misconstrued. Therefore, because of the lack of understanding of the applicable verses, Islamic scholars (both past and present) have recommended that those who wish to apply verse 4:34 within the context of their own marriages tread carefully for fear that they may violate the injunctions contained therein. In today's climate and view on human rights the authors recommend (like the *Fuqaha*) that Muslim husbands do not utilise the third limb of the verse. Muslim husbands should not inflict *any* form of violence upon women for fear of transgressing the bounds set by Allah (s.w.t.). We strongly recommend that Muslims undertake either of the first two elements of verse 4:34 in the context of any marital dispute – to communicate with their wives or seek a temporary separation, or even seek a peaceful divorce (verse 4:128) in order to demonstrate mutual respect and to earn the pleasure of Allah (s.w.t.) in a way that does not injure the feelings of either party, nor violate any other Islamic injunctions.

Certainly, there is no Islamic injunction permitting the use of violence or killing in the name of 'honour' in the matrimonial home. The preoccupation with the wording and interpretation of the Qur'an, which one too often finds, is methodologically unsound and in defiance of the Qur'an itself, where Allah (s.w.t.) has given his own warning that 'by this Book many will be misguided', and the definitively established *Hadith* that 'Whoever interprets the Qur'an according to their own desires [i.e. without the objective hermeneutical approach of the Muslim *Fuqaha*], let them prepare their abode in the Hellfire.' The question of whether domestic violence is permissible in Islam is actually a question of *Fiqh* (i.e. a question for Islamic jurists to rule upon, drawing all of the available tools together, such as the Qur'an and *Sunnah*), as opposed to a *Tafsir* of the Qur'an (i.e. solely a commentary of the Qur'an). Muslims understand Qur'anic verses through the methodology of the *Fuqaha* from the Companions of the Prophet onwards. Muslims throughout Islamic history have not (and should not) take legal rulings directly from the Qur'an because of the dangers of misinterpretation. Perhaps asking the question 'Does the Qur'an Condone Domestic Violence?' is actually inappropriate because the Qur'an itself does not directly provide the answer. While Islamic law is derived from the principles of the Qur'an and the *Ahadith*, not all its details are found there. The details of Islamic legal thought are found in the jurisprudence and literature of the *Fuqaha* and not always directly from the Qur'an. The primary problem that Muslims face in this issue (like many others, for example, suicide bombing) is that they bypass the sound methodology of the *Fuqaha* and attempt to interpret the sacred texts according to their own deficient understandings in highly charged politicised contexts. Muslims can only (and should only) understand the concise, terse and sometimes abrupt terminology utilised in the Qur'an by using only the most sophisticated hermeneutical and linguistic analysis known in history. This exercise is not always undertaken and verse 4:34 provides but one example of the misinterpretations that exist in the Islamic world.

In many senses this chapter has proved extremely difficult for the authors to conceptualise. The authors acknowledge that a classical exegesis of verse 4:34 does appear to permit physical chastisement of women and that this also appears to be the consensus of Islamic scholars generally. However, the authors wish to make it clear that they do not wish to legitimise *any* form of violence towards women, however light (even with a 'toothbrush'). What we have presented here is traditional Qur'anic verses and *Ahadith* of the Prophet Muhammad (p.b.u.h.) on marital discipline, together with the opinions of jurists commenting on the interpretation of the legal verses. The authors wish to make clear their interpretation of verse 4:34 whilst distancing themselves from the interpretations of others. There appears to be an almost absolutist acceptance that the interpretations of verse 4:34 are real enough as this is how the issue is generally viewed by Islamic scholars. There are those, however, who clearly do not recommend acting upon the third limb of the verse. In terms of reading Qur'anic hermeneutics, while the Qur'an is seen as timeless, it is also important for Muslims to view the Qur'an in its current context. The Qur'an was revealed in seventh-century Arabia, and over 1,400 years later the world has moved on. Arguably, there are some aspects of Qu'ranic interpretation that have not. The authors believe that the word of Allah (s.w.t.) as revealed was sent down for humanity to follow but within the context of the Arabian people it was first revealed to. In the last hundred years, the rights of women have developed to the extent that no woman should ever suffer violence at the hands of men. Any form of violence towards women is harmful, even though some Islamic scholars believe that 'gentle' chastisement is permissible. As modern Islamic thinkers, the authors feel and believe it is inappropriate to tolerate such an approach in modern societies. This is also true in terms of piety and *Taqwa* which is why Islamic scholars such as Imam Shafi'I and Imam Fakr Razi have strongly recommended never to strike a woman: *a man who refrains from violence is better than a man who engages in such conduct.*

Notes

1 There is a wealth of literature on this subject, including: Abou El Fadl (2007, 2004); Bonner (2006); Cragg (2005); Esposito (2002); Hoffman (2006); Kepel (2009); Lawrence (2000); and Nelson-Pallmeyer (2003), to name but a few.
2 See, for example, Taqi-ud-Din Al-Hilali and Muhsin Khan (2007); Abdel Haleem (2008); and A.Y. Ali (1987); cf. A. Ali (1984, rev. 1986).

3 See, for example, the various newspaper articles cited in Chapter 6 (by Dr Anna Carline) and Chapter 13 (by Dr Suruchi Thapar-Björkert) in this collection. See also Abou El-Fadl (2001); Anton (2005); Roald (2001); and Wadud (1999).
4 The Islamic commentaries on this issue explain that the verse is for '*ta'dib*' – meaning to 'discipline' the wife. All forms of discipline under Islamic law operate on the principle of deterrence, not of causing pain or exacting retribution.
5 Whenever a verse of the Qur'an is cited in this chapter the English translation will generally be taken from Taqi-ud-Din Al-Hilali and Muhsin Khan (2007), unless otherwise stated.
6 Abdel Haleem (2008) on verse 4:34.
7 A.Y. Ali (1987) on verse 4:34. He implies the sequence of steps and the implied 'soft' meaning of 'beat them (lightly)'.
8 A. Ali (1984, rev. 1986). Ahmed Ali is an author of fiction.
9 Al-Bukhari (1987).
10 As will be discussed shortly, there are also rules in the Qur'an for a wife to deal with a 'disobedient' (*nashuz*) husband.
11 It should be noted that both the Qur'an and Islamic law in general *forbid* domestic violence. However, it seems clear that Islamic law does permit some form of 'symbolic' physical disciplining in very specific situations, within the context of teaching manners and etiquette (*Adab* in Arabic), though it is largely discouraged. The problem within the current debate is the use of emotive words: 'physical violence' as opposed to 'light discipline'. By using the former instead of the latter, one could be judged as misinterpreting the real meaning of verse 4:34 in the Qur'an.
12 It is useful to note that 'disobedience' is not a direct translation of the word *nashuz*, and is therefore probably unhelpful. There is a slight emphasis differential between husbands and wives, and when either transgresses on the rights of the other the Arabic word is '*nashuz*'. However, it is probably best translated as an 'oppressive' (*nashuz*) husband and a 'rebellious' (*nashuz*) wife. Therefore, the word and concept is neither female specific, nor is it limited to women alone.
13 'Ala ad-Din 'Ali (1995, 1: 370).
14 This is not specific to Muslim wives either. Islam permits a Muslim man to marry a Jewish or Christian woman without her having to convert/revert to Islam.
15 For example, many forget that the classical scholar Imam Malik has (by analogy in relation to verse 4:34) extended similar penalties to a husband who *mistreats* his wife. According to Imam Malik, if a husband acts in a 'disobedient' manner, he must first be admonished; after which if he persists, he is to continue paying the wife her maintenance (*Nafaqa*) but she is not required to obey him; finally, he himself may be subjected to physical punishment through the Islamic court system. See Abu Zahra (1997).
16 See Al-Qurtubi (2002, 3:119).
17 For example, many Islamic scholars have translated verse 4:34 and the third limb: 'beat' (Fakhry 2004); 'scourge' (Pickthall 1953); 'beat' (Dawood 1995); 'beat (lightly)' (Taqi-ud-Din Al-Hilali and Muhsin Khan 2007); 'chastise' (Bukhari 1987); 'beat' (Committee of Muslim Translators 2000); and 'beat' (Asad 1980).
18 The word *Idribuhunna* is also used numerous times in the Qur'an in a variety of contexts and sometimes with completely different meanings: see, for example: *To travel, or to get out*: 3:156; 4:101; 38:44; 73:20; 2:273; *To strike*: 2:60,73; 7:160; 8:12; 20:77; 24:31; 26:63; 37:93; 47:4; *To beat*: 8:50; 47:27; *To set up*: 43:58; 57:13; *To give (examples)*: 14:24,45; 16:75,76,112; 18:32,45; 24:35; 30:28,58; 36:78; 9:27,29; 43:17; 59:21; 66:10,11; *To take away, to ignore*: 43:5; *To condemn*: 2:61; *To seal, to draw over*: 18:11; *To cover*: 24:31; and *To explain*: 13:17. See also Pickthall (1953).

19 A. Ali (1984, rev. 1986).
20 However, commenting on the word '*Idribuhunna*,' Imam Sulayman Ibn Umar (famously known as al-Jamal) once stated that the word should be interpreted as: 'Such a strike that breaks not a bone, nor disfigures a limb meaning a strike that is not strong or violent (*Gair Shadid*).' See Al-Jamal (2003, 2: 51), Sulayman Ibn 'Umar ash-Shafi'i.
21 The Famous Malikite Judge Qadi Abu Bakr Ibn al-'Arabi has mentioned in his *Tafsir* that Ata al-Khurasani once said: 'One should not strike her [i.e. his wife], even if he commands her or prohibits her and she refuses, however he should display his anger or displeasure (through means other than striking).' Qadi Abu Bakr then comments: 'This is from the legal opinion of Ata and is from his understanding of the *Shariah* ... it should be known that an act of striking (or hitting) is merely legally permissible; however, it may actually be regarded as being detested via another route – that being the saying of the Prophet Muhammad: "Indeed, I detest for a man that he beat his slave girl when he becomes angry ... "': Abu Bakr Ibn al-'Arabi (2000).
22 The basic rule is strict prohibition, followed by dispensation (*Rukhsa*), in that hitting is generally prohibited, but is legally permitted in cases of *nashuz* as outlined in verse 4:34.
23 Abu Bakr Ibn al-'Arabi (2000).
24 A. Ali (1984, rev. 1986).
25 *Mafatih al-Ghayb* (5:94), Fakhr ad-Din (2002).
26 Narrated from 'Abd Allah ibn Zum'a by Ibn Abi Shayba in his *Musannaf*, Bukhari in his *Sahih* and Muslim in his *Sahih*, as well as others.
27 For a woman to allow a strange man into her private quarters is *khalwa*. This is a euphemism for adulterous behaviour (i.e. wives should not commit adultery). If committed, light discipline is permissible according to Islamic law.
28 Kathir (2000).
29 Narrated from 'Amr ibn al-Ahwas by Imam Nasai in his *Sunan* as mentioned by As-Suyuti (1993, 5:523).
30 *Mafatih al-Ghayb* (5:94), Fakhr ad-Din (2002).
31 Ibn Jarir narrated from 'Ata that he said to Ibn Abbas: 'What is meant by strike without indecent violence?' He replied: 'With a *Miswak* (toothbrush or tooth-stick) or that which is like it.' See As-Suyuti (1993, 5:523).
32 The force utilised by a 'folded scarf' or a 'miswak' is, therefore, purely symbolic. However, it remains unclear whether a woman is herself allowed to 'strike' her husband with a 'folded scarf' or 'miswak' on account of his oppressive and/or adulterous behaviour.
33 Badawi (1995).
34 Narrated by Ahmad in his *Musnad* (4:447) Musnad Imam Ahmad bin Muhammad bin Hanbal – Subject Codified into Chapters (Tabweeb) – Vol. 3 (Arabic Only) (Arabic Edition) (2005) Noor Foundation International, Inc.
35 See Kathir (2000, 1:445), Abu al-Fida Ibn Kathir ad-Dimishqi.
36 See Al-Wahidi (2008), *Asbab al-Nuzul* (4:34).
37 Ibid.
38 See Ibn Kathir (2000, 1:445), Abu al-Fida Ibn Kathir ad-Dimishqi.
39 See n.15.
40 Narrated from 'Aisha, by At-Tirmidhi (1971) is his *Jami* (Chapter on the Obligations of a Man to his Wife).
41 Nawawi and Muhammad Ibn Salih al-Uthaymeen (1998: 137–40).
42 Al-Bukhari (1987, Vol. 8, Hadith No. 68: 42–43).

Bibliography

Abou El Fadl, K. (2001) *Speaking in God's Name: Islamic Law, Authority and Women*, Oxford: OneWorld Press.

——(2007) *The Great Theft: Wrestling Islam from the Extremists*, San Francisco: Harper.

Abou El Fadl, K. et al. (2004) *Islam and the Challenge of Democracy: A Boston Review Book*, Boston: Princeton University Press.

Abdel Haleem, M. A. S. (2008) *The Qur'an (Oxford World's Classics)*, Oxford: Oxford University Press, Re-issue Edition.

Abu Bakr Ibn at 'Arabi, M. (2000) Ahkam al-Quran, Beirut, Lebanon: Dar al-Qutub al-'Ilmiyya.

Abu Hayyan, M. (1993) Tafsir Bahr al-Muhit, Beirut, Lebanon: Dar al-Qutub al-'Ilmiyya.

Abu Dawud, S. (1996) *Sunan*, Beirut, Lebanon: Dar al-Kutub al-'Ilmiyya.

Abu as-Sa'ud, M. (1961), Sharia: Tafsir Abi as-Saud, Riyadh, Saudi Arabic: Maktaba ar-Riyadh al-Hadithiyya, n.d.

Abu Zahra, A. A-R, (1997) Usul al-Fiqh Cairo, Egypt: Dar al-Fikr al-'Arabi, n.d.

Al-Bukhari, M. (1987) *Sahih*, Beirut, Lebanon: Dar Ibn Kathir.

Al-Jamal, S. (2003) Al-Futuhat al-Ilahiyya, Beirut, Lebanon: Dar a-Fikr.

Al-Mahmoud, I. (1990) *How to be Kind to Your Parents*, Al-Firdaus Ltd.

Al-Qurtubi, M. (2002) Al-Jami' li Ahkam al-Quran, Beirut, Lebanon: Dar a-Fikr.

Al-Wahidi, M. (2008) Asbab al-Nuzul Translated by Mokrane Guezzou, US: Fons Vitae.

Ali, A. (1984, rev. 1986) *Al-Qur'an: A Contemporary Translation*, Princeton University Press.

'Ali, A. A-D. (1995) Tafsir al-Hazin, Beirut, Lebanon: Dar al-Qutub al-'Ilmiyya.

Ali, A.Y. (1987) *The Qur'an: Text, Translation & Commentary* (English and Arabic Edition), Tahrike Tarsile Qur'an, 1 January.

Ali as-Sayis, M., As-Subki, A.L. and Ibrahim Kursun, M. (2002) Tafsir Ayat al-Ahkam, Damascus, Syria: Dar Ibn Kathir.

Alkhateeb, M. and Abugideiri, S. (eds) (2007) *Change from Within: Diverse Perspectives on Domestic Violence in Muslim Communities*, Great Falls, VA: Peaceful Families Project.

An-Nasai, A. (1986) *Sunan*, Beirut, Lebanon: Muassasat ar-Risala.

Anton, J. (ed.) (2005) *Walking Together: Working with Women from Diverse Religious and Spiritual Traditions*, Seattle, WA: FaithTrust Institute.

Asad, M. (1980) *The Message of the Quran*, Dar al-Andalus, Gilbralter.

As-Suyuti, A. R. (1993) Ad-Durr al-Mathur, Beirut, Lebanon: Dar a-Fikr.

As-Sawi, A. (2003) Hashiya al-Sawi 'ala Tafsir al-Jalalayn, Beirut, Lebanon: Dar al-Fikr.

At-Tirmidhi, M. (1971) *Sunan*, Beirut, Lebanon: Dar Ihya al-Turath al-'Arabiy, n.d.

Badawi, J. (1995) *Gender Equity in Islam: Basic Principles*, American Trust Publications.

Bonner, M. (2006), Jihad in Islamic History: Doctrines and Practice, Princeton: Princeton University Press.

Bukhari, M. (1987) Sahih Bukhari, India, New Dehli: Kitab Bhavan, translated by Khan, M.

Committee of Muslim Translators (2000) Tafsir of Ibn Kathir, London: Al-Firdous Ltd.

Cragg, K. (2005) Faith at Suicide: Lives Forfeit: Violent Religion – Human Despair, Sussex Academic Press.

Dashti, A. (1994) *23 Years: A Study in the Prophetic Career of Mohammad*, Costa Mesa, CA: Mazda.

Dawood, N. J. (1995) *The Koran*, London: Penguin.

Doi, AR. (1984) *Sharia: The Islamic Law*, London: Taha Publishers.

Esposito, J.L. (2002) *Unholy War: Terror in the Name of Islam*, New York: Oxford University Press.

Fakhr ad-Din, M. (2002) At-Tafsir al-Kabir, Beirut, Lebanon: Dar a-Fikr.

Fakhry, M. (2004) *An Interpretation of the Qur'an: English Translation of the Meanings*, New York: New York University Press.

Guillaume, A. (1955) *The Life of Muhammad*, Oxford: Oxford University Press.

Haqqi, I. (2001) Tafsir Ruh al-Bayan, Beirut, Lebanon: Dar Ahya at-Turath al-'Arabi.

Hatimy, S. (1991) *Women in Islam*, Lahore, Pakistan: Islamic Publications.

Hoffman, J. R. (ed.) (2006) *The Just War and Jihad: Violence in Judaism, Christianity, and Islam*, Amherst, New York: Prometheus Books.

Ibn al-Hajjaj, M. (1954) *Sahih*, Beirut, Lebanon: Dar Ihya al-Turath al-'Arabiy.

Ibn Mundhir, M. (2002) Kitab at-Tafsir al-Quran, Madina, Saudi Arabia: Dar al-Maathir.

Imdad, H. (2004) Imdad al-Karam, Nottingham, England: Al-Karam Publications.

Kathir, I. (2000) *Tafsir of Ibn Kathir*, London: Al-Firdous Ltd.

——(2002) Tafsir al-Quran al-Adhim Beirut, Lebanon: Dar a-Fikr.

Kepel, G. (2009), Jihad: The Trail of Political Islam, IB Tauris.

Lawrence, B. (2000) *Shattering the Myth: Islam Beyond Violence*, Princeton: Princeton University Press.

Misri, A. (1994) *Reliance of the Traveler*, Beltsville, MD: Amana.

Nawawi, I. and Muhammad ibn Salih al-Uthaymeen, Shaykh (1998) *An Explanation of Riyadh Al-Saliheen*, Qur'an and Sunnah Society.

Nelson-Pallmeyer, J. (2003) *Is Religion Killing Us? Violence in the Bible and the Quran*, Harrisburg, PA: Trinity Press International.

Pickthall, M. (1953) *The Meaning of the Glorious Koran*, New York: Mentor.

Roald, A-S. (2001) *Women in Islam: the Western Experience*, New York: Routledge.

Taqi-ud-Din Al-Hilali, M. and Muhsin Khan, M. (2007) *Interpretation of the Meanings of the Noble Qur'an in the English Language: A Summarised Version of At-Tabari, Al-Qurtubi and Ibn Kathir – With Comments from Sahih Al-Bukhari: Summarised in One Volume*, Riyadh: Maktaba Dar-us-Salam.

Wadud, A. (1999) *Qur'an and Woman*, Oxford: Oxford University Press.

Chapter 8

The construction of 'honour' in Indian criminal law

An Indian lawyer's perspective

Geeta Ramaseshan
Criminal Solicitor, India

Introduction

The origin of contemporary criminal law in India can be traced to the colonial period, specifically to the mid-nineteenth century. Three statutes, namely the Penal Code of 1860, the Code of Criminal Procedure of 1898 (amended in 1973) and the Evidence Act of 1872, are the foundation of India's criminal justice system. The Penal Code exhaustively defines 511 offences, and its main strength lies in dealing with crimes against property. However, in the context of offences against the human body, especially in relation to sexual offences, it does not distinguish between different shades or types of crimes.[1] For example, the term 'sexual assault', which is used legally in other jurisdictions, is yet to be formulated in India. As a result of this failure to modify the Penal Code in line with other jurisdictions in offences such as kidnapping, 'seduction', 'enticement', rape and 'outraging the modesty of a woman', the notion that lies behind the law is one of possession and control of the woman by the man to whom she 'belongs'.[2]

'Honour crimes' encompass a variety of different manifestations against women, including 'honour killings', assaults, imprisonment and the interference with the freedom of choice of whom one can marry. In this context, there is a publicly articulated 'justification' that is attributed to a social order claiming to require the preservation of the concept of 'honour' vested only in male (family and/or conjugal) control over women, and specifically women's sexual conduct: actual, suspected or potential.[3] While the term 'honour' is absent in de jure law (i.e. clearly within legislative provisions), the language of the law and the judgements of the criminal courts in India dealing with offences that relate to sexuality often reflect the notion of 'honour' when addressing complex issues, understanding principles of evidence and interpreting them either in favour of the prosecution or defence. This is very problematic, since violence against women is often looked at through the prism of proprietary rights of male members, even though (as some of the cases explained in this chapter indicate) the notion of 'honour' has been used to interpret violence in favour of the victim/survivor. Criminal courts in

India adopt a protectionist approach; such an approach tends to put the burden on the prosecution, and by default on the survivor, to prove her conduct. The Indian legal system has yet to recognise that crimes of honour amount to violence against women and cannot be justified as 'crimes of passion', or those committed in a fit of rage, or so-called honour.

In this chapter, the author explains the various ways in which Indian law is used to criminalise the right of choice in marriages and relationships, and then examines various cases of the Indian Supreme Court in rape, 'outraging the modesty of a woman' and kidnapping from lawful guardianship, where the notion of 'honour' has influenced judicial decisions. The author also addresses the legal and ethical questions that confront such cases and the use of morality as an argument or strategy to safeguard the right of the victim/survivor.[4] The author recognises the importance of understanding the use of criminal law to control same-sex relationships. However, the language of the provisions analysed in this chapter are gender specific; the focus of this paper, therefore, is on heterosexual relationships. Overall, the author analyses these case studies to indicate the approach of Indian criminal courts to the defence arguments on substandard investigations, sentencing and the conduct of the woman, where the notion of honour is introduced.

Of love, marriages, relationships and honour

The author's own understanding of 'honour' and the use of law to address it came when she was a young lawyer and was asked by the state Legal Aid Authority to accompany a twenty-two-year-old man named Mohan to a police station because the family members of a girl called Asha, a 20-year-old woman, had made a complaint against him on the 'charge of outraging her modesty'. According to the complaint, Mohan had stalked Asha when she was on her way to university. He had also written her letters that described her physical attributes and called her on the telephone. The author was a little sceptical about his protestations and initially felt that he had harassed Asha. On sensing that he was doubted, Mohan took out a small bag and emptied its contents showing letters written to him by Asha professing her love for him and pictures of both of them together at the beach. Convinced of his case, the author proceeded with total naivety to the police station, hoping to convince the police that here were two people who loved each other and that the complaint by Asha's family was false.

Asha was not present at the police station, but her father and brothers were. After verbally abusing Mohan in the compound of the police station, Asha's family wanted the Inspector to 'teach Mohan a lesson'. However, they did not want the case to be formally registered as they felt that it would then be formally logged as a crime, resulting in the police taking the case to court (which would then result in their loss of 'control' over the process). Such formality would also have required Asha's presence in court; exposure to cross-examination and the chances of her meeting Mohan in the court premises was what her family wanted to avoid. They also reasoned with the Inspector that the best way to deal with Mohan was to give him a 'good thrashing'. The Inspector did not register the complaint. The author and Mohan managed to speak in private, without the presence of Asha's family. Mohan explained that he and Asha were in love and were planning to get married, but her family objected to the marriage because he and Asha belonged to different castes and it was an issue of 'Manam' and 'Maryadai' (honour, in Tamil) for them.

Mohan also told the Inspector that Asha was kept in confinement and if he could summon her to the police station, the truth would be made known. To prove his point he showed the letters and pictures. The Inspector took them from him. He then proceeded to destroy the letters and pictures, despite the author's strongest protests, and called Asha's family members, informing them that they had nothing to worry about since there was no evidence of Asha's relationship with Mohan. After warning Mohan about his future conduct and advising him to find a woman from his own community, the Inspector informed him that he was also lucky that his own parents were not detained, as they were aware of his relationship with Asha and encouraged it. All the author's protests to the Inspector about his behaviour (and the destruction of evidence) were also of no use. The author never really got to know what happened to Asha and could only hazard a guess at the humiliation or violence she would have been subjected to by her family.

To the Inspector (and Asha's family), Mohan's conduct in keeping letters written by her was indicative of sexual harassment and not an issue of interference with her free choice in marriage or sexual autonomy. Exercising one's freedom of choice in matters of marriage is often met with objections from various individuals, such as the family or the community, that view such conduct as an affront to their honour. The writ of habeas corpus, which is a remedy for securing a person from illegal detention, is frequently used in such cases. Biological families use it for the release of their adult daughters who, they claim, were enticed by their husbands and detained illegally by them. The police, the spouse, his friends and relatives are usually the respondents in such cases. In court, the woman is often coerced or influenced by her family to rejoin them and break off the marriage. In some cases (even when the woman is an adult), Indian courts often confine such women to 'protective custody' so that 'she can have time to ponder over her choice'.[5] Based on a protectionist approach of the law, courts send women (including adult women) to government homes for their supposed safety.[6] In such cases, the constitutional remedy of the writ of habeas corpus is abused; it is used as a coercive measure to punish young persons (especially women) who are viewed as transgressing socially constructed norms of 'honour'.[7]

In October 2009, a 23-year-old Hindu woman from Karnataka, a state in India, converted to Islam in order to marry a Muslim man. Her family discovered her whereabouts and filed a writ of habeas corpus in the Karnataka High Court alleging that she had been forcibly converted to Islam and confined in a Madarassa in the neighbouring state of Kerala. The High Court directed senior police officials of both states to investigate the matter. It also quoted with approval a new terminology of 'love Jihad' (implying that women are being lured into religious conversion by young Muslim men after professing their love for them and marriage), a term coined by Hindu fundamentalist groups.[8] The woman was traced by the police and summoned to court. She informed the judges that she had married and converted on her own accord and was waiting to register her marriage under civil law. Despite her open admissions, the Indian court ordered her to return to her parents' home until the case was investigated. This being a recent case at the time of writing, the Indian court asked the Director-Generals of Police of the two states to file a report by 13 November 2009. According to the judges, 'the facts had national ramifications concerning the security, besides the question of unlawful trafficking, of women'.[9] If one examines the implications of this view, the court appeared to observe that there was no difference between a marriage of choice among adults and trafficking, where young women are lured on false promises of marriage and become victims of a variety of crimes. This reasoning is not only absurd, it also avoids a crucial issue: in such cases, the wishes of the woman are secondary to that of the family when they, out of honour, disagree with her choices about who she wishes to marry. In other words, the writ of habeas corpus is used to control the autonomy of women. It is clearly demonstrated in this case that the woman was 23 years of age and had unequivocally expressed to the judges that she had voluntarily converted to Islam and married her husband on her own accord. The Indian court did not believe her testimony and permitted an investigation into what was clearly false propaganda, ignoring the pleas of a woman who explained that she had exercised her right and freedom of choice to marry a man of her choosing. Indian laws do permit the right of choice of marriage, but in this case, the Indian court criminalised a legal act on the pretext of national security. By linking the construction of 'honour' to the security of the state, a new dimension has been given to the use of violence against women, limiting their powers, authority and control over their own decisions. Such observations severely impact inter-religious marriages which, though legal, are often targeted by fundamentalist violence.

It must be emphasised that habeas corpus is also invoked by husbands for the release of their wives when they are detained by their biological families. At other times, both spouses seek the protection of the court when they are being threatened and harassed by their families. In *Lata Singh v. State of Uttar Pradesh*,[10] the Indian Supreme Court upheld the right of the petitioner to marry a man of her choice, observing that inter-caste marriages were essential to the national interest to potentially help destroy the caste system. However, although the court condemned the violence unleashed in the name of 'honour' (and directed the police in the country generally to protect young people), it condoned 'social sanctions' against such young people. For example, the court observed that if the parents of the boy or girl did not approve of the inter-caste or inter-religious marriage, they were entitled to 'cut off social relations' with their children. This may be considered as the infliction of another form of 'social violence' against persons who transgress the religious-cultural boundaries of Indian social norms, which as a result of this decision appear to be condoned even by the Indian legal system.

The norms of honour and the offence of rape

The offence of rape in India focuses only on the narrow angle of physical penetration of the male organ; any other violent act, such as the use of objects or instruments, is treated as 'outraging the modesty of a woman'. The historic focus on the act of penetration is largely derived from a male pre-occupation with ensuring a woman's chastity and ascertaining the paternity of children.[11] Thus, rape in India is not understood as violence per se but as 'loss of chastity', which in turn has often led to courts addressing the character of the victim/survivor as opposed to the conduct of the offender. Again, since 'loss of chastity' is viewed as affecting the 'honour' of the victim/survivor and her family members, there have been instances when courts have suggested to the victim/survivor that she should marry the perpetrator. Such an approach indicates a preoccupation with marriage and a lack of understanding of sexual violence that results in grave injustice to women. Rape cases in India thus reflect complex and contentious issues, including strong and inhibiting cultural factors, making this a very difficult area for securing justice.

Judgements of the Indian criminal courts have sometimes constructed 'honour' in addressing the principle of evidence and have interpreted it to benefit the survivor of rape. To give an example, it is an accepted principle under Indian criminal law that a crime has to be reported at the earliest instance. However, Indian criminal courts have permitted a delay in registering cases of rape (usually of a few days) on the grounds that the delay could be due to the fact that the 'honour' of the woman and/or that of her family have prevented her/them from approaching the police at the earliest opportunity. While these judgements have no doubt benefited women, and have led to some convictions, the construction of the term 'honour' is extremely problematic since, by linking the offence of rape to notions such as 'honour', 'culture' and 'dignity', these offences are addressed as violations against the wider community and not necessarily against the woman herself. For example, in *Karnel Singh v. State of MP*,[12] a conviction of rape was upheld based solely on the statement of the victim/survivor, though the investigation was found to have been substandard. Addressing the argument of the defence on delay, the judges observed that: ' ... there is no doubt that the investigation was casual and defective. But despite these defects the courts below have recorded their conviction. Are they right? Notwithstanding our unhappiness at the nature of investigation, we hold the accused guilty.'[13] Indian criminal law requires that any charges against the accused must be proved beyond reasonable doubt; a substandard investigation, by implication, would mean that the evidence obtained is not sufficient to sustain a conviction. By convicting the accused solely on the testimony of the 'victim', the ruling transformed the evidential requirement in the context of corroborative evidence. However, in this case, once again the Indian Supreme Court adopted a very protectionist approach based on gender stereotypes. The judges generalised Indian women by male-defined behavioural standards and formed an opinion as if they were superior to women from other cultures, who supposedly would have behaved differently.[14] Consider the following observations: 'In India, women are slow and hesitant to complain of such assaults and if the woman happens to be a married person, she will not do anything without informing her husband. The reluctance to go to the police is because of society's attitude towards such women; it casts doubt and shame upon her rather than comfort and sympathize with her.'[15] Note that the court used the term 'shame', a term often linked to 'honour', rather than using terms such as 'violence' or 'force' against 'vulnerable', 'overpowered' women. These observations provide an understanding on how social norms impact upon a case of rape in India. The question becomes more complex in the context of the criminal justice system that expects women to recount the violent act in a detailed and detached manner, when cultural norms consider talking about sex as taboo, even with close relatives.

Indian criminal law does not provide a definition of incest, nor does it make marital rape a crime, unlike in the United Kingdom. In the case of *State of Himachal Pradesh v. Asha Ram*,[16] the Indian court upheld the conviction of a case relating to an incestuous rape committed by a father. However in so doing, it observed that the father

> is a fortress, refuge and the trustee of his daughter. He ravished the chastity of his daughter, jeopardized her future prospect of getting married, enjoying marital and conjugal life. Not only that, she carries an indelible social stigma on her head and deathless shame as long as she lives.

To address an argument made by the defence (that it was a false case filed under the instigation of her mother) the court observed that:

> No girl of self respect and dignity who is conscious of her chastity having expectations of married life and livelihood, would accuse falsely against any other person of rape, much against her own father,

sacrificing thereby her chastity and also expose the entire family to shame and at the risk of condemnation and ostracization by the society.[17]

The judgement implies that the heinous nature of the crime is not necessarily because of the control a parent has over the child; the father is a trustee and hence can have proprietary rights over the child. In this case, by linking preservation of 'chastity' to self-respect and dignity, the court upholds it as a virtue. The loss of virginity is linked to 'shame' and 'honour' of the family, and it is implicit in the judgement of the court that these are the crucial considerations determining the seriousness of the offence, and not the infliction of violence on the victim.

In the case of *State of Punjab v. Gurmit Singh*,[18] the judgement indicates the approach of the Indian courts when dealing with an improper investigation into a criminal offence. It also provides an understanding of the construction of the term 'stigma.' In this case, the victim aged 16 years was on her way to school when she was forced into a car and gang-raped by three men. The defence argued that as there was an enmity between the two families the allegations made by the victim were false; this was accepted by the original trial court which held that the theory of her rape and abduction were falsely introduced by her father. When the case reached the Supreme Court, it questioned: 'If the investigation officer did not conduct the investigation properly how can that be a ground to discredit the testimony of the prosecutrix? She has no control over the investigation agency and the negligence of the officer cannot affect her testimony.'[19] Such an approach, though it addresses substantive justice and led the court to convict the accused based on the woman's testimony, should have led to an acquittal based on a substandard investigation. The Supreme Court stated that if a defendant could be falsely accused of rape/abduction on account of enmity between families, it was also equally possible that a defendant could have sexually assaulted a prosecutrix in order to exact revenge on a father. An understanding of the social norms is provided in this judgement since, by rejecting the defence's arguments, the Supreme Court considered rape as a 'weapon of revenge' in order to damage the 'honour' of another's family. The Supreme Court held that:

> ... the observations of the trial court are stigmas that have the potential of not only discouraging an even otherwise reluctant victim of sexual assault to bring forth complaint for trial of criminals, thereby making the society suffer by letting criminals escape even a trial. The court should examine the broader probabilities of the case and not get swayed by minor contradictions of insignificant discrepancies. If for some reason the court finds it difficult to place implicit reliance on her testimony, it may look for evidence which may lead assurance to her testimony, short

of corroboration required in the case of an accomplice. The court must be alive to its responsibility and be sensitive while dealing with cases involving sexual molestations.[20]

In this case, the Indian Supreme Court provided a welcomed understanding of the social norms that exist in abduction and rape cases by encouraging trial judges to exercise caution before they reject the testimony of a victim and to understand the complexities when viewing evidence relating to rape.

Kidnapping and seduction

The offence of kidnapping, abduction and inducement of a woman in order to compel her into marriage or seduction into 'illicit sexual intercourse' is an offence under the Penal Code.[21] In order to prove such an offence there must be inducement of the victim; the kidnapping or abduction must take place with the intent that the woman be subjected to sexual intercourse; and the accused must have the knowledge or the intention that the woman be seduced into illicit sexual intercourse as a result of her kidnapping or abduction. The knowledge or intention of the accused, the understanding of 'illicit sexual intercourse' and the notion of seduction are all problematic issues that have resulted in peculiar rulings being delivered by the Indian courts. In a culture where emphasis is placed upon marriage (relationships outside the institution of marriage are prohibited under social norms), family members often invoke this provision to file cases against men and women who elope. It must be said, however, that this law is also used to address the concern of trafficking where women are lured into sex work on promise of marriage.

In *Rajesh and Others v. State of Maharashtra*,[22] four men abducted the victim while she was walking on the road with the objective of marrying her to one of them. The defendants were charged with abduction and the attempted murder of the victim. The victim did not name the defendants in her complaint even though she had recognised them. The trial court and the High Court sentenced the accused to two years imprisonment. On appeal, the Indian Supreme Court was of the opinion that the victim had tried to protect the defendant but nevertheless upheld the conviction and held that the omission on the victim's part of not naming the defendants did not create any doubt regarding their presence at the time of commission of the offence, since other evidence proved crucial and consistent. However, taking note of the age of the victim (who was 18); the fact that one of the defendants wanted to marry her and probably believed that she would; and that they were all college students, the Court reduced the sentence from two years to one.[23] The case demonstrates that a woman's (non)statement or (non)testimony had no relevance in a given situation that resulted in a conviction.

Statutory rape is an offence when the victim is below 16 years of age. The parents are the lawful guardians of the minor, and kidnapping from lawful guardianship is an offence when the victim is below the age of 18 in the case of a female, and 16 if a male. However, this also poses a problem because the age of consent for marriage is 18 years, but marriage of those below 18 is not void under Hindu and Muslim laws. Thus, when young people below the legal age of marriage elope and get married, their marriage is 'legal' even though the biological families file cases of kidnapping from lawful guardianship. *In Kuldeep Mahato v. State of Bihar*,[24] K, a 17-year-old, was forced into a car at knifepoint by the accused, who was known to her. She was then taken to a different city, detained and raped by the accused. K narrated the facts to her father who lodged a complaint. The question of K's age became crucial. In the absence of documents, such as birth certificates, it is only by medical examination such as an ossification test that age is determined. Such a test is on the basis of an examination of the bones and is an approximation (it has a margin of error of about a few months). This often results in both the prosecution and the defence trying to use the examination to their advantage, with the prosecution claiming that the victim is a minor, while the defence contends that she is an adult. In the case currently discussed, the Indian court observed that the victim's evidence did not necessarily indicate that the defendant had kidnapped her with the intention to marry her against her will, or so that she may be forced into 'illicit sexual intercourse'. K was held to be a minor on the date of the offence of kidnapping from lawful guardianship. On the issue of rape the court believed that her movements were not restricted by the defendant to justify the conviction of rape.[25] In this case, the Indian court observed a strict method of interpretation of the law and held that as she was found to be travelling in a vehicle and was a minor for the purpose of kidnapping, the defendant was guilty of that offence. However, since she was above 16 years, the court held that there was no rape and that she had consented to intercourse. Male-defined standards were used in the reasoning: that the victim could have run away and could have sought refuge with neighbours. Such reasoning propagates a myth that a woman can successfully resist a rape if she really wishes to do so.

In relation to the definition of 'seduction', the following case demonstrates how the term is often used in the context of women who are sexually experienced and those who are not. In *Ramesh v. State of Maharashtra*,[26] the victim was a minor below the age of 18 years who was living with her stepfather. At the time of the offence she was married but did not live with her husband. According to the prosecution, ' ... she was accustomed to indulge in promiscuous intercourse with customers for money (sic)'.[27] On the day in question, the accused met her stepfather and asked him to bring the girl with another sex worker to a lodge. The accused was found to have known her age and hence was guilty of the offence. The father was found not guilty of inducement as the victim was 'promiscuous'. In this case, the

Supreme Court defined seduction as the 'surrender of her body by a woman who is otherwise reluctant or unwilling to submit herself to illicit intercourse in consequence of persuasion, flattery, blandishment or importunity, whether such surrender is for the first time or is preceded by similar surrender on earlier occasions'.[28] Though the victim was a minor under the law,

> She offers herself for money – not casually but in the course of her profession as a prostitute – there are no scruples, nor reluctance to be overcome, and surrender by her is not seduction within the Code. It would then be impossible to hold that a person who instigates another to assist a woman following the profession of a prostitute abets him to do an act with intent that she may or with knowledge that she will be seduced to sexual intercourse.[29]

By this reasoning a minor under the control of a male (her stepfather in this instance), even when forced into sex work, is incapable of being seduced under the law. Note that the court in the judgement acknowledged that this provision was enacted to give effect to the International Convention for the Suppression of Traffic in Women and Children of 1910, and yet found a minor who was obviously forced into sex work by her father to be 'promiscuous'. The problem of defining seduction has confronted courts in various ways. Some courts have taken the view that the verb 'seduce' under the law has two senses. In its ordinary sense, it means inducing a woman to stray from the path of virtue for the first time; however, it is also used in the wider sense of inducing a woman to submit to 'illicit sexual intercourse' at any time or any occasion.[30] Other decisions of Indian courts have used the term seduction as 'properly applicable to the first act of illicit intercourse, unless there be proof of a return to chastity on the part of the girl since the "first act"'.[31] In such a view, sexually experienced women cannot be seduced; only the sexually inexperienced can seek the benefit of the law.

Outraging modesty

Cases concerned with sexual assaults are governed by Section 354 of the Penal Code, couched within an extremely archaic term: 'outraging the modesty'. Assaulting or using unlawful force upon a woman with intent or knowledge to outrage her modesty is a criminal offence. Since intention and knowledge are essential ingredients for the act, and since modesty is a social construction, cases under this provision have often resulted in debates as to what constitutes 'modesty'. The following case indicates the extreme confusion that prevails in interpreting the term 'modesty'.

In the case of *State of Punjab v. Major Singh*,[32] a child of seven and a half months was sexually assaulted by the defendant. The injuries inflicted upon the child were proven, but since understanding the term 'modesty' was problematic, a three-member bench of the High Court was charged with the task of interpreting the term. The majority bench took the view that the offence could be complete only if the woman felt that her modesty was outraged, and as the child was of an extremely young age, she was incapable of having her modesty outraged. However, a single judge took the dissenting view that the term implied accepted notions of modesty and not the notions of the woman who was the survivor of the crime. Even though the purpose of this view was laudable (namely to punish the defendant), with the introduction of 'accepted notions', community standards were introduced into the concept of 'modesty' while women's experiences were rejected.

The case was then referred to a three-judge bench of the Indian Supreme Court. The majority view held that the defendant was guilty of the offence; however, they added to the confusion of the term by applying the test of 'reasonableness' in this argument. In the dissenting opinion of one judge:

> The test of the outrage of modesty must be whether a reasonable man will think that the act of the offender was intended to or was known to be likely to outrage the modesty of the woman in question. In considering the question, he must imagine the woman to be a reasonable woman and keep in view all her circumstances concerning her, such as, her station and way of life and the notions of modesty of such a woman.[33]

The introduction of the 'reasonable man' test is a creation of English common law, and is based on a fictitious personification of the court and jury's social judgement. It has also been defined in various ways.[34] The 'reasonable man' has been interpreted as the 'normal man', who would purchase any normal magazine and read it at home, or the 'normal man' who would mow the lawn in his shirt.[35] A presiding judge has to decide what 'reasonable' means and it is inevitable that different judges may have varied opinions on the same question given the elasticity of the term.[36] Though some jurists argue that the reasonable man includes a reasonable woman, in reality it has never included women's experiences and the perspectives of women. Allegations such as provocation, loose morals or ill-reputation and submissiveness viewed through the male gaze become defences in a trial. Indian courts treat this creation of fiction as a subject that is viewed through the male gaze; furthermore, the second judge in the above case rejected the test of a woman's reaction to the crime (i.e. the reaction of a 'reasonable woman'). He said: 'In my judgment any act done to or in the presence of a woman is clearly suggestive of sex according to the common notions of mankind that must fall within the mischief of this section.'[37] Holding that the act of the accused was deliberate, the judge held that he had outraged the child's modesty. The third judge, in order to justify the punishment, interpreted standards of modesty and shame by stating: 'I think the essence of a woman's modesty is her sex writ large on her body. The reaction of the woman is very relevant but its absence is not always decisive.'[38] He also stated,

> ... a female of tender age stands on a different footing and her sexual powers are dormant. The baby has not yet developed a sense of shame and has no awareness of sex. Nevertheless, from her very birth she possesses the modesty which is attributable of her sex.

Such reasoning imposes 'modesty' as a quality that all female children must possess.

Conclusion

An attempt has been made to interpret some of the judgements of the Supreme Court of India. They indicate that the court has transformed rules of corroboration; convicted the accused on the sole testimony of the victim (so long as there is a strong prevalence of probabilities); and given analytical tools to trial courts in understanding evidence, while being conscious of social norms. However, in order to secure justice for victims/survivors, the judgements appear to have accorded 'special legal sanctity' to the construction of honour in criminal law. Feminist jurisprudence has not evolved in the body of Indian judgements. In the absence of the same, these precedents are often quoted with approval by many defence lawyers who use the observations to develop their cross-examinations, resulting in harassment of the survivor when she is giving her evidence and concluding with what appears to be anti-women judgements. Such a focus has resulted in many acquittals, when a survivor's perceived conduct does not conform to social norms.

The definition of the law in rape, seduction and 'outraging the modesty' perpetuates myths and stereotypes.[39] Conscious of this problem, in a subsequent[40] judgement the court expanded modesty to include acts that are an affront to the dignity of women. Campaigns for a comprehensive law on sexual assault and harassment, and the repeal of archaic laws, have yet to fructify. The Indian Supreme Court has developed an impressive jurisprudence on women's human rights. In the absence of legislation, it formulated the concept of sexual harassment in the workplace and defined it using the language of the UN Convention on the Elimination of All Forms of Discrimination Against Women.[41] In so doing, it also made human-rights treaty laws part of domestic law. What is required is the weaving of women's experiences over such precedents so that the construction of 'honour' in such offences has no relevance.

Notes

1 Dhagamwar (1992: 122).
2 Ramanathan (1999: 50).
3 Welchman and Hossain (2005: 4).
4 While my own preference is for the term survivor, the word victim is used in the judgements and legal parlance in India in order to describe women who have faced violence, hence the two terms are used interchangeably in this paper.
5 Observations of a bench of the Madras High Court, in a case where the author was representing a husband who was seeking the release of his wife detained by her family.
6 Such women may also be victims of rape. Their freedom is completely restricted in such homes, and they are detained under an Order of Court. Sometimes, a rape victim who is actually a witness is confined to 'protective custody' while the perpetrator of the crime obtains bail and has no restriction placed on his freedom.
7 The writ of habeas corpus is a constitutional right under Article 32 and 226 of the Indian Constitution.
8 *The Hindu*, 23 October 2009.
9 Ibid.
10 AIR 2006 SC 2522.
11 Agnes (1992).
12 AIR 1995 SC 2472.
13 Ibid.: 2473, paragraph 4.
14 Ramaseshan (2007).
15 AIR 1995 SC 2472, 2474, paragraph 7.
16 JT 2005 (9) 574.
17 Ibid.
18 AIR 1996 SC 1393.
19 Ibid.: 1399, paragraph 7
20 Ibid.: 1403, paragraph 15 and 1404, paragraph 20.
21 Section 366 of the Indian Penal Code.
22 AIR 1998 SC 2724.
23 Ibid.
24 AIR 1998 SC 2694.
25 Ibid.
26 AIR 1962 SC 1908.
27 Ibid.: 1911, paragraph 6.
28 Ibid.: 1912, paragraph 8.
29 Ibid.
30 *Prafullakumar Basu v. Emperor* AIR 1930 Calcutta 209; *Emperor v. Laxman* Bala AIR 1935 Bombay 652; *Suppiah v. Emperor* AIR 1930 Madras 980; and *Pessumal v. Emperor* AIR 1927 Sindh 97.
31 *Emperor v. Baijnath* AIR 1932 Allahabad 409, AIR 1955 Calcutta 100 and AIR 1934 Lahore 227.
32 AIR 1967 SC 63.
33 Ibid.: 65, paragraph 5.
34 See Ramanathan (1999).
35 An American writer quoted by Lord Greer in *Hall v. Brooklands Auto Racing Club* (1933) KB 205, 224.
36 Per Lord Macmillian in *Glasgow Corporation v. Muir* (1943) AC 448, 457.
37 AIR 1967 SC, 67 para 13.
38 Ibid.: 68, paragraphs 16 and 17.

39 For an understanding on such stereotypes, see the Canadian Supreme Court judgment of *R v. Ewanchuck* (1999) SCJ 1, No. 10.
40 *Rupan Deol Bajaj v. KPS Gill* JT 1995 (7) SC 299.
41 *Visaka v. State of Rajasthan* AIR 1997 SC 3011.

Bibliography

Agnes, F. (1992) 'Protecting Women Against Violence? Review of a Decade of Legislation 1980–89', *Economic and Political Weekly*, Vol. 27, No. 17.

Dhagamwar, V. (1992) *Law, Power and Justice – The Protection of Personal Rights in the Indian Penal Code*, London: Sage Publications.

Goonesekere, S. (ed.) (2004) *Violence, Law and Women's Rights in South Asia*, New Delhi: Sage Publications.

Kannabiran, K. (ed.) (2005) *The Violence of Normal Times, Essays on Women's Lived Realities*, New Delhi: Women Unlimited.

Kannabiran, K. and Kannabiran, V. (eds) (2002) *De-Eroticizing Assault: Essays on Modesty, Honour and Power*, Calcutta: Bhatkel and Sen.

Kapur, R. (1996) *Subversive Sites: Feminist Engagements with the Law in India*, New Delhi: Sage Publications.

Menon, N. (2004) *Recovering Subversion Feminist Politics Beyond the Law*, Urbana, IL: Permanent Black.

Mukhopadhyay, S. (ed.) (1998) *In the Name of Justice: Women and Law in Society*, New Delhi: Manohar.

Nair, J, (2000) *Women and Law in Colonial India*, Delhi: Kali for Women.

Ramanathan, U. (1999) 'Reasonable Man, Reasonable Women and Reasonable Expectations', in Dhanda, A. and Parashar, A. (eds) *Engendering Law: Essays in Honour of Lotika Sarkar*, Lucknow: Eastern Book Company.

Ramaseshan (2007) 'Addressing Rape as a Human Rights Violation; The Role of International Human Rights Norms and Instruments', *IWRAW Asia Pacific Occasional Papers Series*, No. 10.

Sagade, J. (2005) *Child Marriage in India, Socio-Legal and Human rights Dimensions*, Oxford: Oxford University Press.

Sarkar, L. and Sivarammaya, B. (eds) (1994) *Women and Law: Contemporary Problems*, New Delhi: Vikas.

Welchman, L. and Hossain, S. (2005) *'Honour': Crimes, Paradigms and Violence Against Women*, London: Zed Books.

Chapter 9

Men's violence and women's responsibility

Mothers' stories about honour violence

Dr Åsa Eldén
Researcher, Swedish Research Institute in Istanbul

Introduction

Umeå, Northern Sweden, 1996. A 16-year-old woman is murdered by her brother and cousin. The two young offenders are convicted of murder and threats. Though witnesses inform the police that the male family members had gathered together and decided that the young woman had to die, these men were not brought to court. The mother of the young woman informed the police about the threats and about the physical violence directed towards her. Her brother-in-law called her shortly after the murder: 'Now it's your turn, whore.'

Dahouk, Iraqi Kurdistan, 1999. A 19-year-old woman who grew up in Sweden is taken to her parents' hometown. She thinks that she is going to marry an elder relative, but instead she is murdered by her father and three uncles. Her mother and sister witness the murder and the sister escapes to Sweden. When two of the uncles return, they are convicted of murder and given life sentences. The sister is the prosecutor's key witness. The mother is too afraid to speak in court with the uncles present. However, she agrees to show a taped interview in which she tells the police about the murder, nodding when asked if this is the truth.

Uppsala, Central Sweden, 2002. A 24-year-old woman is murdered by her father in front of her two sisters and her mother. She had left the family years before and was living with a death threat. Her father is brought to court and charged with murder. One of the sisters testifies against him. In the District Court, the mother uses her right as a close relative not to testify. In the Court of Appeal, she gives her testimony which supports her husband, whose story – as was clear to many – appeared to be a lie.

These three cases, all very well known in Sweden, involve young women murdered by close relatives; young women who have become symbols of women's exposure to terrible acts of violence committed in the name of honour. These three cases also involve other women, particularly sisters and mothers. Female relatives of the murdered young women play important roles in the judicial proceedings following the murders. They risk their lives in support of the murdered woman by testifying against their close male relatives; in some instances, they support the murderer of their own daughters. It is clear that these women, sisters and mothers, all act in different ways. The aim of this chapter is to focus on some of these 'other women', namely the mothers. How can we understand mothers' interpretations of themselves in relation to other women – and to men – in a violent everyday life in which cultural concepts of honour are used?

Honour violence – gendered violence

The author's point of departure when discussing violence committed in the name of honour is to conceptualise this violence as male violence against women (i.e. as a form of gendered violence). This means that in order to be understood, concrete acts of violence must be located in the context in which they take place and be related to the control of, and discrimination against, women.

In her report on violence against women in Palestinian society, Nadera Shaloub-Kevorkian argues that 'honour killings' (in her vocabulary 'femicide') must neither be understood as separate from less severe forms of violence against women, nor from the social, cultural, economic or political context in which they are committed (Shaloub-Kevorkian 2004). Shaloub-Kevorkian uses a widened definition of 'femicide' in which severe acts of violence such as murder or attempted murder are understood as linked to less severe acts such as threats and control.[1] This definition is based on women's accounts about their own experiences of violence, in which seemingly less severe forms of violence (e.g. threats) are equally as frightening as physical assaults. This corresponds with research on violence in other cultural contexts, such as Sweden. For example, a survey on men's violence against Swedish women published in 2001 shows that women's reporting on health issues were higher after experiences of threats (and sexual violence) than after physical violence (Lundgren et al. 2001). In other words, in order to interpret violence and its consequences, severe violations must be related to less severe forms of violence, and to culturally accepted acts that are not defined as violence. In this chapter, these acts are understood within a cultural context of honour.[2] The concrete implication of this will be elaborated in connection with empirical examples consisting of women's interpretations of their lives. The author's point of departure, therefore, is that in an honour-cultural context, a man's honour is connected to what women related to him (by blood or marriage) demonstrate to others: a 'virgin' or a 'whore' (Eldén 2001).[3]

Since the first years of this millennium, in Swedish society honour killings and honour violence have received attention to an extent which cannot be compared to any other form of violence against women. Beginning after the murders explained in the introduction to this chapter (which were presented by politicians as eye-openers), the Swedish Government took a series of initiatives to combat violence in the name of honour. From 2003 to 2007, 180 million Swedish kronor (about €16 million) was set aside for different projects, such as sheltered housing, special units at social-service institutions, preventative work, and so on. After 2007, that amount has been doubled, if not tripled, by the Swedish government. A large number of honour-violence handbooks for professionals have been written and distributed. NGOs and other institutions receive huge amounts of money from the government for various attitude-changing projects among Swedes with immigrant back-ground. These ventures seem to be very uncontroversial, even though they are the largest ventures on violence against women ever launched in Sweden.[4] The magnitude of, and lack of resistance against, initiatives within the field of honour violence (compared to other initiatives concerning vio-lence against women)[5] may of course be interpreted in different ways. One possible interpretation would be that this violence is easy to identify as something 'different' in Swedish society, something that essentially has nothing to do with 'us', but is 'the other's' problem. It is considered to be a problem that 'we' can help 'them' to get rid of.

These debates and political initiatives have been dominated by a focus on young women, something which can be interpreted along the same lines. Individual young women have been portrayed as wanting to lead an 'ordinary Swedish life' like their friends. They have been presented in con-trast to a united 'family' wanting the girls to behave according to their (cultural) rules. 'Other women' (e.g. mothers) in these young women's immediate surroundings have been more or less invisible in this debate, as have internal power relations within the family. As far as attention has been paid to mothers, it has been as perpetrators or co-perpetrators rather than as victims of violence.[6] Mothers are thus described as active in, and directly or indirectly responsible for, the violence to which young women are exposed. This, just as the above-mentioned lack of resistance, may be interpreted as a way of alienating violence committed in the name of honour and portraying it as essentially different from men's violence against women in a Swedish context. Instead of focusing on how men in these cases use violence against women, a 'conflict' between a (culturally foreign) collective and an individual (wanting to be like 'us') becomes the main sub-ject. In doing so, classical colonialist notions of East versus West are reproduced.[7]

The author wishes to follow Welchmann and Hossain when they state that 'women remain the majority of victims and survivors of "crimes of honour"', and therefore suggest that the most fruitful path when formulating strategies to combat this violence is to 'draw on the existing frameworks established to address all manifestations of violence against women' (Welchmann and Hossain 2005a: 6). This, however, does not mean a denial of the fact that men can be victims of violence. Neither does this assert that women are never abusive towards other women, or towards men.

As Purna Sen points out as a feature of honour crimes, there is a potential for women's active participation (Sen 2005). What the author wishes to do is not to deny this activity but to look into it much deeper.

This chapter is an indirect critique of the exclusive focus on young women in the Swedish debate. It is necessary to widen the discussion on gendered violence committed in the name of honour and see connections between different victims in violent everyday life.[8] The author achieves this by focusing on how women talk about other women and men, with a particular interest in the question of women's responsibility for men's violence against women. The empirical material used consists of stories told by mothers exposed to honour violence.[9]

Loyalty between women saves lives ...

The interviewees all live in Sweden. They have been exposed to violence by close male relatives, and they interpret their experiences using concepts which can be placed in a cultural context of honour. At the time of the interviews, none of them were living with the violent men; they had all been able to leave. When talking about the process in which they escaped the violence, solidarity and loyalty between women appears to be an important theme.

In Adele's story, her mother's support saved her life.[10] As a non-married teenager, Adele became pregnant. For several months, she refused to acknowledge the pregnancy, but finally she had to admit to herself that she was pregnant. She decided that she also had to tell her mother. She chose to do so when the two of them were alone together in the doctor's waiting room:

A: So I said to her: 'I am pregnant, that's why we are here today.' She said: 'Have an abortion. You have to have an abortion.' 'But I can't, it's too late to do that.' 'But they will kill you!'
Å: Did she say so?
A: Yes. She's living with them, she knows them, and she knows my dad. She said: 'They will kill you, they will not let you live here.' I said: 'I don't know what to do. I can't change this, make it undone.' She just cried. I was so sad. What had I done to her? I had destroyed her life, now she will suffer for what I have done. They will blame her, and tell her that it's her fault.

Adele and her mother lied to the rest of the family; they said that Adele had a disease which made her belly swollen. Her mother was present when Adele gave birth to her child, and immediately after the delivery the child was sent away to a foster home. The plan was never to let Adele's father and brothers know about the child. 'She saved my life,' Adele concludes, 'if she had said anything it would have been too late.'

Like Adele, Jasmin talks about loyalty between women as saving lives. Her daughter reported her father's physical and sexual abuse to the police, after many years of very severe violence against both Jasmin and the daughter. He was convicted and sentenced to jail for a number of years. This meant that not only the daughter but Jasmin could escape the violence they endured:

J: Every day I thought I would die. But I prayed to God that he wouldn't kill me in front of the children. If he hadn't been in jail today, maybe we would not have been alive. I don't think we would have been alive.

In Jasmin's story, her daughter's acts – leading to the imprisonment of the man who had beaten Jasmin since their first day of marriage – are the reason why they are both alive. During the whole process Jasmin supported her daughter. But this support had a high price.

... but has a price

People in Jasmin's surroundings abandoned her when they found out that she helped her daughter to report what her husband had done.

J: The friends I had, immediately turned their backs on me. They started to call me bad things, saying that I shouldn't have done this.
A: Done what?
J: Helped my daughter to report. She should not have reported her own father ... It's not good. A woman coming from my country shall not support her daughter and put her own husband to jail. She shall instead support her husband, and keep the daughter away or get rid of the daughter. You know how they think.
A: So they said that you betrayed your husband when you supported your daughter?
J: Yes. It was very, very wrong. I should not have done that. Then they started to hunt me, and threaten me.

Jasmin's support of her daughter and her refusal to support her husband against her daughter was met with very strong reactions from the people around her. She was abandoned, harassed, threatened and forced to leave her home and, with help from the social services, was able to hide in another town.

In Adele's case, her mother's support was not unconditional. When telling the story of why her mother stood by her side and saved her, Adele is ambivalent. She is sure her mother did it for her daughter's sake, but also for her own. Adele describes her mother's actions as both life-saving and as a deceit.

A: Why do you think your mother kept quiet about this?
A: Because she knew what would happen to me.
A: She wanted to protect you?
A: Yes, but not only that. She would have suffered as much as I would because of my behaviour. It was my fault. She wanted to protect both of us, not only me. She is my mother, it is her duty to tell me what I can do and what I can't do, what is wrong and what is right.

Adele did not agree on her baby being adopted, so she decided to take her back from the foster home and keep her. By doing this, she lost her mother's support. Her mother stood by her side as long as the pregnancy – what Adele had done – was invisible to the male family members. When it was no longer invisible, Adele was left alone. She wrote a letter in which she told her family about the pregnancy and ran away with the child.

Jasmin was made responsible for her daughter's 'betrayal' of her husband, and her surroundings demanded that she dissociate herself from her daughter. She chose not to, and had to escape and hide from the violence and threats. Adele's mother supported her daughter only as long as she agreed to lie about the pregnancy to male members of the family. She demanded that Adele pretend that her child never existed. When Adele refused to do so, she lost her mother's support.

Men's honour: the limit of loyalty between women

In a cultural context of honour, as employed in the stories of Adele and Jasmin, men's honour is related to what female relatives show to others: their good or bad reputation (Eldén 2001). The crucial meaning of women's reputation may be interpreted in the light of a divided femininity as understood in the tradition of Abraham, that is in cultural contexts rooted in the common tradition of Judaism, Christianity and Islam (Svalastog 1998). In these contexts, at a conceptual level, Madonna/virgin and whore appear as essential and mutually exclusive categories of women. But they may also become concrete in a woman's life. A woman who gets a bad reputation is defined as a whore who can never again be a 'pure' virgin – she has left one category for another. Only when a woman who is branded as a whore no longer exists, socially or physically, can the honour of the collective be restored. Reputation may thus become a question of life and death (Eldén 2004).

In Adele and Jasmin's stories, it is also possible to see how different women's reputations – in these cases mothers and daughters, or in other cases sisters or cousins – must be understood as connected. The behaviour of one woman has an impact on how the (male) surroundings perceive other affiliated women (cf. Shaloub-Kevorkian 1999).[11] A woman who gets a bad reputation and is branded as a whore 'infects' other women. And if a woman is punished because she has stained the honour of the family, this can be seen as a direct threat against her female relatives. As the violent acts directed towards the woman are interpreted as the woman's own fault (her getting a bad reputation), this communicates a message to other women: If you behave in the same way – or if people say you do – you may meet the same fate (Eldén and Westerstrand 2004).

Thus, women are not only made responsible for their own behaviour, but for other women's behaviour as well. Jasmin was threatened and harassed because she supported her daughter. She insisted on being loyal to her daughter and therefore had to escape. Adele said that she was certain that her mother was blamed for her getting pregnant and leaving the family. Her mother's stipulation in supporting Adele was that the pregnancy and the child were kept secret. As a woman's reputation exists only in other people's eyes, and the reputation is considered more 'real' than what has actually happened, visibility (or invisibility) is of vital importance. If Adele's child is known to her male family members, Adele becomes visible as a stained whore. When she decided to keep her child, she lost her mother's support and protection. Adele's mother chose to stay loyal to her husband and sons.

People in Jasmin's surroundings expected her to betray her daughter and stay behind her husband. Jasmin acted differently and therefore had to escape. In these stories, there seems to be a limit of culturally accepted loyalty between women. Women are expected to take responsibility for the behaviour of other women, to control and protect each other in order not to defile the honour of the family. In doing so, they have a space to stand behind and be loyal to each other. But this is true only as long as the loyalty does not make them disloyal to men. If it does, they are obliged to abandon other women and stay behind the interest of the male collective. In the two stories discussed above, what will become of women who are loyal to each other and disloyal to men is obvious: they are seen as 'whores' who – literally or socially – have to be eliminated. But what is at stake if women are disloyal to men? Another interviewee, Diana, will shed light on this question.

Men are violent – but are they responsible for their violent acts?

Diana was brought to Sweden by her husband. Both Diana and her husband had been married before. He was divorced, and his ex-wife and children were living in the same town in Sweden where he settled with Diana. Diana was a widow with one daughter. The couple's arrival in Sweden was the starting point for the abuse. Her story contains systematic violence, in some cases so severe that it resulted in life-threatening injuries. When Diana discusses the reasons behind her husband's violence against her, his former wife (and their joint children) and his mother are given as the reasons for the abuse, rather than the man himself:

D: He hits me all the time. His children were the worst. You should never marry a man with children. When we were asleep, she called. We were never left in peace because she phoned all the time, his ex-wife. And his mother had her opinions; she participated alongside his relatives. They all repeated: 'You came with an open woman, and you even gave her gold.'

Diana understands her husband's conflicts with his ex-wife and his own family as the source of the violence. In Diana's interpretation, these conflicts stem from the fact that his family did not accept her as his new wife and saw his divorce and new marriage as a dishonour to the family. They called Diana a whore and harassed both her and her daughter. In Diana's story, her husband's conflicts with his family and ex-wife appear as the direct cause for him using violence against her:

D: She (the ex-wife) used the children in order to create problems for us. He started to beat me again, dragged me and told me that I should get out. Every time he had fights with his children, he came back and hit me. The problem is ... he and I did not have any problems. The problems always came from his ex-wife and the children. Every time he had problems with them, he hit me.
A: So he listened to them and then he came back to beat you?
D: He was very weak in the relationship with his children and the family. Afterwards, at night, he came and kissed my hands and said 'I'm sorry.'

In Diana's story, her husband is very active in his use of violence against her. At the same time, she describes him as weak. People in his surroundings – in particular women – are portrayed as the ones standing behind the violence, not the man who abuses her. Diana left her husband when he threatened to send her own daughter back. As in Jasmin's story, loyalty to her daughter became a way to escape violence. However, in Diana's interpretation of the violence he used against her, the husband was not a perpetrator in control of his own acts, but a weak man not able to stand up against other women.

The cultural demands of loyalty towards men that appear in Jasmin and Adele's stories are confirmed when Diana interprets her violent experiences. Even though she has left the relationship, she does not blame her husband for the violence. The man who carried out the violent acts is not held responsible for the violence she was exposed to. Instead, she places the responsibility on the women 'behind' him who accuse her of staining the honour of the family, and thus she stays loyal to her husband. Using this as a point of departure, the author argues that one function of the cultural demands on women to show loyalty to men and disloyalty to each other is to avoid acknowledging men's responsibility for their violent acts.

One may see Diana, Jasmin and Adele as *cultural agents* in the sense that they use culturally meaningful statements when interpreting their own experiences (Brantsæter 2001). The normative demands of disloyalty between women and women's loyalty to men can – as has been done above – be interpreted within a framework of honour-cultural demands, in which women are expected to act according to the interests of the male collective in order to uphold the honour of the family. But could they also be interpreted as a confirmation of the cultural demands that dominate the country in which these three women are living (i.e. Swedish understandings of violence and men's non-responsibility)?

Women's loyalty to men: a demand crossing cultural boundaries

Apart from describing other women as responsible for the violence her husband exposed her to, Diana presents other explanations. Among these are, for example, her husband's psychological weakness and addiction to gambling. As shown above, she also draws a picture of her husband as weak and powerless in relation to people in his surroundings. Thus it is fruitful to interpret Diana as a cultural agent using culturally accepted explanations of men's violence in a Swedish context. A dominant understanding of violence in Swedish political initiatives and research is that violence is committed by men who – in different ways – are deviant (Wendt Höjer 2002; Mellberg 2004; SOU 2004). When searching for explanations as to why men use violence against women, the main question concerns the difference between violent men and other men. The answers differ: violent men express powerlessness; they are mentally ill; in different ways socially disadvantageous; they suffer from unhappy childhoods; or they are addicted to alcohol or the use of drugs. As mentioned above, the Swedish debate on honour violence fits well into this understanding of violence as a form of deviance. In this debate, individual and social deviance has been replaced by cultural issues: violence against women becomes a problem that is associated with foreign cultures.

What these approaches have in common is that they present the perpetrator as deviant in the sense that he is dissociated from the average Swedish man. According to a strong self-image, this average man is supposed to be gender equal. However, statistics provide a different story. According to the (so far) most comprehensive survey on men's violence against women in Sweden, published in 2001, the number of women reporting exposure to violence (physical violence, sexual violence and threats) by a man during their lifetime is 46 per cent (Lundgren et al. 2001). If almost every second woman has been exposed to violence, many men in Sweden are perpetrators. This shows a gap between the self-image of Swedish men as gender equal and the everyday experiences of women and men.

In her Mission to Sweden in 2006, the UN Special Rapporteur on Violence Against Women concluded that the gender equality agenda has not been effective in regard to violence against women. In her interpretation, Swedish society shows reluctance in 'addressing the deeply rooted unequal power relations between women and men which underlie the continuation of diverse forms of violence against women' (Ertürk 2007: 2; cf. Wendt-Höjer 2002).

Instead of seriously questioning the underlying cultural patterns of a country where so many women are still exposed to violence, in spite of many political initiatives supposedly promoting gender equality, violence in Swedish society is interpreted as an alien phenomenon. This makes men's violence appear a marginal problem, a problem for very few men and women. Violence is 'their' problem, not 'ours' (Lundgren 2004). Furthermore, the deviant-based explanations remove the man's responsibility for using violence. It is not the man who hits, rapes or murders – it is a foreign culture, an unhappy childhood, sickness, lack of education, alcohol or anabolic steroids. When the responsibility for the violence women are exposed to is located outside the individual man, the most obvious link between different cases of men's violence against women is lost: the fact is that these are crimes committed by men directed against women. Violence is located outside a gender-cultural context in which men are ranked higher than women, and is neither understood as an expression of gender power relations, nor as a means to uphold them.

Here, one can see a link between cultural demands on women in contexts characterised by upholding the honour of the family, and contexts characterised by upholding a self-image of gender equality. In both contexts, women are expected to show loyalty to the male collective. As shown above, in an honour-cultural context, women are expected to show disloyalty towards each other and loyalty to men in order to protect the honour of the family. In a context which has a strong self-image that stresses gender equality as more or less already achieved, women are expected to show loyalty to men in order to uphold this image. Hence, individual men are not seen as responsible for their behaviour (as they are assumed to be gender equal). And their violent acts are not perceived as acts committed in a cultural context giving men the right to dominate women (as this context is assumed to have reached gender equality) (cf. Lundgren and Westerstrand 2005). In both cases, the cultural demands function in a similar way: they take away men's responsibility for violence against women.

Women's responsibility: being loyal

What about women's responsibility? Does the author's argument imply a suggestion that women hold no responsibility for their actions in situations in which men use violence? The answer is no, of course. Throughout this chapter the author has tried to discuss both activity and responsibility, but from a perspective that makes visible the context of the violence and that does not make women responsible for men's acts.

In recent years, there has been a growing awareness in Sweden of the connection between violence directed towards women and their children. Research has shown the severe consequences for children living in families where their fathers are violent towards their mothers, and political initiatives that have been taken in order to come to terms with this (see Mellberg 2002; Eriksson et al. 2005). Government institutions and related agencies now need to use this knowledge the other way around. In cases of honour violence, Swedish society has chosen to put most, if not all, attention on the vulnerability of young women and daughters. It is the author's firm conviction that a relevant point of departure when professionals and others meet these young women is to ask whether there are other abused women in the family (i.e. mothers and sisters). Doing this generates knowledge about the connections in women's exposure to violence – mothers and their children, children and their mothers.

Conclusion

The focus on women as co-perpetrators of men's honour violence against women may in many cases be a blind alley. This focus redirects the questions and actions, and removes men's individual responsibility for their violent acts, while it makes the gender-cultural context in which the violence takes place invisible. However, this does not mean that it is irrelevant to talk about women's activity in, and responsibility for, violence directed towards other women.

A path more fruitful than blaming women for men's violence would be to understand women's responsibility in terms of loyalty. As shown in this chapter, women meet cultural demands of loyalty to men in an honour-cultural context as well as in a context in which gender equality is an ideal. Women are thus made responsible for showing loyalty to the male collective and for hiding men's responsibility for their violent acts. And when men's responsibility is hidden, this gives them leeway to continue using violence against women.

In the empirical examples presented in this chapter – the interviews and the briefly sketched legal cases – disloyalty to men has shown women a way to escape the violence and made it possible to punish men for their violent acts. This is not an easy path, but it may be a necessary one, in order to change cultural demands of upholding the strength of the (honour-cultural or gender-equal) male collective, and to seriously combat violence against women.

Notes

1 This is in line with Liz Kelly's concept 'the continuum of violence', which was introduced in 1988 and has since been widely used in feminist research on violence against women. Kelly uses this concept in order to make visible the connections between severe violence and less severe violence and control (Kelly 1988). Using this understanding, violence is not treated as an isolated phenomenon, but as taking place in a context which – more or less openly – accepts men's right to use violence against women. This understanding is also the point of departure for United Nation's work against violence (see e.g. UN 1993).

2 The author sees culture as created through human acts and interpretations, carried out in contexts where the individual relates to frames of interpretations which may be more or less normative (cf. Geertz 1973; Lundgren 2001).

3 For an overview on how honour is linked to violence and used in different cultural and national contexts, see Welchmann and Hossain (2005b).

4 In 2007, the Swedish government announced initiatives to combat violence against women, honour violence and violence among same-sex couples, which, all in all, are much larger: 800 million Swedish kronor (Regeringens skrivelse 2007/08:39).

5 For a presentation of the resistance against Swedish initiatives on violence against women, see for example SOU 2004.

6 This pattern appears, for example, in handbooks on honour violence that are widespread among professionals within social services, the police and the courts. These have a strong focus on young women (often using the term *flicka*, 'girl', which has old-fashioned associations), while grown-up women are seldom referred to as victims of violence. Another example is how the Swedish government's latest action plan to combat 'honour related violence and oppression' stresses that women may be direct perpetrators in cases of honour violence, as well as indirect supporters of the violent acts (Regeringens skrivelse 2007/08:39).

7 For a classical analysis on the East-West dichotomy, see Said (1978).

8 In the article *Hederns försvarare* (Defenders of Honour), Jenny Westerstrand and I show connections between different victims of violence in a legal case of an honour killing and how these are relevant before, as well as after, the killing. We also argue that different perpetrators must be understood together in order to make violence and the responsibility for violence legally visible (Eldén and Westerstrand 2004).

9 These interviews have been conducted within the project *Spänningsfyllt moderskap* ('Tense motherhood'), financed by the Research section of the Nordic Council of Ministers (*NordForsk*).

10 All names and other details which might make possible an identification of the interviewees have been changed.

11 Nadera Shaloub-Kevorkian's research on violence against women in a Palestinian context contains stories that are very similar to Adele's and Jasmin's. For instance, the mother of a raped girl says: 'An honourable woman knows how to raise her

daughters. Mothers are to be held responsible for any dishonourable behaviour by their daughters' (Shaloub-Kevorkian 1999: 162).

Bibliography

Brantsæter, M. (2001) *Møter med menn dømt for seksuelle overgrep mot barn*. Oslo: Oslo University.

Eldén, Å. (2001) '"Om hon lever vill människor se mer och mer". Rykten, splittrad kvinnlighet och heder bland unga kvinnor från Mellanöstern', in *Sociologisk forskning* 3–4 2001.

——(2004) 'Life-and-Death Honour. Young Womens Violent Stories About Reputation, Virginity and Honour – In a Swedish Context', in Mojab, S. and Abdo, N. *Violence in The Name of Honour – Theoretical and Political Challenges*. Istanbul: Istanbul Bilgi University Press.

Eldén, Å. and Westerstrand, J. (2004) 'Hederns försvarare. Den rättsliga hanteringen av ett hedersmord', in *Kvinnovetenskaplig tidskrift* no. 3, 2004.

Eriksson, M. et al. (2005) *Tackling Men's Violence in Families. Nordic Issues and Dilemmas*. Bristol: Policy Press.

Ertürk, Y. (2007) *Mission to Sweden. Report of the Special Rapporteur on violence against women*. Human Rights Council A/HRC/4/34/Add.3.

Geertz, C. (1973) *The Interpretation of Cultures*, New York: Basic Books.

Kelly, L. (1988) *Surviving Sexual Violence*, Minneapolis: University of Minnesota Press.

Lundgren, E. (2001) *Ekte kvinne? Identitet på kryss of tvers*, Oslo: Pax forlag.

——(2004) *The Process of Normalizing Violence*, Stockholm: ROKS.

Lundgren, E. and Westerstrand, J. (2005) 'Behövs en sammanhållen våldsförståelse?', in *Socialmedicinsk tidskrift* No. 6 2005.

Mellberg, N. (2002) *När det overkliga blir verklighet. Mödrars situation när deras barn utsätts för sexuella övergrepp av fäder*. Umeå: Boréa.

——(2004) *Mäns våld mot kvinnor: synliga mödrar och osynliga barn*. Uppsala: Uppsala universitet.

Regeringens skrivelse 2007/08:39 *Handlingsplan för att bekämpa mäns våld mot kvinnor, hedersrelaterat våld och förtryck samt våld i samkönade relationer.*

Said, E. (1978) *Orientalism*. London: Routledge.

Sen, P. (2005) 'Crimes of Honour. Value and Meaning', in Welchman, L. and Hossain, S. (eds) *'Honour': Crimes, Paradigms and Violence Against Women*. London and New York: Zed Books.

Shaloub-Kevorkian, N. (1999) 'Towards a Cultural Definition of Rape: Dilemmas in Dealing with Rape Victims in Palestinian Society', in *Women Studies International Forum*, No. 2 1999.

——(2004) *Mapping and Analyzing the Landscape of Femicide in Palestinian Society*, Jerusalem: UNIFEM and Women's Center for Legal Aid and Counselling.

SOU 2004:121 *Slag i luften. En utredning om myndigheter, mansvåld och makt. Betänkande av utredningen om kvinnofridsuppdragen.*

Svalastog, A-L (1998) *Det var ikke meningen … Om konstruksjon av kjønn ved abortinngrep, et feministteoretisk bidrag*. Uppsala: Uppsala University.

UN (1993) *The Declaration on the Elimination of Violence Against Women*. A/RES/48/104.

Welchmann, L. and Hossain, S. (2005a) 'Honour, Rights and Wrongs', in Welchman, L. and Hossain, S. (eds) *'Honour': Crimes, Paradigms and Violence Against Women*. London and New York: Zed Books.

Welchman, L. and Hossain, S. (2005b) (eds) *'Honour': Crimes, Paradigms and Violence Against Women*. London and New York: Zed Books.

Wendt Höjer, M. (2002) *Rädslans politik. Våld och sexualitet i den svenska demokratin*. Stockholm: Liber.

Chapter 10

Lack of due diligence

Judgements of crimes of honour in Turkey

Dr Leylâ Pervizat
*Lecturer in Gender Studies and Intra-Family Violence at
the Halic University, Istanbul, Turkey*

Introduction

Crimes of honour are women's human-rights violations. These specific forms of violations, killing women in the name of honour (and the various forms of violence resulting from honour codes) are widespread in Turkey. This highly sensitive and controversial issue is discussed in this chapter from a variety of perspectives: the lack of due diligence and legal and cultural punishments (despite the recent developments on the eradication of these crimes of honour) is the main focus of this chapter. First, the author attempts to address the terms used, namely *honour* and *custom,* in dealing with honour crimes in Turkey. An ongoing volatile political environment, the effects of the armed conflict in gender relations and their effect on these types of gender-based violence must be kept in mind when analysing these different terminologies. What breaches the code of honour, how breaches are handled differently in various circumstances, and what 'cleans the dirt on the family name' are detailed and explained. Most importantly, the sequence of events and different factors leading to an 'honour killing' are also presented. All of these issues (addressed in the second part of this chapter) are illustrated with a case study from Şanlıurfa. Although the case took place some time ago, it is still a very typical example of what happens in crimes-of-honour cases in Turkey. The transgression of the social codes, restoring honour within the family, the court procedures adopted and the final verdict of the court highlight some very crucial issues in cases like the one selected for discussion. The chapter finally addresses the reforms made in an attempt to eradicate the practice of HRV in Turkey in recent times.

What *makes* an honour killing?

The concept of honour (*namus*) denotes a series of codes which include different variables in its content as well as different implementation procedures, in controlling and regulating women's sexuality, their lives, their choices and their autonomy, all within a hegemonic masculine order in which we live.

All of these codes, their procedures for implementation and their implications change over time and space within any given culture. Thus, these codes are not static; on the contrary, they are embodied within ever-changing qualities and standards. Within this constantly changing framework, the concept of honour in Turkey's context is almost exclusively related to the women, their bodies, sexualities and lives. Thus, crimes of honour are the result of actual and/or perceived transgression of these boundaries, and individuals who are perceived to have violated these values and standards (which sometimes are at odds even with the social traditions and norms of the society in which they live) are subjected to crimes of honour.[1] What constitutes the transgression of these codes, and what are the specific implications for each transgression, vary according to the geographical location and/or the socioeconomic context of each transgressor. The transgression can be as minor as telephoning the local radio station and requesting a favourite song be played (and the request being witnessed by members of the family); or going to the corner shop to get chewing gum in Şanlıurfa; or even a (married) woman asking a stranger at a shopping mall what the time is (even while she is shopping with her husband) in İzmir, one of the developed cities in the Aegean region. All of these violations have the concept of honour at the heart of the application of violence. When these kinds of transgressions occur, it is believed that they create a stain on the family honour. The remedies for cleansing the stain on the family honour, it is believed, must be achieved (and depend on the severity of the situation). Of course, within the hegemonic masculine order in which we live, the honour cleansers are usually men. However, an important point must be made here given the nature of the discussions taking place around this subject. While the one who 'pulls the trigger' in the name of honour may be a man or a young male, the role of women in these executions must be appreciated diligently if law enforcement and other legal agencies want to eradicate these crimes. Women, like sisters or mothers-in-law, are extremely powerful players in the aiding and abetting of executions, as well as the commission of offences leading up to executions. This issue must be carefully appreciated, no matter how much it may offend feminists or members of women's movements. The roles of both men and women are very controversial in debates on honour violence. While executing a woman is seen as a rite of passage into manhood for some young men or boys (who may avoid much tougher sentences at trial due to child-protection laws), it is clear that not all young boys are eager to kill their sisters; likewise, not every woman is eager to help another woman in this situation.

The punishments for transgressing the boundaries of honour are generally the public execution of female children and women. Quite often there is a public display element to these cold-blooded executions, closely followed by locals visiting perpetrators after a murder has been carried out, with locals even sending 'get well' wishes if, for some reason, those perpetrators find themselves in hospital. In other words, the injured party or the victim here is not viewed as the girl or woman, but the man who needed to follow a code to 'eliminate the woman so the family honour can be restored'. In such circumstances, the honour code perceives that a man carries the pain and burden of a woman's transgressions, and his duty to carry out an execution is caused by the 'fault of this woman'.

In Turkey's context, there is another crucial angle to this debate. Some people view that the term custom (töre)[2] must be used and/or replace the term honour in debating these executions and the codes relating to these executions. There are several reasons for the insistence of this debate: one pertains to the traditional roles of women and keeping these values intact in the midst of the modernisation process. Some women's organisations do not advocate the abolition of certain honour codes (as well as their implications). Although they are against the execution of women in the name of honour, they still believe in (and wish to hold on to) the concept of honour as a way 'to make our daughters citizens with good morals'. Even though they may seem or sound progressive, the reason(s) behind holding on to the concept of honour reveal a quite traditional and patriarchal view towards women's sexuality. Other proponents of this view believe that these types of executions will disappear with the eradication of the feudal system. If one examines this argument, one must assume that the feudal wars resulting from land disputes, blood feuds and/or animal ownership are exactly same as controlling women's sexuality. What is important in custom killings is the maintenance of the order within the tribal structure and the feudal system. A generalisation would stipulate that mostly men kill other men in such killings. Although women may also be victims of custom killings, this does not relate to the expression of women's autonomy in terms of their bodies and lives, nor their opposition against the society in which they live in terms of the 'individualisation of women'. Crimes of honour are a control system regulating women's sexualities; custom killings may disappear with the modernisation of society, as is widely noted in the western parts of the country, but the control of women's sexuality within the honour code still strongly continues. This is simply because the essence of the honour concept is the control of women by society, and patriarchal males are reluctant to let go of this aspect of the honour dynamic.

Another dimension to the discussion of the custom versus honour debate in Turkey is also thought-provoking: some high-ranking authorities have made explicit declarations stating that 'these killings do not include Turkey in general' but 'are restricted to only South-eastern Anatolia'. Here, the intended political message is that 'backward Kurds are killing their women', and the rest of Turkey does not have a problem with crimes of honour, or HRV. Their political opinion is that this is a Kurdish problem and that it can be solved once the region is developed economically. However, problems with these arguments (as every feminist researcher is well aware) are that violence against women and incidents of femicide do not disappear through the abolition of feudalism. Patriarchy and hegemonic masculine orders persist, although they may change their forms and adapt different practices and cultural conditions towards controlling women. Whether crimes of honour are a Kurdish practice, only belonging to the Kurdish culture, can be explained away by looking into the gender and women based statistics in the country. However, the state regularly fails to provide comprehensive statistics on gender and women-related issues. While this is an urgent issue concerning women's rights that requires addressing, the authorities are being questioned more and more on crimes of honour. Responding to a written deposition from a Member of the Parliament, Fatma Kurtalan, the Ministry of Justice reported that in the first six months of 2009 alone, 953 women were murdered in the country with the majority of cases suspected to be the result of honour killings and honour related violence.

Furthermore, the establishment of an independent Kurdish women's movement in the region during the armed conflict and the atrocities endured by women require additional consideration. The ongoing 30-year-long conflict in Turkey has had a major, disproportionate impact upon women. Severe poverty in one of the poorest regions in the country can be considered itself as a form of violence. Nationalist politics, coupled with the feudal system, have made women's lives extremely difficult. The armed conflict has affected women's human-rights issues, and specifically honour killings, and how local men respond to interventions from the state, women's movement groups and the media as 'outside' institutions. The powerful militarism, nationalist movements, politics and policies hinder the creation of a prosperous and peaceful existence, as well as failing to maximise women's rights. Women's lives and bodies have become the battleground where men demonstrate their manhood; the control of women becomes a primary indicator of manhood, power, strength and hegemony. The control and authority exercised over women results in severe forms of violence and the violation of women's rights. However, a recent development is the continuing struggle by powerful independent women's movements in Turkey, which are able to address many issues and continue to help local women to become the creators of their own lives.

A case of then ...

The case of Gönül Aslan illustrates a very well-known example of a woman's transgression of accepted social norms; the decision-making process of the family council about the appropriate punishment; the execution process; and the thought process of the judiciary and the courts in relation to crimes of honour (Şanlıurfa, Dec.: 1998/170). Gönül's situation began as a *typical* case of forced marriage which resulted in an attempted murder case in the name of honour. A detailed look into the specifics of this case demonstrates how the state did not, with due diligence, prosecute it, and how there is gender-based persecution of women who disobey the social norms in which they live. The legal and social punishments for these types of cases are very clearly documented in the author's doctoral dissertation, which was written after analysing 200 cases. The case is just another example of the sentences provided by Turkish courts. However, this nearly 12-year-old case is slightly different from the other cases the author has been collating. Since the victim survived attempted murder and told her story to the media, it captured the public's attention and made this third-page news into a 'colourful story' to document. Moreover, the ratio of the judgement and the ruling of the case by the Turkish court has one of the most interesting uses of language and semantics amongst the cases the author has collected. It simply demonstrates the state's active role in permitting violence in these types of cases.

Gönül Aslan, after surviving the attempt on her life, explained the following at the preliminary hearing at the Office of the Public Prosecutor of the Republic. She was forced to marry Sakıp Aslan, her paternal cousin (i.e. her father's brother's son) in a religious wedding. She was not happy with the marriage and ran away with Nihat Türk, whom she had been seeing for a while. Her family found them in Aydın and brought her back home to Antalya. After the family committee decision, the male members of the family decided to kill her. Her sister, Sevgi Aslan, notified her about the outcome of the decision of the family. The perpetrators, exclusively male family members and namely Sakıp, Osman, Abdullah and Mahmut, set off with her in a car driven by Hacı. The journey started in Antalya and lasted until they had arrived in Viranşehir, Şanlıurfa. Initially, Mahmut asked his son, Ali, to commit the execution, but Ali declined. So there was a lengthy debate on how and who should murder the woman before, and during, the journey. Allegedly, they were also asking Gönül to reconcile with her husband. They stopped at the side of the Euphrates, a big river running through several countries in the region. Abdullah Aslan wrapped a scarf around her neck; Sakıp held the sides of the scarf; and both pulled the ends of the scarf to suffocate her. Because of the suffocation, she passed out and was thrown into water. She soon came to her senses after hitting the water; she did not remember how she was thrown into the river. She heard the perpetrators were talking amongst themselves about whether she was dead or not; in a moment of desperation, she pretended that she was dead. She did not know for how long the river would drag her along. She later got out of the river by holding onto the tree branches in the water and asked help from a man at a nearby gas station.

Of course, this 'colourful story' led to a trial, followed closely by the media at the time. First, the court never took into account that this was a forced-marriage case, although there were lengthy discussions about the issue of religious weddings. In the judgement, the judge ruled that this was not a forced marriage:

> It is not true that the complaining injured party was married to her
> accused husband Sakıp Aslan against her own volition. The contrary is
> clearly illustrated by the wedding photographs and statements ... Sakıp
> had seen Gönül before and liked her and asked her to marry, the injured
> Gönül had agreed and she had married him of her own volition.

In this case, a woman's autonomy, her free choices and free will, were clearly
unrecognised by the state and the Turkish courts. Even after she had told
officials that this was a forced marriage, her words were not taken into
account and were ignored. Marriages in Turkey are widely arranged and
decided by parents, mainly in less developed areas but also in more developed areas, and are forced upon young children and adults. Most often, the
woman (as well as the man) might not have much say about the marriage.
The judge's statement in this case reflects a prevailing view in society that
disregards women's rights as well as international agreements Turkey has
signed on the freedom of women. Moreover, the issue of handling the testimonies of women is a very important concern, which is currently receiving
legal attention by women's human-rights lawyers in Turkey. As was stated in
the judgement, all of the defendants and witnesses changed their testimony
at the trial after the initial interrogation process at the Prosecutor's Office.
The issue has two extremely troubling sides which require urgent intervention and analysis. First of all (and earlier on in the author's research into
these cases), it was extremely revealing for the author to discover (after such
a detailed and premeditated execution process) that some of the perpetrators
did not attempt to cover their tracks, or make up a better story, to avoid
being put on trial. This appears to be a common pattern, not only in this
case, but also in other cases in the author's research. It is assumed that the
true intent of not attempting to hide or change stories about 'how the
execution process was undertaken' relates to the perpetrators' assumption
that they had 'the right to cleanse the dirt from the family honour'. The perpetrators treated the entire process as their 'given and granted right'. The
reason for their honesty at the initial periods of the investigations stemmed
from this understanding, and it was noted that the perpetrators had difficulty
understanding why the state was intervening in such cases. In other words,
when it concerns the issue of honour, society is the judge, jury and executioner,
not the state. Perpetrators of crimes of honour expect that the state should
understand and give necessary permission to the 'defenders of such honour'.[3]

Second, as was the situation with Ali and Sevgi Aslan, some of the witnesses changed their testimonies during the trial. Ali, a male relative, may
have had different reasons for changing his testimony than Gönül's sister,
Sevgi. Ali's change can be explained by the fear of being prosecuted. However, for Sevgi (the victim's sister), the reasons for changing her testimony
were substantially different. As a woman, she must obey the orders of the
male members of the family, otherwise defying the family code may bring

about a similar punishment to Gönül's. Not only would she be expelled from her family, but the family might also execute her. So, under coercion, intimidation and duress, changing testimony is more common for women in these cases than for men. Still, the current situation in Turkey is an inadequate protection of witnesses within the legal system in relation to HRV.

On the question of premeditation, the judge also went to great lengths to explain how the attempted murder of Gönül was not a premeditated action, by declaring that: ' ... when the file was examined it was agreed that the incident did not include the elements of premeditation.' Explicitly, the Turkish judge denied the existence of evidence, as well as the testimonies of witnesses, that the acts were premeditated leading up to the failed execution. As mentioned earlier, the male members of the family 'picked her up in Aydın and brought her back to Antalya'. The family had a meeting, and it was decided that the victim was 'a disgrace to the family'. Male members of the family then drove her to Viranşehir, Şanlıurfa. Travelling from/to all of these cities, and deciding upon the nature of the execution with her father present, must have taken days, as noted by the victim as well as in the initial testimonies of the defendants and witnesses. Aydın is a province in the Aegean region of Turkey; Antalya is in the Mediterranean region, and Viranşehir is in the Southeastern region. In a country as big as Turkey, this involves several days of travelling. Unfortunately, the court disregarded this evidence in its ruling that the acts were not premeditated:

> According to the content of the file, the talks carried out by the elders stating that it was a matter of honour and that it had to be cleansed was not considered sufficient for premeditation, in order for it to be sufficient it is necessary that a decision is taken on who would commit the murder and how it would be committed, preparations are made, the plan is executed, and the act is concluded calmly without giving up, and these are not present in the incident at hand, thus the act is not considered as a full attempt at murder with criminal intention.

The judge insisted that the element of composure and premeditation was non-existent in this case by stating:

> ' ... this girl is a disgrace, let's throw her into Fırat;' acting on this suggestion the vehicle was stopped and the act was committed ... It is illustrated by the content of the file that the very short time that elapsed between the adoption of the idea of throwing her into the water and the implementation of it by the accused is not enough for imperturbability necessary for premeditation and that the incident materialised with criminal intention ... If the decision of murder was taken imperturbably by the family council, which would provide the condition for pre-meditation, there would be nothing that would prevent the immediate

execution of it since the injured was in the same house with the accused, thus it appears that such a decision was not taken beforehand, it was only discussed that it was a matter of honour, the idea of killing the injured by throwing her into Fırat came up in the vehicle and was immediately implemented.

Another highly interesting point is the 'issue regarding culture'. In court, the judiciary denied Gönül's declaration on 'being forced into marriage'; Sevgi changed her testimony based on 'cultural factors' because of family and societal pressure and because of the long and prevalent history of crimes of honour in the country. However, while the judge disregarded the cultural elements of the execution process of honour killings on the one hand, on the other he acknowledged the 'unchaste behaviour of Gönül' and 'the judiciary's role in dealing with moral issues':

> ... the injured was not forced to marry her husband the accused Sakıp Aslan, it is obvious that the injured did not comply with the principle of honesty and loyalty based on the moral principles determined by both the Civil Law and the society, and she made a habit of that, she constantly provoked and humiliated her husband and her family by such conduct of hers, under these circumstances the law cannot credit an understanding which considers illegitimate and immoral relations normal.

What this aspect of the judgement demonstrates is that women are the property and the display of familial honour; if there is a stain on the family it is her fault that she brought about the stain to her family, yet it is the perpetrator's responsibility to 'cleanse' it. The perpetrators, who are overwhelmingly men, are viewed and understood as the victims, yet the chastity of a woman is what is really on trial in this case. Furthermore, the court treated the perpetrators extremely leniently for supposedly 'correcting the transgressions of women' by making explicit statements about the virtue of the women:

> The fact that the testimony of the complaining injured victim could not be taken despite all the investigation conducted during the process of trial, and although her place was known by the relevant units of the State, and her refusal of giving her testimony in order to help the proceedings of the court cannot be explained all by the lack of security concerning her life. Her testimony could have been taken in any place out of Şanlıurfa on an indefinite day and then she could have been placed under protection. Again, however, the complaining injured victim did not do this and she used the process of trial as a means of revenge on the accused, and this is incompatible with the principles of justice and equity. Thus, our court hesitates to consider the claims of the

complaining injured victim as sincere ... The rules of law concerning severe provocation on behalf of the accused were applied, but not on the ground that the accused exhibited good conduct during the investigation and trials.

And the following excerpt clearly demonstrates the judiciary's attitude towards women's human-rights issues, specifically towards crimes of honour in Turkey:

It is not possible in any way that the judiciary might have formed an opinion under the influence of any sex, or any ideology protecting that sex, or the media which tries to evaluate and promote the incident in terms of its inadequate legal and social dimensions ... The most convenient method compatible with the norms of the criminal court is to evaluate each case within its unique concrete and objective conditions and to differentiate each punishment by taking into consideration the site of the crime, the social, psychological and societal status of the perpetrators. The judiciary and in this sense our court has no mission of 'intimidating the society' for the matter of the elimination of custom and honour killings ... Although such murders and attempted murders are committed in similar conditions, if not the same, not only in Şanlıurfa but all around our country, it is meaningful that recently, especially Şanlıurfa, started to be mentioned with 'Custom and Honour Killings' in a way which causes excitement, and the province started to be remembered with these features only (emphasis added).

In their verdict, the Turkish court acquitted Ali and Osman Aslan. Abdullah, Sakıp, and Mahmut Aslan were sentenced to four years, five months and 11 days each. Hacı Aslan, the driver, was sentenced to two years, two months and 20 days. These lenient punishments for defendants in cases like these, as well as the explicit statements of the Turkish court in this case, demonstrate a serious lack of due diligence in prosecuting and punishing honour-killing cases and granting lenient sentences to the perpetrators of those who clearly infringe on women's rights.

... and now?

So what has changed, and what is the current situation in Turkey? Turkey has made significant attempts *on paper* to eradicate crimes of honour in the country. To all intents and purposes, these reforms are extremely important and are significant steps, and some have international implications too. However, a majority of these recent positive steps at reform are yet to be implemented on a national level. The issue took a significant turn in November 2002 with the attempted execution of Şemse Allak by stoning, known as *recm*. At the time, the people of Turkey thought that *recm* was a practice belonging to the neighbouring countries in the region, and the news of Şemse's case helped move the issue from the third page to headlines on the first page of daily newspapers. The issue also became a top priority for the European Union (EU) and its officials, since Turkey was in the midst of an accession process. All this led to serious and widespread debates, especially during the drafting of the Turkish Penal Code. Even with strong pressure from women's movements and from EU Officials, the new Penal Code does not consider drafting rules issuing stricter sentences for perpetrators of crimes of honour. The new Penal Code, however, does include a reference to custom killings in its language.[4] The cultural and political significance of the difference between these terms has already been addressed above.

Furthermore, on 4 July 2007, the Prime Minister's Office issued a declaration entitled 'Preventive Measures for Violence Against Children and Women and for Custom and Honour Killings'.[5] This is a powerful, seven-page document, outlining the role of the government in eradicating crimes of honour, if it is implemented. The declaration came after the investigations of the Parliamentary Commission responsible for researching honour and custom killings.[6] Moreover, the Women's Status General Directorate stated that it would conduct a nationwide research project on gender and violence. The General Directorate of Police also issued statistics regarding custom and honour killings.[7] The Presidency of Religious Affairs also issued a press release on 8 March 2004 stating that 'crimes of honour have no place in the Koran and the Islamic religion'.[8]

In the autumn of 2004, the government made yet another surprising attempt in the international arena towards highlighting its objective of eradicating crimes of honour. Turkey, for the first time in its history since its inception 87 years ago, undertook a main resolution on women's rights regarding crimes of honour at the United Nations General Assembly Third Committee (UN A/C.3/59/L.25: 15 October 2004). The resolution was sponsored jointly by Turkey and the United Kingdom and had eight co-sponsors from the Organisation of the Islamic Countries.[9] In addition, Turkey has been co-sponsoring a resolution on extra-judicial executions (i.e. honour killings) at the United Nations Commission on Human Rights since 2000.[10]

However, while these are all very important steps, Cemil Çiçek, the Minister of Justice at the time, did not at any stage mention any of these international attempts during his public speeches. AKP (the Justice and Development Party), the ruling party, cannot and will not alienate its own constituency by talking about women's rights issues as human-rights issues, or labelling crimes of honour as forms of extra-judicial execution, although the state has signed international instruments at the UN. The conservative government of the AKP, also known as practitioners of 'mild Islam', hold very traditional views regarding women.[11] The reforms the party recommended after winning the elections in the autumn of 2002 are not social and cultural reforms maximising women's human-rights issues; they are more legal-orientated economic and political reforms without gender-based perspectives, even with the adoption of new Penal Code. Unfortunately, the author's preliminary findings on the current developments concerning the new Penal Code demonstrate that a lack of due diligence is still persisting in the handling of crimes of honour in the country by the authorities since the adoption of the new Penal Code.[12]

Conclusion

Crimes of honour are seen as major forms of violence against women, but not as violations of women's human rights in Turkey. There is great interest in discussing crimes of honour in general, by government officials as well as by the public. However, this discussion, whether intentionally or not, fails to discuss the concept of crimes of honour in the context of women's sexuality and women's human rights. While recent developments are greatly encouraging and hopeful, the nature of cases and the way they are handled does not inspire confidence: cases of crimes of honour in Turkey are still not prosecuted with due diligence at a judicial level and there is substantial work that needs to be done about the cultural transformation regarding women's human-rights issues. There is still a long way to go towards the eradication of crimes of honour in Turkey.

Notes

1 The author adopts this definition of honour killings in her research after reading a Pakistani woman's application on the grounds for fear of murder in the name of honour to the British authorities: see *Islam v. Secretary of State for the Home Department; Regina v. Immigration Appeal Tribunal and Another, ex parte Shah* (Conjoined Appeals) 25 March 1999.

2 *Sözlerin Soyağacı: Çağdaş Türkçenin Etimolojik Sözlüğü* (Sevan Nişanyan, Adam Yayınları 2003) mentions the two origins of the word *töre* (custom). First, it has the meaning of customs (*adet*) and morals (*ahlak*), as used in 1942. It derives from Mongolian. In Mongolian, it means traditional Mongolian Law. In old Turkish, it is used as *törü*, meaning law, organisation, order and custom. It should also be noted that *Törü* or *töre* actually originates from the name Torah, which is the Old Testament. In addition to these meanings, *tör* in Mongolian also means the state.

3 This is one of the major changes in recent years after the public campaigns and awareness-raising activities conducted by feminist activists, especially during the reform process of the Turkish Penal Code. The judges are more and more pointing towards gender inequalities and violence against women in their judgements these days.

4 The Turkish Penal Code No: 5237 accepted on 26 October 2004, became effective on 1 June 2005. The Code was published in the Official Gazette No: 25611 on 12 October 2004. It is generally considered very progressive on many

areas of women's rights, recognising the individuality of women and their bodily rights.

5 Prime Ministerial Declaration Number 2006/17, Ankara, Turkey. The author believes that this Declaration is very comprehensive if it is to be implemented.

6 Officially titled and numbered: *Töre ve Namus Cinayetleri ile Kadınlara ve Çocuklara Yönelik Şiddetin Sebeplerinin Araştırılarak Alınması Gereken Önlemlerin Belirlenmesi Amacıyla Kurulan Meclis Araştırması Komisyonu 10/148, 182, 187, 284, 285.* The author also testified before this Commission on 18 October 2005. Unfortunately, the author believes that the members of the Commission were driven by political ambitions and the prospect of personal gains, and some of the experts sitting on the Commission were not sufficiently experienced to appreciate the issues. In the end, the report was obscured for political reasons, and by lack of expertise. However, this Commission led the way to the drafting of the Prime Ministerial Declaration, explained above.

7 The National Police Department published its research at the time on its web page (http://www.egm.gov.tr), though the research is now no longer accessible. The statistics can be found in the extensive report of the Parliamentary Commission.

8 See http://www.diyanet.gov.tr/english/default.asp.

9 United Nations General Assembly Resolution A/C.3/59/L.25: 15 October 2004. The resolution in 19 different languages can be obtained at http://www.wunrn.com/reference/crimes_honor.htm.

10 http://ap.ohchr.org/documents/E/CHR/resolutions/E-CN_4-RES-2000-31.doc.

11 At the time of writing, Turkey is going through major political reforms, including the reconciliation of the Kurdish issue of some 30 years.

12 While the author notes some major improvements at some of the courts in Diyarbakır, the Supreme Court in Turkey recently appeared to inadvertently approve the execution of women and girls in the name of honour by demanding 'good proof of family committee decisions' as part of its review of evidence at trials: http://www.bianet.org/bianet/kadin/109544-kadinlarin-katillerini-yargitay-koruyor (accessed on 7 May 2009.)

Bibliography

Prime Ministerial Declaration *Töre ve Namus Cinayetleri ile Kadınlara ve Çocuklara Yönelik Şiddetin Sebeplerinin Araştırılarak Alınması Gereken Önlemlerin Belirlenmesi Amacıyla Kurulan Meclis Araştırması Komisyonu* 2006/17, Ankara, Turkey.

ŞanlıUrfa Criminal Court Decision No: 1998/170.

Nişanyan, S. *Sözlerin Soyağacı: Çağdaş Türkçenin Etimolojik Sözlüğü* İstanbul: Adam Yayınları, 2003.

The Turkish Penal Code, No: 5237.

United Nations Commission on Human Rights 60th Session, Resolution 2000/31.

United Nations General Assembly Resolution, A/C.3/59/L.25, 15 October 2004.

Press Release of The Republic of Turkey Presidency of Religious Affairs Press and Human Relations Office on March 8 2004, World Women's Day. Available at http://www.diyanet.gov.tr/english (accessed on 30 September 2009).

Chapter 11

A comparative study of the reform work conducted in Asia and Europe to combat violence and 'so-called' honour murders[*]

Rana Husseini
Author, Senior News Reporter and Human Rights Activist,
Amman, Jordan

Introduction

'So-called' honour crimes and honour-related violence (HRV) against women are deeply rooted in history and date back to ancient civilizations across many continents. Global statistics of honour killing or murders are also very disturbing: in 2000, the United Nations Population Fund estimated that every year over 5,000 women die in honour killings around the world.[1] Honour crimes are reported to take place in many countries, permeating all religions and all social classes. This chapter will provide a commentary on the problem of HRV in those societies with the most recent activism against the rising trend of the phenomenon, including over a decade's work by governments and activists in Europe attempting to minimise the number of HRV crimes, amending laws on punishments for perpetrators of such crimes and offering professional help to 'migrant' communities, where the vast majority of these crimes take place.

The reform work

Some societies appear to have made inroads into transforming people's attitudes about HRV, as well as the legal handling of perpetrators of such crimes (by initially treating these types of killings as 'normal' murders). Murders in the name of 'so-called' honour were in the past (and are still) considered as being the accepted punishment for a female accused of sexual infidelity. However, while some societies create and enforce laws against domestic abusers, other societies remain somewhat inactive; they are still fighting to enforce social and legal reforms to protect women as victims of violence. Reform efforts have been documented in some countries, mainly in the Third World, where the general attitude is to hold women responsible for acts of adultery or fornication and inflict punishment upon them, while at the same time these societies turn a blind eye towards male adulterers who engage in sexual activities (and are not punished or rebuked even for their transgressions). The legal system plays an important role in reinforcing these oppressive attitudes when men who are convicted of murders in the name of 'so-called' honour are met with especially lenient sentences. In countries such as Jordan (until, perhaps, recently) and Egypt, those who commit crimes of honour appeared to have very lenient sentences imposed upon them (e.g. some get away with as little as three months imprisonment for killing a sister or daughter in the name of honour). It is worth noting at this juncture that in many countries, activism and government actions occurred following a specific case that created a public outcry in the community and forced individuals, groups and the government to campaign seriously against these crimes. Activism within these countries began in the mid-1990s and continues to this day.

Jordan and the surrounding region

In Jordan approximately 20 women are killed annually in the name of honour. A strong movement began in the mid-1990s to amend some of the laws that appear to provide lenient custodial sentences to perpetrators of honour killings. It began with a series of articles in local newspapers as well as seminars and workshops organised by women's rights groups. Religious figures, the Jordanian Royal family, women's rights organisations and other leaders in the community began to speak openly against these crimes. The activism by these individuals, the media and non-governmental organisations (NGOs) grabbed international media attention, and several documentaries were produced on the issue by the end of the 1990s, on Jordan and other countries within the region. The international attention prompted a group of young activists to form a local committee named 'The Jordanian National Committee to Eliminate So-Called Honor Crimes'. The Committee focused on campaigns, collecting signatures, distributing pamphlets and raising awareness regarding the discriminatory clauses in the legal system, the right of life, the right to a fair trial and the negative consequences of these crimes upon women and their families. The Committee's aim was to collect 50,000 signatures, a specific number needed in order for the Jordanian Parliament to present an amendment to the law in Jordan. The long-term objective was to start a new trend in Jordan of involving civic society in activities such as signing petitions and presenting them to Parliament on serious and important issues such as HRV. The petition was the first of its kind and nature in the history of the Kingdom.

The Committee, with its tireless campaign, only managed to collect a little over 15,000 signatures, and the draft law that the government proposed (to enforce much stricter punishment against perpetrators of honour killings) was defeated twice in the Lower House. However, the continued efforts of activism in Jordan eventually began to bear fruit. Awareness on the issues increased people's attention and changed attitudes about accepting and/or encouraging these types of murders; as time passed, more and more people began to show their rejection of these murders and violence against women in general. There were also reports of change in attitudes amongst the Jordanian judiciary, in terms of passing tougher punishments against perpetrators. Criminal prosecutors began taking the prosecution of murders more seriously, expanding their investigations when the case appeared to involve a murdered woman or a woman who appeared to be killed in suspicious circumstances (such as disappearances, accidents or suicides).

There is still the occasional demonstration of lenient sentences imposed upon men convicted of honour crimes in Jordan. However, the most important reform is the reference by the Criminal Court's Attorney-General, who is able (much like the A-G for the United Kingdom, in relation to the Court of Appeal) to appeal against a sentence at the Cassation Court if it appears to him that a sentence imposed by a criminal court is somewhat unduly lenient. In July 2009, the presiding judge at the Criminal Court in Jordan announced the formation of a special tribunal to handle cases of honour killings. The judge justified the decision of forming such a specialised tribunal based on inconsistencies in verdicts issued by the four tribunals at the Criminal Court. Three months later, in October 2009, the Criminal Court's newly established tribunal handed two men a 15-year prison sentence each for killing their siblings in two separate murders that were related to family honour. The court, in a judicial precedent, rejected the victim's family's request to drop charges against the defendants, a right that would have reduced the sentence by half. This is the strictest sentence ever issued by a Jordanian court to date against a defendant who killed in the name of 'so-called' honour.

Work in Syria against honour crimes is relatively new, but much has been done since the phenomenon came into the public arena and addressed by local NGOs and the international media. Recent numbers that have emerged from Syria and have been reported by activists estimate that between 200 to 300 honour killings take place in Syria each year.[2] A local organisation named 'Syrian Women Observatory' launched a nationwide campaign entitled 'Stop Women Killing ... Stop Honor Crimes' in 2006, demanding the abolition of laws that provide lenient sentences for killers. The campaign called for an end to the brutal killing of women and called on religious leaders (and decision-makers) to take a stand against crimes of honour.[3] It was the murder of 16-year-old Zahra Abdo in January 2007 that prompted local organisations in Syria to speak up against crimes of honour.[4] Zahra was abducted from her village and raped by a man. She was later locked behind bars by the authorities to protect her from her family. One of her cousins married Zahra to help secure her release from prison. This peaceful solution did not appease her family. One day, her elder brother stabbed her to death after her husband left for work.[5] More recently, Syria's Grand Mufti Cleric Ahmad Hassoun, for the first time, publicly condemned honour crimes against women in Damascus. He described honour crimes as un-Islamic, called for the protection of abused women and requested a change in the laws that do not adequately punish honour killers.[6] In July 2009, media agencies reported that Syrian President Bashar Assad also ordered the cancellation of an Article that offered exemption in penalties to offenders like honour killers. While activists say that such a shift in policy is positive, perpetrators of crimes of honour are still able to escape stricter sentences; this is because Syrian criminal law, while aborting plans for the exemption clause, still retains a special reduction clause that reduces an honour killer's sentence in certain circumstances, such as provocation.

Other countries such as Pakistan, Turkey and Palestine have also wit-nessed public movements and the involvement of civil society, individuals and governments to abolish honour crimes by introducing draft laws that eradicate codes and practices that support the imposition of lenient sentences upon perpetrators and to raise public awareness regarding this issue. According to a study prepared by UNICEF and a group of Pakistani law-yers, there were 1,261 murders committed in the name of honour in 2003, including 930 murders against women, 316 against men, eight against female minors and seven against male minors.[7] Law Coordinator for the Shirkat Gah Women's Resource Centre in Pakistan, Sohail Akbar Warraich, said in a paper that these murders have been part of Pakistan's society and legal history for centuries.[8] Warraich pointed out that honour crimes occur in all four provinces of Pakistan and in the tribal areas adjoining the border with Afghanistan, adding that, traditionally, the practice enjoys social sanction, originating from social procedures for accusing and punishing individuals for extramarital sexual activities.[9]

Some well-known activists in Pakistan are sisters Asma Jahangir and Hina Jilani. It was in their office that Samia Sarwar was killed by her family in April 1999. Sarwar was visiting their office seeking a divorce from her abu-sive husband. Although both women started their activism in the 1980s by opening a shelter and offering a hotline for abused women, the murder of Sarwar prompted a public outcry among Pakistani civil society. Demonstra-tors marched to the Lahore High Court, where several prominent citizens addressed the gathering, vowing not to 'let Samia's blood be spilt in vain'. Asma Jahangir proposed to build a monument outside her office honouring the memory of women killed in the name of 'honour'. Asma Jahangir and Hina Jilani were strongly criticised by many conservatives after the two condemned the murder of Sarwar. Jahangir's response to her critics was to call on the government to open new investigations in almost 300 cases of honour killings reported in Pakistan in 1998. According to Amnesty Inter-national, no action was ever taken on the issue.[10] However, the Pakistani government's reaction abroad was much more evident than it was back at home. A representative from the Pakistani government condemned the killing of Samia Sarwar before the UN Human Rights Commission in Geneva shortly after her murder. The minister of women's development made a statement in Washington on 10 April 1999, four days after Samia's death, pledging the government's commitment to women's rights in Pakistan.[11] Jahangir said that the many documentaries covering crimes of HRV against women helped make news of the case and gave international recognition to the issue.[12] *Time* magazine described Jahangir as 'A small lady – with a large job. Back home, people are starting to recognize that a voice capable of challenging authority is invaluable.'[13]

Turkey

Turkey is another country that has placed crimes of honour on the top of its agenda and of its NGOs. Researchers and activists estimate that the reported number of women and girls murdered in the name of honour is approximately 200 per annum, though the real statistics might reveal something higher.[14] Turkish women groups have been working hard to eradicate some of the laws that allow the imposition of lenient sentences on honour killers in such murders, and their efforts have resulted in the amendments of certain articles to the Turkish Penal Code that once used to grant sentence reductions to honour killers under Turkish criminal law, namely provocation.[15] For example, women's lobby groups helped to bring about an amendment in the Turkish Penal Code (Article 38) that incriminates any person who forces another person to commit a crime, by punishing them with the same sentence as the perpetrator. If the person so incited is a minor, the sentence of the inciter is increased.[16] Women's movements and other related organisations also reported positive changes in attitudes towards crimes of honour amongst members of the public and within judicial decisions; perpetrators of two honour killings each received life-imprisonment sentences for their 'so-called' honour crimes.[17]

Palestine

Palestinian women's groups in the West Bank and Gaza also began their struggle early in the 1990s to combat crimes of honour and approached the problem openly.[18] Maha Abdo, a social worker in the West Bank, said ' ... for years we did not want our dirty laundry hung in public. These issues were not discussed. But it is out now because of the growing awareness amongst Palestinian women.'[19] Palestinian activists reported early work on the issue of honour crimes. One such activist, Aida Touma-Sliman, stated in an essay that the first demonstration against honour crimes inside Palestinian society in Israel was held in 1990 and was organised by the Al-Fanar Organization in protest at the murder of a young village woman by her father.[20] According to Touma-Sliman, the father killed his daughter after discovering that she was pregnant out of wedlock, with the knowledge that the incident was caused by one of the victim's family members.[21] During the main trial, the head of the Higher Follow-Up Committee (representing Palestinian minorities in Israel and also a local mayor) justified the father's action, saying ' ... the father had no choice because it was the only way he could continue to live in an honorable manner ... these are our traditions, and that is how we act.'[22] His statements outraged many Palestinian activists and groups, pushing the Al-Fanar Organisation and a group of activists and intellectuals to circulate a petition and to run paid advertisements in the local papers, calling for the resignation of the official who provided the testimony in court.[23] In her accounts, Touma-Sliman said the resignation did not happen. However, more importantly, the ordeal created a momentum and established the visibility of the challenge against crimes of honour in Palestine up to this date.[24]

The running of paid advertisements, the petitions, the organisation of demonstrations and the support amongst Palestinian politicians, police officials and the public at large forced the press and media to take note of the issue of honour crimes (and the criticisms of the treatment of women).[25] Three years later, an organisation named Al-Badeel (a coalition of organisations and individuals) was established by ten women and human-rights activists to fight family honour murders inside Palestinian society within Israel.[26] In a paper presented at a regional conference on the issue of honour crimes in Palestine, Touma-Sliman said Al-Badeel began its activities following a horrific murder that shook Palestinian society. In 1991, a father and son murdered and burnt their daughter (and sister) who became pregnant out of wedlock. Touma-Sliman explained that hundreds of people marched against the killing. Subsequently after the court case, it was revealed that actually the father had raped his daughter, and she had become pregnant with his child. Fearing his crimes might be exposed he murdered his daughter and burnt her body with the help of his son. Since this high-profile case, men and women in Palestine have marched on the streets whenever a suspected honour crime has taken place in Palestinian society. Al-Badeel played an important role in raising awareness of these issues.[27]

As with the legal difficulties encountered in Jordan, Palestinian women's groups attempted to fight crimes of honour and amend those laws which offered lenient sentences to honour killers. These amendments were presented to the Palestinian Parliament, but were quashed by those deputies and officials who argued that ' ... reform will lead to a collapse in the moral fabric of society'.[28] *The Guardian* newspaper published a news report that quoted official statistics released by the Palestinian Women's Affairs Ministry: approximately 20 Palestinian women and young girls were killed in 2004 (and 50 were reported as suicide cases, mostly suicide committed by force) for supposedly threatening familial honour.[29] The turning point in the coverage of the Arabic press of the issue of HRV was in 1995, following the murder of Ibtihaj Hasson. It was reported that village people and relatives stood next to her dead body clapping and cheering her murder. 'This tragic and ugly scene was the impetus behind a wave of articles by intellectuals and human-rights activists condemning both this murder and honor crimes in general,' Touma-Sliman said.[30] She said that prior to this incident, the coverage of these crimes by the media was brief and buried within inside pages, with very limited information about these crimes.[31]

The European Union

Meanwhile, many European countries, including Germany, Sweden, France and Denmark, began experiencing their own share of honour crimes and HRV in the 1990s. The countries making up the European community have undertaken extensive work and have offered professional protection and services for victims of domestic violence; unfortunately, many have chosen to overlook the issue when it concerns ethnic minorities and migrant communities, with some governments viewing HRV as a culturally based phenomenon separate from Western value systems and therefore a private matter. However, after some very violent incidents, particularly those related to HRV, European countries have increasingly become concerned about crimes of honour, forced marriages and other forms of oppression against women within immigrant communities. Previously, murders committed in the name of family honour within immigrant communities were reported, but there were no clear definitions and no statistics about these crimes in many European countries. It was therefore very difficult to even discuss or observe patterns of HRV in terms of a specific form of oppression and violence against women. Many governments and local NGOs decided to take action by enforcing laws that protect vulnerable migrants, offering services and raising awareness in relation to these issues. Asma Jahangir has stated that the activism undertaken in Third World countries, such as Jordan and Pakistan, by women, NGOs and activists, has contributed to the raising of awareness in Western communities (and the European community overall) of the abuses perpetrated within migrant communities living in Western societies. She said:

> Western countries did not believe these crimes were happening in their own communities and thought they were immune and that it only happened in our part of the world, until they were confronted with two horrifying so-called honour murders committed within migrants in their own communities.[32]

Sweden offers a very good example of the courageous activism and interest taken in HRV, and it should be regarded as one of the leading countries to have highlighted this problem and to have conducted extensive work to combat this form of violence. One of the most successful activities undertaken in Sweden was to support a group of young migrant men who toured the country and who in turn addressed their male peers to refrain from practicing any form of violence against their female relatives (for more detail, see Chapter 13 by Suruchi Thapar-Björkert in this collection). The murder of Fadime Sahindal in Sweden triggered the attention of many European governments, NGOs, police forces and human-rights activists. While many conferences took place before Fadime's death (since she herself was an activist on the issue in 2001), greater media attention about HRV occurred after her death. Her murder in January 2002 stirred a public debate in Sweden, which drew attention to the difficulties that migrant girls and women in families with strong patriarchal honour norms in Sweden face, in the form of threats of violence and abuse undertaken by men in their families.

In 2004, a conference was organised by Kvinnoforum, a Swedish women's organisation, in which the organisers attempted to tackle the phenomenon of HRV from a global perspective by exchanging notes with their Middle Eastern counterparts on how they handled this phenomenon in their respective countries.[33] The President of Kvinnoforum and the organiser of the event, Bam Bjorling, referred to Fadime who sought help at their centre: 'We had to deal with this issue especially that many young girls came for help or teachers at schools were visiting us to report the disappearance of some girls or girls that were forced into marriage.'[34] One of the most important works undertaken that has helped achieve a significant impact on the cause of honour crimes is the Swedish project 'Elektra' that is entitled 'The Sharaf Heroes Project' ('The Heroes of Honour Project'). It aims to directly influence boys and young men who control girls, including their sisters and other female relatives. The Sharaf Heroes Project started in 2004 and aimed to engage boys and young men in questioning the 'honour culture' and actively take a stand against crimes of honour. The participants were trained to talk to other boys and young men, and were considered role models for an alternative point of view.[35] Eight young Swedish boys from immigrant backgrounds lectured twice at conferences the author attended in Sweden. Their activities aimed at pointing out the fact that young men can act as role models, as peers to help change attitudes towards violence carried out in the name of honour. The group also performed theatrical plays at schools and led discussion groups at high schools.[36]

The County Administration of Sweden has presented a study that appears to show that approximately 1,500 immigrant girls may have been exposed to HRV between 2002 and 2004.[37] In a paper on HRV and cross-cultural encounters and power conflict that was presented to the conference organised by Kvinnoforum, Professor Mehrdad Darvishpour pointed out that there is a generational conflict in existence amongst immigrant families living in Europe because the youth have a stronger will and a better opportunity to integrate into new Western society and become influenced by Western norms, unlike their parents. Parents, on the other hand, are afraid that their children are 'becoming Swedish' or 'becoming European' and conflicts can arise within the family.[38] Professor Darvishpour also provided his own interpretation of this conflict when he said: ' ... males in immigrant families tend to live in the past, women live in present and their children live in the future.'[39] According to interviews in Sweden, immigrant girls and boys expressed concern over a change of attitude in their parents' behaviour after arriving in Sweden, which sociologists attribute to the parents' loss of power over their children, who are able to integrate in society and learn the language faster than their parents.[40] Overall, the awareness and activism undertaken in Sweden has borne fruit; the courts and police forces, for example, now take crimes of honour very seriously and consider such crimes as a violation against women's rights. This is no less demonstrated in the case of Fadime Sahindal, where the Uppsala District Court sentenced her father Rahmi to life imprisonment on 3 April 2002, after considering his action as ruthless and a 'pure execution'.

In the United Kingdom, work to combat crimes of honour began in the late 1990s. According to the European Report on HRV, UK police responded with mixed reactions to domestic violence in general in the 1970s. The understanding was such that 'there was a culture of policemen siding with male perpetrators'.[41] The general attitude that prevailed at the time was that 'a bit of domestic' was not regarded as a real crime, and 'an Englishman's home is his castle', regardless of what he did. However, this changed with a shift in legal policies concerning women, the increase of women recruits in the police force, lobbying by women's rights groups and a change in public awareness in general.[42] The UK's early attempts to address crimes of honour in the 1990s were with a project that focused on strategies to address such crimes. This was initiated in 1999 and jointly coordinated by the Centre of Islamic and Middle Eastern Laws (CIMEL) at the School of Oriental and African Studies at the University of London and the International Centre for the Legal Protection of Human Rights (INTERIGHTS).[43] The project aimed at supporting people working in the field relating to HRV and murder, whilst facilitating a network and cooperation amongst lawyers, activists, academics and others to combat the rising phenomenon of honour crimes in the UK and globally.[44] In 2001, the London Metropolitan Police initiated a campaign entitled 'Enough is Enough – Domestic Violence Strategy'. The project provided extensive guidelines for the police force concerning relations with the public, whilst utilising human-rights language both as a philosophical tool and as a legal tool underpinning the fight against these forms of violence.[45] In its review of honour killings, the London Metropolitan Police

Multi-Agency Violence Murder Review in 2003 stated that practitioners and academics had yet to devise an appropriate definition for these types of killings, arguing that there was no 'honour' in 'honour killings' and related murders.[46]

It was estimated that there were 20 honour-based crimes committed in the UK between 1997 and 2002, with the police estimating that around 12 honour-related murders are committed against women in Muslim, Sikh and Christian families in the UK annually.[47] The term 'honour killings' received greater media attention in 2003 when Kurdish-Muslim immigrant Heshu Yones, 16, was killed by her father for betraying the family honour by dating a boy outside wedlock. With this great attention, the Metropolitan Police announced in 2004 that it was reviewing 117 murder cases (52 in London and 65 in other parts of England and Wales) over the previous decade in order to establish whether or not 'honour' was a contributing factor to these deaths, so as to understand the phenomenon as a risk indicator.[48] And in 2007, a 70-year-old grandmother was sentenced to life imprisonment for ordering the honour killing of her daughter-in-law. Other family members were complicit and involved in the murder and were also sentenced to long terms of imprisonment.[49]

In Germany, the Terre des Femmes Organization conducted a report on crimes of honour in Germany, pointing out that the issue was and remained a marginalised topic, although counselling services and crisis centres were beginning to deal with these issues.[50] However, a different issue relating to HRV against female migrants in Germany came to light. In 2002, Terre des Femmes began a campaign against forced marriages in Germany, reacting to the story of Turkish women who were increasingly becoming vocal about their stories of being forced into marriages against their will.[51] The campaign was covered extensively in the media and pressure was placed on the German government and other political parties to take action against these human-rights violations.[52] Based on the success of their campaign against forced marriages, in November 2004 Terre des Femmes launched a similar campaign entitled 'No to Crimes in the Name of Honour', addressing the issue of honour crimes in Germany.[53] The aim was to install mechanisms for the prevention of these crimes at both national and international levels through the amendment of laws. The organisation also pushed for the application of appropriate legal proceedings against perpetrators who commit such crimes in the name of honour. According to Terre des Femmes, there were approximately 40 cases of murder or attempted murder in the name of honour in Germany between 2002 and 2004.[54] The German courts asserted that they took any act threatening the right to life of any woman extremely seriously, and in April 2006, a German court sentenced a 19-year-old Turkish male to nine years and three months imprisonment for shooting his older sister in a crime of honour at a bus stop in a Berlin suburb.[55]

Many other recommendations and declarations have been made during European conferences held on the subject, including clauses that support working actively on preventing the mitigation of HRV (within the context of perpetrators) at the European and Member State level, with a constant engagement between Member State institutions and NGOs and coordination of such efforts through mechanisms provided by the European Union.[56] Perhaps an important recommendation for reform is the nature of policies adopted in relation to migrant and ethnic communities living in the European community. One must seek to improve living, working and educational conditions of minority groups, whilst at the same time eliminating any discrimination that many may still face, if there is to be any success in the combat against HRV. Poor housing, work opportunities and education will only harbour and infest patriarchal views and the mistreatment of women and further isolate minority groups from mainstream society. Likewise, ethnic and migrant groups must respect the culture and rules of the society they are now living in and must also demonstrate a willingness to adapt as much as possible. It is necessary to provide immigrant communities with the necessary tools for integration, in order to avoid conflicts or the need to resort to 'double-lives', where children live a European life at school or work but are forced to lead different lives at home.

Conclusion

It is clear that European activists concerned with the rising trend of HRV have begun convincing parliaments, legislators and governments to seriously address the issues crimes of honour pose and to amend laws in order to provide protection to women and migrant children. These amendments have included stricter custodial punishments for families who force their daughters to undergo female genital mutilation (FGM) operations and perpetrators of honour crimes, regardless of the 'cultural and traditional excuses' (such as provocation) that honour killers usually hide behind. Other amendments include increasing the legal age of marriage in order to prevent forced marriages on young migrant men and women alike. There needs to be a continuous drive on the part of governments, NGOs and activists working in this area to raise greater public awareness of HRV. It is important for these institutions and governments to address the common cultural belief systems held by migrant communities that still accept and encourage these crimes. They should lobby for legislation that provides better protection for women, to improve social services for abused women and to empower women psychologically and emotionally. Within this framework, men should also be encouraged (and invited) to join any efforts that support this difficult task, helping to highlight the unjustified practices involved in HRV that clearly violate the rights of women, including the rights to life, liberty and security. Clearly HRV invokes women's human-rights issues. The importance of the role of men is clearly demonstrated in the Sharaf Heroes Project, where men can and do make a difference in changing attitudes towards crimes of honour. NGOs in particular should push to make the murder of each and every woman in the name of 'so-called' honour a national issue. Media and news reporters, including myself, should therefore continue to play an important role in raising awareness regarding these murders; they should constantly report cases of honour killings and HRV to raise awareness and empower women. However (and perhaps most importantly), there needs to be more in-depth academic research on the root causes of HRV and honour killings, including how such crimes begin; the consequences of such actions and crimes upon the entire family, including the close/immediate family (e.g. mothers, sisters, daughters, and so on) and extended family members; and the psychological impact on honour killers when they are driven to commit crimes of honour. Thankfully, this book (as do other books on this subject) continues this process of academic research into the phenomenon of HRV and honour killings.

Notes

* The author uses the word 'so-called' on purpose. The author wishes to point out that we should refrain from using the word 'honour' because when we refer to honour killings and HRV, we could in one sense be interpreted as justifying such murders and, of course, there is no 'honour' in any honour killing. Activists around the world have been working tirelessly to change this and to make a difference. The author is of the opinion that we should focus our attention upon terminology and show that honour killings are unacceptable socially, morally and religiously. That is why the author uses the term 'so-called' when referring to honour killings.

1 See Karamanou (2002).
2 See Elass (2007).
3 Ibid.
4 Ibid.
5 Ibid.
6 Ibid.
7 See Zeidan (2004).
8 See Welchmann and Hossein (2005).
9 Ibid.: 79.
10 Amnesty International (1999: 21).
11 Ibid.: 39.
12 Cuomo (2000: 237).
13 See McGirk (2003).
14 See Moore (2001).
15 Turkish Civil and Penal Code Reforms (2005: 62).
16 Ibid.: 63.
17 Ibid.: 63–64.
18 See Curtius (1995).
19 Ibid.
20 Welchmann and Hossain (2005: 193).
21 Ibid.
22 Ibid.
23 Ibid.

24 Ibid.
25 Ibid.: 194.
26 Ibid.: 193.
27 Ibid.: 194.
28 McGreal (2005: 18).
29 Ibid.
30 Welchmann and Hossain (2005: 195).
31 Ibid.
32 Phone Interview with United Nations Special Rapporteur on Freedom of Religion or Belief of the Commission on Human Rights Asma Jahangir in Pakistan, 10 November 2006.
33 *Honor-Related Violence with a Global Perspective* (2004: 9).
34 Ibid.
35 *Honor-Related Violence, European Resource Book and Good Practice* (2005: 64).
36 Ibid.: 96.
37 Ibid.: 30.
38 Ibid.
39 Ibid.
40 Ibid.: 45–46.
41 Ibid.: 108.
42 Ibid.
43 Ibid.: 113.
44 Ibid.
45 *Honor-Related Violence with a Global Perspective* (2004: 113).
46 *Honor-Related Violence, European Resource Book and Good Practice* (2005: 98).
47 BBC News (2004).
48 *Honor-Related Violence with a Global Perspective* (2004: 32).
49 *The Daily Mail* (2007), 19 September.
50 *Honor-Related Violence with a Global Perspective* (2004: 75).
51 DAPHNE – Program 2003/2004 (2004: 3).
52 Ibid.
53 Ibid.
54 Ibid.: 8.
55 BBC News (2006), 13 April.
56 *Honor-Related Violence with a Global Perspective* (2004: 110).

Bibliography

Amnesty International, Pakistan (22 September 1999) Violence against Women in the Name of Honour, AI Index: ASA 33/17/99.

Cuomo, K. (2000) *Speak Truth to Power, Human Rights Defenders who are Changing the World*, New York: Crown.

Curtius, M. (1995) 'Palestinian Women Fight to Outlaw West Bank's Honor Killings', *The Sydney Morning Herald*, 14 March.

DAPHNE – Program 2003/2004 (2004) Report prepared Terre Des Femmes, as part of the EU-funded project that is led by the Swedish organization Kvinnoforum, Shehrazad – Combating Violence in the Name of Honour.

Elass, R. (2007) '"Honor" Killing Spurs Outcry in Syria, A 16-year-old's Killing Spurred the Country's Grand Mufti to Call for Legal Reform and Protections', *The Christian Science Monitor*, 14 February. Available at http://www.csmonitor.com/2007/0214/p07s02-wome.html.

Europe Tackles (2004) 'Honour Killing', BBC News World Edition, 22 June.

'Grandmother Jailed for Life Over Honour Killing of "Cheating" Daughter-in-Law', (2007) *The Daily Mail*, 19 September. Available at http://www.dailymail.co.uk.

'"Honour Killing" Brother Jailed, A 19-year-old Turkish Man has been Jailed for Nine Years and Three Months by a German Court for Shooting his Sister in a So-Called "Honor Killings"', (2006) BBC News, 13 April.

Honor-Related Violence with a Global Perspective: Mitigation and Prevention in Europe, (7–8 October 2004) Organized by Kvinnoforum/Foundation of Women's Forum, Stockholm, Sweden.

Honor-Related Violence (2005) European Resource Book and Good Practice, Based on the European Project 'Prevention of Violence against Women and Girls in Patriarchal Families', Kvinnoforum, Stockholm.

Karamanou, A. (2002) 'Women the Target of Fundamentalists', *Al-Raida*, Vol. 19, No. 97–98.

McGirk, T, (2003) 'Asma Jahangir, The Pocket Protector', *Time Magazine Online*. Available at http://www.time.com/time/asia/2003/heroes/asma_jahangir.html.

McGreal, C. (2005) 'Murder in the Name of Family Honor', *Guardian Weekly*, 1–7 July.

Moore, M. (2001) 'Honour Killings Follow Women to the City', *Washington Post Service*, 9 August.

Turkish Civil and Penal Code Reforms from a Gender Perspective, The Success of Two Nationwide Campaigns, Women for Women's Human Rights (2005).

Welchman, L. and Hossein, S. (eds) (2005) *'Honour': Crimes, Paradigms, and Violence Against Women*, London: Zed Books.

Zeidan, A., (2004) 'Voices Calls for a Law that Protects Pakistani Women and their Rights, 1261 Honor Crimes Last Year and the Tribal System is Responsible', *Al-Hayat*, Society section, 7 February.

Chapter 12

Ending honour crimes in sub-Saharan Africa

Looking at a long hard death

Nancy Kaymar Stafford, JD, LLM
Legal Consultant, USA

Introduction

Throughout the world women and girls are killed, injured or otherwise degraded in the name of family 'honour'. Honour crimes are also committed in sub-Saharan African countries, where a cycle of violence is often ingrained in the community culture. However, because honour crimes in sub-Saharan Africa do not normally result in death, as they do in other parts of the world, they are generally overlooked as cultural practices, or family issues rather than crimes that warrant government intervention and punishment. Indeed, a review of publications related to honour crimes rarely mentions sub-Saharan Africa. One must question why so little attention is paid to honour violence in this part of the world and how it differs from honour violence in other regions.

Honour crimes stem from the patriarchal notion that a woman's chastity or virtue is somehow tied to her family's honour. Historically, men have been considered masters over their wives (and children), free to discipline and demand obedience from them because of the man's status as head of household. Therefore, if there is the mere hint of impropriety on the part of a female member of the household, the family – and particularly its male head – is dishonoured. The family must then find a way to restore its reputation. Often the answer is violence against the woman, to punish her and prove to the local community that the man is in control of his family.

When one looks at the concept of honour crimes in relation to sub-Saharan Africa, this typical paradigm, of crimes committed in reaction to actual or perceived family dishonour caused by the woman's actions, does not work. Often in sub-Saharan Africa one sees violence as atonement for a family 'sin', something the woman herself had no control over and was not a part of. Therefore, one must look at an expanded definition of honour, and look not only at an action that impacts the dignity of the man or the family, but also at the concept of the dignity of the woman in order to understand honour crimes in sub-Saharan Africa. Examining honour crimes in this manner, one must read traditional customary practices as crimes of honour.

These practices often result in violence against women. The fact that these practices have until recently been contained within the community – whether for protection of the community, tribe or individual family – has made it difficult to identify some of the practices and their impact on women. However, a crime that attacks the dignity of a woman within a family, simply because of her status as a woman, *is* an honour crime and as such these practices must be considered crimes of honour.

This chapter will look at the background of crimes of honour in sub-Saharan Africa. The author will address some customary practices throughout the region and discuss why these should be considered crimes of honour – or more aptly, honour/dignity crimes.[1] The author will also consider the laws that are currently in place to prohibit crimes of honour. The author will explain that ending behaviour that is embedded in tradition is not simple: cultural practices die a long, hard death. As such, it is imperative that governments take the first step to protect women from all culture-related violence. With that in mind, the last part of this chapter will look at the state's responsibility for protecting its female citizens from crimes of honour. Protection does not merely mean enacting legislation to prohibit these crimes. In this instance, laws alone are not enough. States in which honour violence occurs must take steps to address the underlying issues or root causes of honour crimes through a comprehensive approach involving legal reform, social services and public education.

Cultural patterns that permit honour crimes

'Violence against women is closely linked to the regulation of sexuality' (Coomaraswamy 2005: xi). In sub-Saharan Africa, the regulation of sexuality generally is manifest from one of four sources: patriarchy, religion, colonialism and economic inequality. These sources tend to overlap and are tied to the concept of machismo.

Patriarchy, religion and colonialism

The impact of patriarchy, religion and colonialism can be grouped together when discussing the root causes of honour crimes. Patriarchal and religious foundations for honour violence are archaic and make over-broad generalisations about the status of women, preaching woman's obedience to man. Colonialism implemented these religious and patriarchal norms (for example, see generally Merry 2003). There is an assumption that women lack capacity and should be treated as property. A man, be it a husband, father or brother, must step in and chastise a woman if she steps outside the cultural norm in order to restore the family (or his) honour. Strangely, under traditional patriarchal and religious paradigms, there is also an underlying assumption that men cannot control their sexual urges in the presence of 'enticing' women. Courtney Howland (1997: 283) points out that for the five major religions – Buddhism, Christianity, Judaism, Hinduism and Islam – the religious 'legal structures regard women's sexuality as potentially evil and destructive of men'. Men are given a 'divine mandate to exercise authority over women' (ibid.) for the good of the entire community. Unfortunately, 'women who are victimized by male dominance are blamed for the violence perpetrated against them' (Parrot 2006: 42). In short, women are often blamed for men's inability to control their sexual urges.

From the author's own experience, religion in sub-Saharan Africa tends to manifest itself as a blend of various branches of Christianity and animism. As one local Ghanaian explained it, 'that way we have all bases covered'. Women suffer under both belief systems. Animism by its nature is laden with customs and practices that harm the dignity of women (see generally Dow 2000). Likewise, Christianity is fraught with patriarchal views, beginning with the Fall of Adam. Martha Fineman (2009) put it best when she stated:

> Historically, and in accordance with the church's approach to marriage, legal and other texts analogized the relationship between husband and wife to other 'natural' hierarchical arrangements. Thus, a man was enthroned as head of the family, just as Jesus reigned as the head of the church and the King was the head of the state. The respective positions of husband and wife were rigidly distinct and patriarchally ordered – husband's role, as frail wife's protector, was deemed 'divinely ordained'.
>
> (Fineman and Worthington 2009:2)

During the period of colonization, the British brought their patriarchal notions and religious, primarily Christian, beliefs with them to Africa. The British system of governance and the British common law were imported into the African system. In order to develop a sustainable legal system, the common law needs to be 'capable of evolving in the light of changing social, economic and cultural developments' (see the English House of Lords case of *R v. R* (1992) 1 AC 599, 616). This did not generally occur in Africa. The common law may have evolved in Britain, but these developments did not trickle down to its colonial territories. A prime example of this is the crime of marital rape in Ghana.[2] The British judiciary began questioning the validity of a marital rape exemption as early as 1888 and officially declared the exemption invalid in 1991 (Stafford 2008: 65). However, the Ghanaian criminal code continues the exclusion today (ibid.).

When most countries in sub-Saharan Africa became independent they were left with a mix of statutory law, customary law, proclamations from the colonial powers, religious law and local tribal law. The failure to update the law to reflect current social conditions aids in maintaining subordinate gender roles in the family. Even where the laws have been promulgated, a seeming lack of willingness to properly enforce these laws, evidenced by the fact that honour crimes continue despite them, leaves women with a lower social and familial status, subordinating them to their male counterparts and leaving them vulnerable to honour violence.[3] Moreover, according to Mary Wandia, Africa women's rights coordinator for ActionAid International, 'many communities are complicit in excusing or condoning violence against women, and in so doing, tacitly approve of the abuse'. Neighbours and friends may hesitate to intervene in abusive relationships because marital relations are often considered a 'private matter' (Kimani 2007).

Economic inequality

'Historically, women in most cultures in Africa have been economically independent from their male counterparts, even enjoying great economic prestige' (Ofori-Baodu 2005: 349). This was prior to colonialism. The colonial masters overlooked women's economic potential. Laws were crafted to ensure training, education and access to credit for men with little thought of the role that women could play in the economy (ibid.). Moreover, during the colonial period customary law was interpreted solely by men. Taking a page from their own history, the colonial powers could not consider expanding rights to African women that they were denying to Western women. Hence, as men became the sole arbiters of the customary law, it began to favour the male position. Women were denied the right to inherit property from their husbands, to own clan land and to acquire assets of their own. They were put in a position of complete dependence on the male members of the family. Women were equated with children under the law and in customary practice. They needed to be cared for and were incapable of rational thought or action.

As will be seen in the next section, placing a woman in a situation of destitution, vulnerability and helplessness makes the cultural 'price' of noncompliance great. She has no choice but to accept her fate and the violence that comes along with it. *Trokosi* and *ngozi* imprison young girls into futures of sexual violence and lack of dignity, with no education or hope for independence from their male captors. Bride price, *lobola* and widowhood rites keep women tied to the man's family directly because of the economic and social implications that would result if they chose not to comply. The following will outline these traditional customary practices that foster the concept of honour and perpetuate a cycle of violence for women.

Cases of honour crimes in sub-Saharan Africa

When most people think of honour crimes, they picture a woman throwing herself on her husband's funeral pyre, or a jealous husband killing his wife because she was seen alone in the company of another man. Indeed, these are horrible examples of honour crimes committed against women in many societies. In sub-Saharan Africa, however, honour crimes are more insidious.

They appear to be merely the customary practices of certain communities or ethnic groups. In reality, they are acts that destroy women's dignity to the benefit of men's dignity. The following outlines some of the detrimental cultural practices that take place in sub-Saharan Africa and why these crimes against women's physical integrity and dignity should be considered honour crimes and must be addressed as crimes by African states.

Girls as compensation in Ghana and Zimbabwe

Dori Agale is approximately 30 years old and was recently released after 25 years in the *trokosi* system in Ghana (Grand Rapids Press 2007: D8). *Trokosi*, which literally means 'slaves of the gods' in the local Ewe language, is a traditional practice whereby '[v]irgin girls, often under 10 years old, are given by their families to work as slaves in religious shrines to appease the gods for crimes committed by relatives' (Center for Reproductive Rights 2003: 46). Dori's family handed her over to the local priest 'under threat of a death curse' (Grand Rapids Press 2007: D8). Originally she worked as a field hand, but when she reached puberty she became a sexual slave as well. A local non-governmental organisation, International Needs Network, estimates that there are 5,000 trokosi woman and girls still enslaved in Ghana's trokosi shrines (International Needs Network 2006: 2).

Ghana criminalised *trokosi* under section 314A of the Criminal Code (Cap 29) in 1998. It states:

> (1) Whoever (a) sends to or receives at any place any person; or (b) participates in or is concerned in any ritual or customary activity in respect of any person with the purpose of subjecting that person to any form of ritual or customary servitude or any form of forced labour related to a customary ritual commits an offence and shall be liable on conviction to imprisonment for a term not less than three years.

Ghana recently reported to the United Nations Committee on the Rights of the Child, the body responsible for the implementation of a state's obligations under the United Nations' Convention on the Rights of the Child (CRC). During the meeting, Committee member Ms Ouedraogo, the representative from Burkina Faso, noted her concern that: 'the practice of Trokosi still occurred even though legislation had been adopted to prohibit it' (United Nations 2006: 3). The Ghanaian representative, Ms Mahama, replied that the 'Government in cooperation with civil society organizations was making concerted efforts to eliminate the practice' (ibid.). However, 'because of the deeply rooted religious beliefs, villagers fear that if they do not obey the trokosi practice, they will anger the war-gods and bring unending bad luck upon their families' (Parrot and Cummings 2006: 118). *Trokosi* is an animist belief that continues to perpetuate violence against women in order to benefit the greater family unit. *Trokosi is* a crime of honour.

Likewise, a study conducted by the World Health Organization (WHO) found that families in Zimbabwe continue the ritual of *ngozi* or *[Kuripa] Ngozi,* the practice 'whereby a girl can be given to a family as compensation for a death of a man caused by a member of the girl's family' (WHO 2002: 157). Making matters worse, 'on reaching puberty the girl is expected to have sexual intercourse with the brother or father of the deceased person, so as to produce a son to replace the one who died' (ibid.). While there is no prohibition of *ngozi* under Zimbabwean law, rape is prohibited under the Sexual Offences Act, Chapter 9: 21. Section 8 of that law states:

(1) Any person who, whether or not married to the other person, without the consent of that other person – (a) with the male organ, penetrates any part of the other person's body; or (b) with any object other than the male organ, penetrates the other person's genitalia or anus; or (c) engages in fellatio or cunnilingus with the other person; shall be guilty of an offence and liable, subject to section sixteen … [regarding HIV] … to the penalties provided by law for rape. (2) Penetration to any degree shall be sufficient for the purpose of paragraphs (a) and (b) of subsection (1).

Moreover, Article 14 of the Constitution of Zimbabwe (2000) states that 'No person shall be held in slavery or servitude or required to perform forced labour'. But the practice continues, with girls being treated as compensation to the dead man's family. *Ngozi is* a crime of honour. The practices of *trokosi* and *ngozi* in Ghana and Zimbabwe, respectively, are both crimes of honour. Women and girls are being enslaved by their families in order to atone for a crime, social infraction or animist belief. The enslavement results in restoration of the family's honour. It is not atonement for a sin or crime committed by the woman or even a perceived sin or crime committed by the woman. Indeed, she has nothing to do with the underlying crime. This ritual enslavement robs a woman of her most basic rights and of her dignity.

Widowhood rites in Uganda and Liberia

In Uganda, a woman who is widowed is often required to marry her husband's brother. 'Because customary law views a wife as an outsider to her husband's clan, if she wishes to remain in her home with her children, she may have to submit to being 'inherited' by one of her deceased husband's relatives' (Faulk 2006: 453). Although the Ugandan Constitution (1995), Article 31, states that '[m]en and women of the age of eighteen years and above, have the right to marry and to found a family and are entitled to equal rights in marriage, during marriage and at its dissolution', the practice nevertheless continues. Ms Harriet Musoke (2007), a Senior Principal

Lecturer at the Law Development Centre in Kampala, Uganda, notes that widow inheritance is still practiced in rural parts of Uganda. There has been some opposition to the practice, particularly if a person has died of AIDS. However, in the rural areas of Uganda many people believe AIDS is the result of witchcraft and continue the practice of widow inheritance undeterred by the risk of AIDS (ibid.).

Similarly, there are reports of Liberian widows being compelled to marry relatives of their late husbands (Carter Center 2007: 1). If they do not, family members require them to forfeit any property from their late husbands. This is in contrast to the Domestic Relations Law of Liberia of 1973 (Title 9), subsection 2.1, which notes that marriage is a civil status 'to which the consent of parties capable of making such a contract is essential'. One could argue that a woman has a choice to either lose all of the household possessions or marry a family member, and therefore enters into marriage with her late husband's relative freely. But does she really? Subsection 7.2 of the Domestic Relations Law states that a marriage is voidable if at the time of the marriage either party 'consented to such marriage by reason of force, duress or fraud'. The prospect of destitution and losing one's children would clearly qualify as duress. Again, the woman is in a situation of utter reliance on her husband's clan and does not have the luxury of voiding the marriage and losing all of her property and economic support.

The tradition of widow inheritance *is* again a crime of honour. Although it may originally have been established to protect widows from destitution, the practice has evolved into one of patriarchal domination. A man's family would be dishonoured if his widow broke with the community or was allowed to live within it without association to his clan. Women are shackled to their former husband's family. They often cannot return to their own family, and even if they could, their children are considered part of the male clan and would have to remain with the husband's family.

Bride price / lobola in Zimbabwe and Namibia

The system of bride price is still well practiced in sub-Saharan Africa. Although sometimes referred to as *bogadi, bohali, analobolo, roora, malowolo, impango* and *sionda*, the term *lobola* will be used in this chapter. *Lobola* is a 'patriarchal ideology where men dominate the marriage process and control the decision-making power' (Women and Law in Southern Africa 2002: 8). *Lobola* requires a husband to purchase his wife, generally at the time of marriage, with cattle or other assets which are given to her family. This payment for the woman 'signifies the transfer of the woman's reproductive and productive rights to the man's group, thus locating the children born in a marriage in the father's family' (ibid.: 17).

Lobola is an interesting phenomenon when speaking of honour because the honour of the family can be held by the husband or by the woman's family depending on whether she has married. For example, in some countries, like Zimbabwe, if an unmarried girl is raped – and therefore her family dishonoured – the perpetrator can pay *lobola* to her parents and therefore avoid prosecution (Herald 2007). This basically compensates the parents for future lost income, since she is now tainted merchandise. However, if the woman is already married she is blamed for dishonouring her husband by having sex with another man, even if she was raped. She may be beaten or abandoned as a result.

In Namibia, the original role of *lobola* was to strengthen family relationships, not to give power to a man over his wife (Thomas 2007: 606). However, as women have gained equality and become more educated, with greater employment potential, the price of *lobola* has increased. A recent survey found that, 'a significant number of young men ... felt that having made such a high payment they were entitled to greater control over their wives, and greater power and entitlement within the household' (ibid.: 609). Namibia passed the Combating of Domestic Violence Act (Act No. 4) in 2003. The Act, in section 4(1), permits a person who has suffered physical or sexual abuse in domestic relationships, including customary marriages, 'to apply for a protection order against another person in that domestic relationship'. However, because of the *lobola* payment, and the potential for having to repay it if the relationship deteriorates, women feel that they are unable to protect themselves against this violence.

Lobola is paid to a woman's family by her husband; not to the woman herself. It is meant to honour the parents and represents compensation for raising their daughter. The daughter, however, is treated like chattel that can be bought and sold. Once with the husband, if the daughter wishes to leave the marriage – for example, because of excessive abuse by the husband or his taking of additional wives – the *lobola* must be repaid. Given the economic hardships faced by most families in sub-Saharan Africa, it is unlikely that the assets given to the parents will still be available. It would bring shame upon the family if the daughter left her marriage and *lobola* was not repaid. Often the family will discourage her from leaving her husband and not allow her to return to her clan for just this reason. She is fully economically tied to her husband, lacking all dignity as an individual person. She is held in the marital relationship for the honour of her family, and for her economic well-being. Again, *lobola is* a crime of honour.

Regional and international standards

The above is just a small sampling of traditional practices that represent honour crimes in sub-Saharan Africa. Honour crimes are brutal, senseless crimes that should be prohibited by a country's internal laws, as well as condemned by the international community. But merely enacting a law is not enough. Often this most grievous form of violence against women goes virtually unpunished by national legal systems, despite laws prohibiting it, as is seen above. When states refuse to prevent, investigate and punish these crimes, they fail to sufficiently protect their female citizens, thus giving tacit approval to these crimes and reinforcing the culture of violence within the family. International law is clear that cultural practices that result in violence against women cannot stand. The following outlines some of the regional and international standards that address honour crimes.

The African Charter

The African [Banjul] Charter on Human and Peoples' Rights (African Charter) outlines several provisions related to honour crimes, including: equality before and equal protection of the law (Article 3); respect for the life and integrity of the person (Article 4); the right to liberty and security of the person (Article 6); and the elimination by the state of every discrimination against women, as stipulated in international declarations and conventions (Article 18). Moreover, Article 1 of the African Charter requires that 'Member States of the Organization of African Unity parties to the present Charter shall recognize the rights, duties and freedoms enshrined in this Charter and shall undertake to adopt legislative or other measures to give effect to them'. Article 2 requires that all people be afforded the rights under the African Charter without distinction, including sex.

Interestingly, the African Charter is the only human-rights treaty to not only give rights but to outline a person's duties. These provisions may be used to perpetuate cultural practices that propagate honour crimes. Article 27 requires that the rights and freedoms of each individual shall be exercised with due regard to the rights of others, collective security, morality and common interest. While Article 29 states that individuals have the duty 'to preserve the harmonious development of the family and to work for the cohesion and respect of the family; [and] to respect his parents at all times', some would argue that the woman's right to dignity and to the security of the person is offset by the right to maintain the culture and morality of the population. This tension between the particularism of cultural relativism and the universalist concept of human rights has long been debated. Significant critical analysis has been written on this topic and therefore will not be repeated here. Suffice to say, the author believes strongly that the universal principles of human rights – and the protection of the individual they afford – far outweigh any cultural right that interferes.

UN system

The United Nations Human Rights Committee (HRC), the committee charged with interpreting the International Covenant on Civil and Political Rights (ICCPR), addressed honour crimes directly. In its General Comment

28 the HRC notes that: '[t]he commission of so-called 'honour crimes' which remain unpunished constitutes a serious violation of the ICCPR and in particular of articles 6 (right to life), 14 (equality before the law) and 26 (equal protection of the law, and prohibition on discrimination based on sex)' (United Nations 2000).

Likewise, the Committee on the Elimination of Discrimination against Women, the body charged with interpreting the Convention for the Elimination of All Forms of Discrimination against Women (CEDAW), noted in its General Recommendation 12 that Articles 2 (general elimination of discrimination against women), 5 (modification of cultural practices that discriminate), 11 (discrimination in employment), 12 (discrimination in healthcare), and 16 (equality in marriage and family) of CEDAW 'require the States parties to act to protect women against violence of any kind occurring within the family, at the work place or in any other area of social life' (United Nations 1989). Clearly, this would include instances of honour violence. Moreover, General Recommendation 19 is vital to the issue of violence resulting from customary practices. This recommendation states that:

> Traditional attitudes by which women are regarded as subordinate to men or as having stereotyped roles perpetuate widespread practices involving violence or coercion, such as family violence and abuse, forced marriage, dowry deaths, acid attacks and female circumcision. Such prejudices and practices may justify gender-based violence as a form of protection or control of women. The effect of such violence on the physical and mental integrity of women is to deprive them of the equal enjoyment, exercise and knowledge of human rights and fundamental freedoms.
>
> (United Nations 1992)

The recommendation goes on to state that '[r]ural women are at risk of gender-based violence because of traditional attitudes regarding the subordinate role of women that persist in many rural communities' (ibid.) and that:

> Family violence is one of the most insidious forms of violence against women. It is prevalent in all societies. Within family relationships women of all ages are subjected to violence of all kinds, including battering, rape, other forms of sexual assault, mental and other forms of violence, which are perpetuated by traditional attitudes. Lack of economic independence forces many women to stay in violent relationships.
>
> (Ibid.)

While the Committee does not specifically cite any of the traditional practices noted above as honour violence, or indeed as gender-based violence, it is clear from the Committee's comments that, had they considered them, these types of crimes against women would fall under the practices prohibited under CEDAW. The fact that the violence resulting from traditional practices comes from within the family makes it just all the more insidious.

The Velasquez Rodriquez case

There is international precedent for holding states accountable for the human-rights violations of private parties if the state fails to prevent, investigate and punish the crime. In the Velasquez Rodriquez Case, the Inter-American Court of Human Rights noted that 'The exercise of public authority has certain limits which derive from the fact that human rights are inherent attributes of human dignity and are, therefore, superior to the power of the State.' (Velasquez 1989: Para. 165) This means that the state is required to respect the obligations set forth in a treaty to which it is a party. In order to respect these obligations, each person within a state's jurisdiction must be able to freely and fully exercise all of the rights recognised within the human-rights treaties to which the state is obligated. 'As a consequence of this obligation, the States must prevent, investigate and punish any violation of the rights recognized by [a human-rights treaty] and, moreover, if possible attempt to restore the right violated and provide compensation as warranted for damages resulting from the violation' (ibid.: Para. 166).

The state is not directly imputable for the human-rights violations but may be held responsible in the international community 'not because of the act itself, but because of the lack of due diligence to prevent the violation or to respond to it as required' by international law (ibid.: Para. 172). The state does not have to have sanctioned the violation, although clearly in some of the sub-Saharan African cases it has. What matters is that there was a violation of an international human-rights obligation and that the state 'allowed the act to take place without taking measures to prevent it or to punish those responsible' (ibid.: Para. 173).

The Human Rights Committee confirmed a state's obligation to prevent, investigate and punish in the case of *Delgado-Paéz v. Colombia* (1990). It is clearly an international standard that must be upheld by states that are party to the ICCPR, and its reasoning should be applied to all human-rights treaties. Therefore, under this standard, states are required to protect women from acts of violence in the name of honour and acts that attack their dignity. States are aware of these traditional cultural practices and as such are obligated to prevent the crimes if possible, to investigate crimes of honour which they are clearly aware of and to punish perpetrators.

Conclusion

It is important to understand the root causes of honour violence when seeking to end the inequitable treatment that women face. A long history of patriarchy, colonialism, cultural and religious traditions, coupled with economic disparity, have had a crippling effect on women's positions in sub-Saharan African society. Women have been left in a vulnerable position where they are often treated more like property than like people. The need for the dominant members of society – men – to regulate women, particularly in relation to their sexuality, has resulted in harmful customary practices that are an affront to women's dignity. These practices result in the commodification of women. Enslaving girls (*trokosi*); using girls as compensation (*ngozi*); forced marriage for widows; and bride price (*lobola*) are just a few examples of traditional practices that should be considered honour crimes. As seen in this chapter, these practices are used to control the acts of women and maintain family honour. Passing legislation to secure gender equality and prohibit violence against women is the first step to ending honour crimes in the sub-Saharan context. The ability to enforce such legislation is an important second step. When women are required to travel long distances at great expense to secure their rights, they are less likely to do so. When laws are equalised to give women the same rights as men, dangerous customary practices still continue 'for fear of social sanctions' (Women and Law in Southern Africa 2002: 28).

Clearly, at this point, the laws are not stopping the practices that result in honour violence against women. However, having these laws is a very important first step. Promulgating laws, and the public debate that is usually part of the process, reaps great educational advantages. It starts the dialogue, and it recognises that traditional practices that deny women's dignity are crimes against their honour. NGOs and others can use that information to educate judges, lawyers and women themselves about their rights. They can implement policies on the ground that it will give women the economic fortitude and personal empowerment to stand up for their rights. The bottom line is that honour violence is a crime. It is a crime against women – their dignity and their person – and it is prohibited under international law. Custom, tradition and family honour cannot be used as means for continuing this cycle of violence against women and keeping them physically and economically subordinate. Cultural practices may die a long, hard death, but they will not die at all if governments and the international community do not take the steps needed to protect women from this type of violence.

Notes

1 Please note this chapter does not address the issue of female genital mutilation/ female genital cutting (FGM/FGC). Although the practice continues throughout the subcontinent, it has been examined extensively elsewhere and therefore will not be engaged with in this chapter. The author would like to note that she strongly believes FGM/FGC is a crime of honour as it is used primarily to ensure the virtue of women and retain control over their sexuality (and thus the family honour).

2 In fact, marital rape in Ghana is a legal impossibility, since there is no crime of rape within a marriage. Acknowledging this fact, the author uses the term to mean a married man having sexual relations with his wife against her will.
3 The second section of this chapter will provide concrete examples of laws and constitutional protections that should stem the incidences of honour crimes, but have not.

Bibliography

African [Banjul] Charter on Human and Peoples' Rights (1982), adopted 27 June 1981, OAU Doc. CAB/LEG/67/3 rev. 5, 21 I.L.M. 58, entered into force 21 October 1986.

Carter Center (2007), 'The Modia Drama Club takes Bong County', *The Carter Center Record*, Issue 1, 16 April 2007.

Center for Reproductive Law and Policy (2003), 'Ghana', in *Women of the World: Laws and Policies Affecting their Reproductive Rights – Anglophone Africa*, New York: Center for Reproductive Law and Policy.

Constitution of the Republic of Uganda (1995), available at http://www.parliament.go.ug/images/constitution_1995.pdf.

Constitution of Zimbabwe (2000), available at http://www.chr.up.ac.za/hr_docs/constitutions/docs/ZimbabweC(rev).doc.

Convention on the Elimination of All Forms of Discrimination against Women, ratification and accession by General Assembly resolution 34/180 of 18 December 1979, entered into force 3 September 1981.

Coomsaraswamy, R. (2005) 'Preface', in Welchman, L. and Hossain, S. (eds) *'Honour': Crimes, Paradigms, and Violence Against Women*, London: Zed Books.

Delgado-Paéz v Colombia (12 July 1990), Case No. United Nations Human Rights Committee.

Dow, U. (2000), *Far and Beyond*, San Francisco: Aunt Lute Books.

Faulk, G (ed.) (2006) 'Inheritance Law in Uganda: The Plight of Widows and Children', *Georgetown Journal of Gender and the Law*, Vol. 7, 451.

Fineman, M. A. and Worthington, K. (2009) *What is Right for Children? The Competing Paradigms of Religion and Human Rights*, London: Ashgate.

Grand Rapids Press (6 October 2007), *Couple Work to free Slaves in Ghana*.

The Herald (21 April 2007), *Zimbabwe: Expose all Sexual Abuse Cases*.

Howland, C.W. (1997) 'The Challenge of Religious Fundamentalism to the Liberty and Equality Rights of Women: An Analysis under the United Nations Charter', *Columbia Journal of Transnational Law*, Vol. 35, 271.

International Covenant on Civil and Political Rights, ratification and accession by General Assembly resolution 2200A (XXI) of 16 December 1966, entered into force 23 March 1976.

International Needs Network (26 October 2006), *The Chosen Ones: Slavery in the Name of God*. Available at http://www.ineeds.org.uk (accessed 22 February 2008).

Kimani, M. (July 2007), 'Taking on Violence Against Women in Africa', *Africa Renewal*, 21. Available at http://www.un.org/ecosocdev/geninfo/afrec/vol21no2/212-violence-against-women.html (accessed 30 October 2009).

Merry S. E. (Spring 2003), 'From Law and Colonialism to Law and Globalization: Martin Chanock. Law, Custom, and Social Order: The Colonial Experience in Malawi and Zambia', *Law and Social Inquiry*, Vol. 28, 569.

Musoke, H. (2007) 'Question', private email (17 December 2007).

Ofori-Baodu, G. (2005), 'Ghanaian Women, the Law and Economic Power', in Bond, J. (ed.) *Voices of African Women: Women's Rights in Ghana, Uganda, and Tanzania*, Durham, NC: Carolina Academic Press.

Parrot, A. and Cummings, N. (2006), *Forsaken Females: The Global Brutalization of Women*, New York: Rowan and Littlefield.

R v. R [1992] 1 AC 559 (HL).

Stafford, N. K. (2008) 'Permission for Domestic Violence: Marital Rape in Ghanaian Marriages', *Women's Rights Law Reporter*, Vol. 63, 63.

Thomas, F. (2007), 'Global Rights, Local Realities: Negotiating Gender Equality and Sexual Rights in the Caprivi Region, Namibia', *Culture, Health & Sexuality*, Vol. 9, No. 6, 399.

United Nations (Eighth Session 1989), *General Recommendation No. 12: Violence Against Women*.

United Nations (Eleventh Session 1992), *General Recommendation No. 19: Violence Against Women*.

United Nations (20 March 2000), *General Comment No. 28: Equality of Rights Between Men and Women (Article 3)*, CCPR/C/21/Rev.1/Add.10.

United Nations (26 January 2006), *Summary Report of the 1093rd Meeting, Committee on the Rights of the Child*, CRC/C/SR.1093.

Velasquez Rodriquez Case (1988) Series C, 28 ILM 291 (1989); Inter-American Court of Human Rights. 29 July 1988.

Women and Law in Southern Africa (2002), *Lobola: Its Implications for Women's Reproductive Rights*, Harare, Zimbabwe: Weaver Press.

World Health Organization (2002), *World Report on Violence and Health*, Geneva: World Health Organization.

Chapter 13

Conversations across borders

Men and honour-related violence in the UK and Sweden

Dr Suruchi Thapar-Björkert

Senior Lecturer in Sociology, University of Bristol

This chapter engages with debates on honour-related violence (HRV) in the UK and Sweden and positions these debates within the broader context of media representations and multiculturalism. The chapter highlights two interrelated arguments. First, though academic and policy interventions have made HRV more visible, they have inadvertently reproduced an anti-male rhetoric that fails to expose the vulnerability of men and the shifting subject positions that men can occupy in relation to HRV: as perpetrators, as victims, as observers or as agents of change. Second, these interventions fail to acknowledge that male initiatives to challenge practices of HRV are extremely important to break cycles of gendered violence. In relation to the latter, the paper critically engages with the *Sharaf Heroes Project*, a unique male intervention in Sweden that works preventatively with young boys and men towards challenging and changing attitudes on honour-related violence.

Introduction

Critical engagement with media representations and discourses on multi-culturalism have challenged the ways in which ethnic-minority cultures and ethnic-minority women are positioned in relation to Western liberal democracies and white Western women. However, these debates have inadvertently focussed on dichotomous constructions of either female 'victimhood' or the vilification of ethnic-minority men as 'violent' (see Volpp 2001 and Razack 2008). In particular, ethnic-minority men seem to occupy a fixed subjectivity within these debates – as a 'perpetrator'. Consequently, this has drowned progressive initiatives emerging from within ethnic-minority communities. This chapter will thus highlight a significant gap in these analyses – the role of men as initiators of progressive strategies to combat HRV.

This chapter will be divided in the following way. In the first section, I will briefly analyse some comparative definitions and conceptualisations of HRV. In the second section, I will analyse media representations in relation to HRV. The third section will outline some of the fragile links between multiculturalism and gendered violence. In the fourth section, I will critically engage with the unique efforts of a specific men's project, the *Sharaf Heroes Project*.

Methodologies and definitions

The research on which this chapter is based emerged from a Swedish government-funded project (2004–5): 'State policy, strategies and implementation in combating patriarchal and "honour-related" violence in U.K., Sweden and Turkey'. In-depth qualitative interviews were conducted with an array of stakeholders in statutory and voluntary organisations in the UK, Sweden and Turkey, though this chapter draws on interview data from the UK and Sweden only. Professionals working at the interface of policy and practice were specifically interviewed, and this data was analysed in conjunction with Swedish government factsheets, reports from Swedish County Administrative Boards and media representations in broadsheets and tabloids. Only the names of respondents who requested anonymity have been changed.

Nearly all respondents expressed difficulties and ambiguities in defining and conceptualising what constitutes HRV. Indeed, the difficulties in defining HRV have had implications for state intervention in terms of policies and prosecution, and in devising appropriate methodologies to measure the extent of the problem. In 2002, following the murder of Fadime Sahindal (a 26-year-old girl of Kurdish ethnicity), the Swedish government (2002)[1] identified HRV as a practice confined to 'strongly patriarchal families'. This position was broadened in 2003/2004 and HRV conceptualised as a practice where 'the everyday lives of girls and young women ... are subject to extreme rigorous control, lack of freedom, coercion, threats and violence ... by their families'.[2] This definition was supported by governmental bodies such as the County Administrative Boards (Länsstyrelsen) and the National Board of Health and Welfare (Socialstyrelsen), who highlighted the importance of identifying the specific characteristics of HRV in order to avoid conflation with general 'patriarchal violence'. A narrower definition 'minimizes the risk of making invisible those exposed to violence with an explicit honour motive and with the support and acceptance of the collective'.[3]

In the UK, organisations such as *Southall Black Sisters* conceptualise HRV as a form of domestic violence since ' ... singling out honour killings risks promoting a racist agenda rather than gender equality' (Gupta and Hutchinson[4] 2005: 8; see also Gupta 2003: 3). However, Diana Nammi from the Iranian and Kurdish Women's Rights Organisation (*IKWRO*) argues that to incorporate honour killings under the umbrella of domestic violence is wrong because 'honour killing is a deliberate act, a planned killing and the perpetrator is actively looking to kill'.[5] Increasingly, honour violence is being discussed in terms of forced marriages since 'forced marriages have an element of honour in them ... honour is used to justify violence and the burden of honour is placed on women' (interview with Vinay Talwar, Forced Marriages Unit, August 2005).[6] I would suggest that the most convincing approach is violence against women (VAW), which states that acts committed in the name of honour (such as FGM and honour killings) are not that different from other acts of violence against women (Kelly and Lovett 2005). Keeler (2001) points out that if we limit our focus, we will not be able to develop an overall accurate understanding of violence against women, but will contribute to the invisibility of one or more aspects of it (Keeler 2001: 7). Also an 'integrated approach' does not differentiate between violence against women in black, minority and ethnic (BME) communities and in dominant white communities, since differentiations could reinforce power relations between men and women of different ethnicities (see Beckett and Macey 2001; Meeto and Mirza 2007).

Media representations in the UK and Sweden

Discussions on oppression and violence against 'women of foreign origin' or 'immigrant women' were brought to public attention in the 1990s with the murders of Sara, Pela Atroshi and Fadime Sahindal in Sweden. When Sara (a 15-year-old of Kurdish ethnicity) was murdered in 1996, the focus was more on the *individual*. Sara's brother (who committed the murder along with his cousin) was described as a 'difficult boy' (*strulig kille*) and the rector of his former school described him as broken (*trasig*), from a hard background (*jobbig backgrund*) and with large knowledge displacements (*stora kunskapsluckor*).[7] When Pela Atroshi (a 19-year-old of Kurdish ethnicity) and Fadime Sahindal were murdered, media debates projected the idea of 'culture' – how the concept of 'honour' was something that belonged to the 'Kurdish culture'. For example, the murder of Pela Atroshi was referred to as 'the Kurd murder'[8], and the planned killing of Pela in Dahouk (a Kurdish part of Iraq) reinforced the perceived differences between 'Kurdish culture' and 'Swedish culture'. The uncles (Swedish citizens) who killed Pela were tried in the Swedish court for murder and given life sentences, whereas Pela's father was tried in a local court in Dahouk and sentenced to five months in jail on parole. This, also 'highlighted the distance between gendered norms and legal practices in the immigrant's country of origin and those practiced in Sweden' (Hellgren and Hobson 2008: 391).

In all three cases, a debate on immigrant men and boys who 'can't accept the girls' wishes to choose their own lives' was raised. A discourse of 'modernity' where Pela and Fadime were murdered 'because they want to live their lives as modern women ... in modern Sweden' was juxtaposed to a discourse of an archaic 'tradition' adopted by their Kurdish community (see *Aftonbladet*, 23 January 2002: 29).[9] Similarly, an article in *The New York Times* (July 2002), 'Lost in Sweden: A Kurdish Daughter is Sacrificed', portrays Fadime as 'a symbol of second generation immigrant success' but one whose 'very desire for independence ... turn[ed] her into the tragic emblem of a European society's failure to bridge the gap in attitudes between its own culture and those of its newer arrivals'. Kamali (2003) argues that a cultural explanation is commonly provided when speaking of honour violence, while 'culture' is never mentioned in connection with 'Swedish' men beating 'Swedish' women (2003: 23).[10] Kamali suggests that a more productive way to approach these issues would be to focus on structural forms of systematic discrimination and their exclusionary consequences for immigrant communities.

Other analyses also contest these culturalist explanations (see Larsson and Englund 2004). *Uppsala Nya Tidning* (2002), a local newspaper from the same town that the Sahindal family lived in, published an article which emphasised how violence perpetrated by 'immigrant men' was projected as a consequence of a lack of 'integration' within Swedish culture (cited in Reimers 2007: 247). For example, it was stated that 'Fadime's father, Rahmi Sahindal, had little interest in *becoming Swedish* (and) ... clung hard to their Kurdish identity, living as part of a patriarchal clan' (*New York Times*, July 2002). Thus non-integrated foreign men are threats to women, 'not primarily owing to these men's gender, but to their culture' (Reimers 2007: 247).

The difficulties associated with culturalist-essentialist explanations were reflected in media debates on honour killings in the UK, which has adversely heightened the sense of insecurity and fear of the 'Other' (Majid and Hanif 2003). Wide coverage was provided by the tabloid press in the UK (*Daily Mail* 2003; *The Sun* 2003) following the death of Rukhsana Naz from Derby in 1998 and Heshu Yones in 2002. Honour killings were projected as a feature specific to the 'Other' ethnic minorities in Britain, evident in phrases such as a 'clash of cultures', 'fanaticism in other faiths', and 'barbarism' (*Daily Mirror* 2003). For example, the UK judge in the Yones murder trial, Neil Denison (QC), stated: 'In my view the case was a tragic story of irreconcilable *cultural differences* (my emphasis) between traditional Kurdish values and the values of Western society' (*The Independent*, 30 September 2003). Such statements, made by a UK judge, have in the past influenced the judiciary and the police to proceed cautiously in relation to 'murders' where cultural practices are involved, and have fuelled the belief that there are irreconcilable differences between the cultural values of some ethnic groups and the values of the Western host society.

However, repetitive physical, sexual and emotional abuse is a feature of life for many white majority British women, as it is for women within minority cultures. Dobash and Dobash (1992) narrate some horrific incidents of women being kicked, raped and punched, exemplified in statements such as: 'I had a poker thrown at me because his tea was too weak – he just takes it for granted ... if you are married, you'll have to accept. It's part of being a wife' (Dobash and Dobash 1992: 3).

Both incidents are part of the same patriarchal culture; both may in their own manner be culturally sanctioned (e.g. as punishment for not performing the cultural expectations of a wife or not being an obedient daughter).

Some common themes emerge in these discursive representations. First, the cultures are presented as neatly, prediscursively individuated from each other, such that the insistence on 'difference' that accompanies the 'production' of distinct 'cultures' appears unproblematic; and the central or constitutive components of a 'culture' are assumed to be 'unchanging givens'. This then reinforces 'essential differences' between Western cultures and non-Western cultures (Narayan 2000: 95; Rosenberg 2005). Second, existing scholarship has pointed towards the prevalence of gendered and sexualised violence in the white Swedish population (and in the UK) which is not approached/discussed in a cultural and essentialist manner (Mulinari 2004; Apkinar, 2003; Kurkiala 2003).[11] Incidents of domestic and sexual violence in the West are frequently thought to 'reflect the behaviour of a few deviants – rather than as part of our culture'. In contrast violence in immigrant communities 'are thought to characterise the culture of entire nations' (Volpp 2001: 1186). Third, overemphasis of one form of violence over the other obscures and normalises white women's experiences of violence and highlights violence in minority cultures as 'peculiar'. Furthermore, it compartmentalises violence as a feature of either gender or culture.

Let us now examine how similar ambiguities and tensions in relation to culture, gender and violence are inherent within the liberal multicultural projects. The debates presented in the next section could be seen to be more relevant to the UK, since in Sweden, arguably, 'not minority rights but integration has been the mainframe' (Hellgren and Hobson 2008).

Tensions within multiculturalism

Multiculturalism is about cultural diversity, that is, culturally derived differences, and 'although members can share their society's dominant system of meanings and values ... they can carve out "semi-autonomous" spaces within it' (Parekh 2000: 3). Multicultural approaches emphasise a person's 'right to be different' (Kymlicka 1995), and in the language of multicultural politics, 'cultures' are commonly conjoined with 'communities'. What 'community' lends to 'culture' is the implication of an organic association of people with shared interests, experiences and 'social closeness' (Uguris 2000: 53). Thus the 'cultural community' of multiculturalism is a fixed, bounded and unified collective of shared (cultural) experience and (cultural) needs. What the 'cultural community obscures', however, are the tensions, conflicts and differential power relations within social groups. Arguably the first violence encountered in our examination of multiculturalism is the symbolic violence of this misrecognition and oversimplification of what would be a dynamic and evolving form. It is in this context that the political theorist Susan Moller Okin (1999) explores the supposed irreconcilable tensions between feminism and multiculturalism in her essay 'Is Multiculturalism Bad for Women?' More specifically, Okin questions the claim made by multiculturalism (within the context of liberal democracies) that 'minority cultures or ways of life are not sufficiently protected by the practice of ensuring the individual rights of their members, and ... should be protected through special group rights or privileges (Okin 1999: 10–11; Spinner–Halev 2001; Pollitt 1999). Though Okin's (1999) analysis highlights widening gender inequalities (particularly in the private (domestic) sphere), through the preservation of cultural group rights, nonetheless, her analysis serves as a point of departure for many scholars who argue that there is a presumption within Okin's analysis that, first, minority cultures are more 'patriarchal, sexist than Western liberal cultures' and second, her analysis assumes 'internal homogeneity' within communities. (Volpp 2001: 1185–90). It is argued that feminism/multiculturalism is premised on a binary logic that parallels the limitations created by projecting cultural relativism and universalism as irreconcilable (Rao 1995) and, in these binary constructions, 'the values of Western liberalism are reified, defined as the opposite of culture' (Volpp 2001: 1203).

Importantly, the critique of media representations and the tensions inherent within feminism v. multiculturalism debates reflect a certain node of convergence. In both cases, the argument is against an essentialised and internally homogenous 'cultural' identity, which promotes 'culturalisation of differences' (Ålund 1999) or presents Western women as the embodiment of liberation. I want to extend this idea, specifically in relation to honour violence, which to some extent has become invisible in these dominant debates. First, as individuals we occupy locations of multiple (and conflicting) identities (see Uguris 2000; Beckett and Macey 2001) and reductively opposing 'race' and 'gender' (as Okin's analysis does) suggests that women in minority cultures need to get rid of their 'cultures' in order to eliminate gendered oppression. An excessive focus on cultural practices conceals the hidden structural forces which shape gendered oppression (for example colonialism, globalisation). If cultural violence (violence of cultural practices) is the subject of discussion then we need to understand its workings in association with structural violence, which shapes gendered positionalities. Second, 'gender' (and gendered subordination) in these debates often means 'women', or when the concept of gender is evoked relationally, it is about women as 'victims' and men as 'oppressors'. Not surprisingly, in most analyses of honour violence, men occupy a fixed 'perpetrator' identity and even when men act differently, for example as agents of emancipatory change, their efforts are not taken seriously.

Where are the men?

The greatest hesitation among organisations, academics and activists in the British context has been to involve men in combating violence. Though practitioners in the UK recognise that men can be victims of honour violence, they suggest that men and women face honour violence differently. As Saba Johri from *Imkaan*[12] states:

> men also come under pressure for upholding honour and respectability but not to the same degree that women are expected to uphold. Women experience penalties for transgression that may not be imposed on men.
>
> (Interview with Saba Johri, *Imkaan*, August 2005)

Similarly, the *Southall Black Sisters* argue that men tend to have greater power within the community and are able to escape some 'honour' pressures. When men transgress, the family is quicker to forgive them. Men also have more economic freedom than women, and can take decisions to leave their family more easily than women, if it becomes difficult for them. Nasir Afzal from Crown Prosecution Service (CPS) suggests that 'even when the male was a victim of honour violence, the motivation for the attack was the woman ... but the bulk of cases would involve women' (Interview with Nasir Afzal, CPS, August 2005). Ian Lewis from Renaissance Chambers argues that in the context of HRV:

> There are male victims ... males who are associated with the female ... in an adulterous relationship or an elopement, the male victim would not be the immediate family member but the man outside the family, the outsider who is threatening the honour of the family by associating with the woman victim ...
>
> (Ian Lewis, Renaissance Chambers)

In a recent trial in the UK, 19-year-old Arash Ghorbani-Zarin was found stabbed 46 times in a car in Rosehill in Oxford. The Iranian Muslim had a relationship with the sister (Miss Begum) of his killers, brothers Mohammad Rahman, 19, and Mamnoor Rahman, 16. They were allegedly ordered to kill Mr. Ghorbani-Zarin, due to the 'shame and dishonour' brought to the family by his relationship with Miss Begum, whose father had planned for her to have an arranged marriage (BBC News [TV], 4 November 2005).

Despite acknowledgement of male 'victimhood' in UK there is no organised involvement of men in combating violence. There are 'male dominated organisations' such as *The Muslim Parliament* and *The Council of Sikh Temples*, who have spoken out eloquently on the subject of HRV, but they are very different from the men's groups in Sweden (Nasir Afzal, CPS).

These organisations have argued that religious faith cannot be used for committing violence. As Afzal comments:

> There are very few males who stand up on the stage that condemn the issue of HRV ... but there is a desperate need in U.K. to have male role models but these role models should come from the community themselves.
>
> (Nasir Afzal, CPS)

In relation to this, even the role of 'self-styled' community leaders has been questioned by organisations such as the *Southall Black Sisters*, who see these leaders as presenting 'the most patriarchal and conservative forces in the community' (Siddiqui 2005: 270). Community leaders, as self-styled gate-keepers, it has been argued, can often use the liberal discourse of multi-culturalism to support acts of oppressive behaviour and physical violence towards young women and young boys (see Johal 2003).

However, despite these ambivalences, we need to create political spaces where the community leaders can see HRV as a breach of women's rights without associating any interventions to that effect as an attack on the community's culture or religion. Moreover, if we are combating what we recognise as gender-based violence, then men should be given an opportunity to share that political responsibility.[13] This is important for three reasons. First, an overemphasis on men as perpetrators could lead to men being projected as always a part of the *problem* rather than as part of the *solution*. Commenting on specific endeavours to build a dialogue between men on the subject of violence, Lise Berg, the former Swedish cabinet minister,[14] argues that 'men must be just as involved in the work of creating gender-equality' (Berg 2004: 199). If transforming gender relations can help end gender-based violence then ' ... one of the most urgent tasks is for men to change men, ourselves and other men' (Hearn 1998: 2; Connell 2003; Ferguson et al. 2004).

Second, viewing honour violence 'as a problem created by men' does not enable us to analyse the various subject positions that men can occupy in relation to HRV: as perpetrators, as victims, as 'silent' witnesses and as combatants. Men are culpable in honour violence and also vulnerable to that violence (Sundaram and Jackson 2006). Men can be and are victims of HRV, especially in terms of sexual orientation;[15] they can be punished for economic violations (e.g. theft); for associating with women victims (Siddiqui 2005) or men can be victims of gender patriarchal norms which discipline younger members of the family, irrespective of their gender. Men are often coerced to kill their own sisters, and many men commit crimes under fear or threat of violence. They often dare not say 'no' because of cultural pressures, and in some families men who adopt a 'modern, unprejudiced approach' towards their sisters can be ostracized (Al-Baldawi 2004: 152). Rana Husseini, in the context of Jordan, states, 'men are also victims ... the family comes and tells them that if you do not kill her ... people are going to look down on you ... they are going to spit on us' (Husseini 2004: 17). Men can also be forced to marry their cousins or girls 'they don't love'. Often younger male members of the family are expected to 'own' the honour killing, thus protecting the 'real' perpetrator, such as the father or the mother (Wikan 2005). Kandiyoti (1996) argues that intergenerational dynamics between men often position younger men in a 'one down position'.

Third, if we acknowledge that honour violence is associated with the exercise of power by men over women, then not engaging with men would mean operating through two static and oppositional models of under-standing – men as having power and women as powerless. Thus to view HRV solely as a women's issue, or to focus on women only, is not a sustainable solution. Campanile (2001: 141) argues that if you need to 'build equal relations', then it 'is not a struggle of women against men, or young people against adults, but rather a question of everyone taking on the responsibility for deconstructing domination and building equal relations'.

The lack of political will to involve men (and especially ethnic-minority men) in the UK, or support endeavours that prevent gender-based violence, have to some extent been addressed in Sweden and, in relation to this, let us now examine a male initiative in Sweden, The *Sharaf Heroes Project*. The Swedish government supported the organizing of men against violence, and since January 2003, 11 million SEK has been distributed to associations testing new methods and models to prevent and combat violence in the name of honour.[16]

The Sharaf Heroes (Sharaf Hjältar) Project in Sweden

In 2005, the former Swedish minister, Jens Orback,[17] called for a joint meeting of various men's organizations,[18] to build a common platform and a sustainable effort to tackle 'patriarchal violence'.[19] He stated:

> Men must learn to see how they are themselves part of the problem. Men have to take responsibility ... men cannot remain neutral. If men don't see the superiority and subordination they are a part of, and don't commit themselves to break down structures, these structures will remain.
>
> (Jens Orback)[20]

What is implicit in Orback's arguments[21] is that an approach should be devised to combat both direct violence (direct physical assaults and killings), and structural violence (power inequalities in social structures and oppression). Otherwise, as Galtung (1969: 172) has argued, ' ... (we may) be catching the small fry and letting the big fish loose'.

The *Sharaf Heroes Project* (SHP) cannot be regarded as a men's organisation but rather a men's project that works preventatively to change attitudes towards honour violence. It is organized on a 'voluntary' basis, and the initiative comes from an established group, *Elektra*, at Fryshuset in Stockholm.[22] The first group was created in 2003 by Arhe Hamednaca (of Eritrean ethnicity) and Ahmet Benhur Turkoglu, who conceptualised honour violence as 'honour related life' since it is the entire life that is 'controlled and oppressed'. Supporting the expanded definition of the Swedish Government factsheet (2004), which identifies men as perpetrators and victims of violence, Arhe Hamednaca states:

> The worst thing that could happen to a boy, when a sister commits a crime ... is that the entire family sits down and decides that it is his task to kill the girl. He is forced to do it. And I think that most of them do it against their own will ... The grade of victimhood may not be the same as the girls', but they are victims too.

SHP aim to work preventatively to educate young men and boys to become role models, who work within the families in the 'segregated immigrant-dominated areas' which adhere to an 'honour culture'. As Ahmet Behur Turkoglu, with reference to the work of young boys, states:

> The families are influenced and treat their children differently. And that is because of one individual in the family ... they change the attitudes of their friends. ... some of them cheered when Fadime was killed. But now they fight for women's rights. So the change may happen.

The school is seen as an important site to create a 'Sharaf Heroes group' as schools can provide a 'neutral zone' for discussions about integration, gender equality and family relations' (Al-Baldawi 2004: 153). Moreover, schools offer a hospitable terrain to nurture a gendered dialogue, between young people, on the subject of violence. Kaufman (2001: 11) argues that 'children are often socialised into expectations of behaviour by our society at a young age'. It is within the school 'that the basic values of our society are transmitted; it is here that girls and boys learn about the equal rights and responsibilities of all people' (Berg 2004: 198). Kickis Åhré Älgamo from *Rikskriminalen* suggests that the government should implement the *Sharaf Heroes Project* in every school arguing that, 'one needs to have 100% of the community to combat violence, not only 50%'.[23]

Though the efforts of SHP are remarkable, few men and boys choose to voluntarily commit themselves against the oppression of women. During an interview conducted in August 2005, Azam Karai at *Linnamottagningen* provides two main reasons why men do not organise voluntarily (for e.g. Kvinnors nätverk). First, there is still a wide belief that HRV 'mainly concerns the woman ... and not [the men] directly'. This is a reflection of the embedded patriarchal attitudes where men think that since violence affects women only, it is the responsibility of women to organise against it. Second, the social stigma attached to men working on this issue deters men. For example, men working on HRV have been referred to as 'without honour', 'whore customers', 'fags', and their identity and sexuality as 'real men' has been questioned. Berkowitz (2004) reiterates that men who work to end violence against women are challenging the dominant culture and the understandings of masculinity that maintains it. Male activists are 'often met with suspicion, homophobia and other questions about their masculinity' (2004: 4). To digress from a specific gendered construction of 'masculinity' (specific roles, behaviour and codes of conduct) may heighten men's vulnerabilities (Esplen 2006). For example, they may be made to feel less of a man by other males in the community, ostracised by the community or even subjected to violence. Thus men can experience power and powerlessness at the same time (for example, powerlessness in front of other men and power in relation to one's sister), and this still needs to be recognised. At the same time if only women 'own' violence, then they encounter the risk of isolating themselves in a struggle that can be enriched through men's involvement. Talking specifically about changing attitudes of young men, Crooks et al. (2007: 218), working within a pro-feminist framework, identify three ways that men can engage in anti-violence initiatives: first, through treatment programmes for batterers, which are integrated into a responsive criminal justice system; second, through playing an active role in addressing violence against women in their professional and personal lives; and third, men can make a personal commitment to be part of the solution for ending violence against women.

Both Hamednaca and Turkoglu suggest that their positionality as immigrant men has facilitated their interaction with, and the dissemination of ideas among, their audiences. They have been able to approach youths in 'suburbs, ghettoes such as Norsborg, Hallunda and youth recreation centres', which they argue would have been difficult for a 'Swede'. They argue that a 'Swede' would encounter hostility from 'immigrants' (for example at youth recreation centres) since they *do not know* enough about 'their (immigrants) way of life'. On the other hand, the SHP themselves have received a mixed reception from the public. They have been threatened, and many social groups have viewed their efforts as 'working against culture and religion'. They have encountered statements such as: 'You are a traitor; you betray your own people; you betray the culture you grew up in ... and our women should not play sex as Swedish women'. More pertinently, women have spoken against their efforts and defended their religion and culture, which challenges the discursive representations of HRV in which women are projected as in need of 'saving' from 'barbaric', 'fanatic' men (see Razack 2008). Elden (2004: 93–5) refers to the 'cultural context of honour' as a normative framework of interpretation in which the behaviour of the individual (woman) cannot be separated from the honour of the collective (of men). She argues that Arab and Kurdish women in Sweden use the concepts of 'Swedish', 'Arab' and 'Kurdish' as 'contrasts', and though the substance of the contrast remains constant, its loading may alternate between 'positive' (safety, community, love) and 'negative' (limitations, constraint, subjection).

Though SHP has received international attention, it generates mixed reactions among individuals from both statutory and voluntary organisations in the UK. For example, some individuals working in organisations such as *Imkaan* see SHP as 'vigilantes', and though this organisation views the contribution of men as important, they emphasise that 'men's engagement should not be at the cost of women's involvement'. Even the subject of representation can become contested – 'who speaks on behalf of whom?'

Engagements/disengagements: the Sharaf Heroes Project

The *Sharaf Heroes Project* is a 'preventative measure' and, as argued elsewhere (Thapar-Bjorkert 2006), 'protective' measures (such as sheltered housing and professional/psychological treatment) have to be placed in conjunction with 'preventative' measures for combating HRV. Some distinguishing features of the SHP work can be identified as follows: first, they have broadened the definition of HRV from physical acts of violence to include everyday forms of 'oppression' as forms of violence. This is important because coercion, intimidation and the threat of violence reflect the insidious workings of symbolic and structural violence, which is often unrecognisable. Ahre Hamednaca explains that there are a lot of 'girls of foreign origin' who do not have the right to determine their own lives. They may not always be exposed to violence, but they are controlled and monitored in other ways. However, it's only when a girl resists that a situation erupts in violence and then becomes more public and visible to society. Thus Hamednaca claims that it is wrong to mix up 'honour related life' with 'patriarchal violence', which he claims affects women of Swedish ethnicity. He states:

> … the Swedish woman of today – she has the basics, she can choose her future … whether to get an education, whether to leave home, whether to get a husband, children … But the other part: the woman living under honour related life. She has no chance. She is oppressed from the start. Somebody owns her. She does not own her body. That is the difference.

Second, Hamednaca explains 'patriarchal violence' as more 'individual', as opposed to HRV, which involves the 'collective':

> ... the difference is that when Kalle kills Kerstin it is individual. He does it himself ... But honour related violence is collective ... the entire family sits down and decides that I should do it [kill the girl/woman] against my will to save the family honour.
>
> (Interview with Ahre Hamednaca, August 2005)

SHP has usefully highlighted the opportunities and basic needs available to women of Swedish ethnicity, which are denied to immigrant women living 'under honour related life'. In relation to violence Hamednaca reiterates the 'individual'/white/Swedish versus the collective/ethnic/minority dichotomy. While this is not untrue, it is still difficult to conceptualise both these forms of violence as anything different than patriarchal violence.

Third, SHP is critical about the ways in which HRV has been explained as a 'clash of cultures'[24] and would prefer to understand the problem as a 'clash with universal human rights'.

> I don't think that my culture clashes with your culture. When I speak of the rights of children and the rights of women ... that is not Swedish culture to me. That is universal rights, you see?
>
> (Ahre Hamednaca)

The human-rights discourse is important for a number of reasons: first, it bridges the 'space between race and gender, without trampling on the rights of black and minority communities' (Siddiqui 2005: 279). Second, assertions for human rights on an international plane break down culturally relativist arguments and foreground social justice for all, irrespective of class, race and gender. But there are difficulties with the SHP proposal of upholding human rights. First, the human-rights discourse incorporates a broad canvas of rights and legislations, and it is often difficult to disentangle human-rights violations committed by representatives of the state and those that are committed by non-state actors. As An-Na'im (2005) points out, 'human rights are by definition intended to protect people against excess or abuse of the powers of the state ... crimes like homicide are not human rights violations unless committed by agents of the state'. Though women's rights advocates have challenged this distinction, An-Na'im argues that 'the human rights approach should be seen as only one option among others' (An-Na'im 2005: 71). The human-rights approach should supplement, not undermine, alternative approaches. Second, although human rights are universal in form and intention, they are particular in their use, bounded in scope and scale by cultural norms and geopolitical situations. Arguably, it could be useful to relate human rights to values that are recognised by the community itself, and a more persuasive (through cross-cultural human-rights dialogue), rather than a compulsive strategy in promoting human rights, would not meet as strong a resistance as the absolutist universalist approach (Scheinin 2002).

Assigning the category 'oppressed' to individuals who perceive their social reality differently can be disempowering as well. I illustrate this through a conversation that Ahmet Hamednaca had with a girl in Rosengård, in Malmö, who did not want to be perceived as oppressed and opposed the ideas of the SHP:

AHMET: Here I come, fighting for the rights of woman and then I get attacked by a girl. As soon as I started to talk to her, I understand that they are so oppressed – *they don't understand that they are oppressed* (my emphasis).

GIRL: I'm getting married soon.

AHMET: Oh yeah, that's good! Have you been going out for long?

GIRL: No.

AHMET: But then how are you going to get married?

GIRL: Well, dad showed me three guys and I got to choose which one to marry!

AHMET: That is her freedom – to choose one out of three. That's her interpretation of freedom. That just gives a quick picture of how they live.

The analysis of this exchange is problematic as we cannot impose ideas of freedom and equality on individuals whom *we* perceive as 'victims'. The meanings of 'freedom' and 'equality' are subjective and time-contingent. Individuals in different societies, and of different ethnicities within one country, can understand 'oppression' differently.

I also consider their understanding of 'the family' problematic. According to Hamednaca, many of the young girls and boys he meets do not associate positive qualities with being 'Swedish'. He states:

You don't defend yourself but you defend your family. Because you are brought up to defend the family. The family is the most important thing, more important than society, in their opinion. That is why. And the first argument you hear when talking to boys is: 'But what do you mean? Should I make my sister a whore? Let her out to fuck whoever she wants? Is that what they're after?' If it is a girl, it is the same. 'What, are we bad because we don't behave like Swedish girls?'

Several ideas are entangled in the above quotations. First, I do not think it is problematic, as Hamednaca thinks, that his respondents defend their families. Making judgements or adopting an oppositional discourse on (to) the 'defence of the family' can be perceived as a 'cultural attack' by some immigrant groups. Also we need to bear in mind that familial networks are often the chief building blocks of social capital for immigrant communities, even though, paradoxically, most HRV is carried out by family members. There is also a risk that if some affluent families move away from 'deprived' residential areas, they leave behind a section of the Swedish population who could be in a less advantageous position (for example, less affluent or experiencing problems associated with marginalisation). The latter, then, are seen as representative of 'Swedishness', and this could explain the heightened insecurity of specific immigrant communities residing in these neighbourhoods. In this social context, it is understandable that if an 'immigrant' girl has a 'Swedish' friend, she might risk getting a bad reputation, and may generate problems in her immediate family and wider immigrant community. As Hamednaca affirms:

> So in these areas there is a rumour that if these immigrant girls have Swedish friends, then the girl gets a bad reputation. And she will find it difficult to get married in the future. So they didn't want their daughters to have anything to do with the Swedish girl, which is a pity.

The *Sharaf Heroes Project* is an initiative that comes from individuals from within the community and aims at engaging with the community. However, it is also important to emphasise that ethnic-minority communities are not homogenous entities but have differences on the basis of gender, generation, socioeconomic background, nature of migration and current position in the labour market. These larger structural issues can impact differently on individuals within the community and can influence their attitudes towards violence.

Conclusion

For a sustainable struggle against gender-based violence, a more concerted effort needs to be made at both academic and policy-related levels to facilitate and sustain a shift from 'mainstreaming gender' (which unfortunately led to approaches centred on women only) to 'mainstreaming men'. We need to create political spaces for male initiatives, to see men as agents of change and as participants in reform and potential allies in search of gender justice. If one of the aims of our struggle against gendered violence is to create a new model for empowered women, then we also need a new model of masculinity – one that sustains itself, not through dominance over women, but through collaboration.

Male projects that promote gender-equitable behaviour among men should be politically supported since they can be 'lonely' voices in the field of violence. Securing gender equality is not about disempowering men but working *with them* to dismantle power hierarchies. In the UK there is still hesitation to involve men in combating violence. In contrast, the SHP in Sweden is a positive initiative to combat HRV, even though it is ambiguous and contradictory.

Acknowledgements

The funding for this research was provided by the Swedish Integration Board. I am indebted to Carin Persson, Erika Sallander, Erik Olsson and Christer Gustavsson for their contributions, advice and guidance in this project. Sincere thanks to Dr Gurchathen Sanghera for his critical comments on an earlier version of this paper.

Notes

1 *Regeringens insatser för utsatta flickor i patriarkala familjer*, factsheet, February 2002.
2 *Regeringens insatser för ungdomar som riskerar hedersrelaterat våld*, factsheet, November 2004.
3 Länsstyrelsen i Stockholms län (2005)18 projekt till stöd för flickor och unga kvinnor.
4 Barristers at Renaissance Chambers, a leading family law cohort that includes a team of immigration practitioners.
5 Personal interview with Diana Nammi, September 2005.
6 Forced Marriage Unit (FMU) interfaces between the Home Office (HO) and Foreign and Commonwealth Office (FCO). Also see *The Independent*, 'A Question of Honour' (10 February 2008).
7 See *Dagens Nyheter* (22 December 1996) and *Svenska Dagbladet* (17 December 1996).
8 See *Expressen*, 21 January 2000.
9 In the British media the rationale provided is that of 'a crisis of modernity'. Patel (1997) describes how in the early nineties in Britain, an Asian man established himself as a 'bounty hunter', offering his services to local Asian families whose daughters and wives had chosen of their own right to move away. Quality newspapers referred to him as a 'mediator' who was 'salvaging' Asian marriage from the 'crisis in modernity'.
10 'Ny utredning om diskriminering, integration och makt', Pressmeddelande, 22 December 2003, Justitiedepartementet.
11 In a report for National Council For Crime Prevention (BRÅ 2002: 14), Lotta Nilsson, points out that in four counties in Sweden, Stockholm, Gotland, Dalarna and Östergötland, 1 per cent of working women were exposed to violence within intimate relationships in a given year.
12 *Imkaan* is a national policy, training and research initiative in the UK, dedicated to providing support and advocacy to the specialist refuge sector, supporting Asian woman and children experiencing violence.
13 There have been initiatives to involve men such as the *White Ribbon Campaign*, initiated in Canada in 1991: http://www.whiteribbon.ca.
14 State Secretary for Integration, Democracy, Gender Equality and Sports.
15 *Regeringens insatser för ungdomar som riskerar hedersrelaterat våld*, factsheet, November 2004.
16 *Initiatives to help young people at risk of violence and oppression in the name of honour*, factsheet, January 2007.
17 Minister for Democracy, Metropolitan Affairs, Integration and Gender Equality.
18 The national organisation, 'Mens Network' (Manliga Nätverket), serves as an infrastructure for organisations in other parts of Sweden (such as Piteå, Malmö, Lund, Västervik) to combat men's violence against women.
19 'Ny plattforn för män mot kvinnovåld', *Dagens Nyheter*, 20050318.

20 Inbjudan till presskonferens – 'Män om mäns våld mot kvinnor', Press-meddelande, 17 March 2005.
21 Ny plattforn för män mot kvinnovåld, *Dagens Nyheter* (050318).
22 http://www.elektra.nu/db/artiklar/sharaf.htm.
23 Interview with Kickis Åhré Älgamo, September 2005.
24 Interestingly, a psychotherapist from Save the Children (Rädda Barnen), Sweden, states that they use the phrase: 'Are you a girl, living in two cultures and want to talk about it?' ('är du flicka, lever i två kulturer och behöver prata om det?'). The psychotherapist believes that girls and boys do not want to conceptualize their lived realities in terms of 'honour violence'.

Bibliography

Akpinar, A. (2003) 'The Honour/Shame Complex Re-visited: Violence Against Women in the Migration Context', *Women's Studies International Forum*, Vol. 26, No. 5, 425.
Al-Baldawi, R. (2004) 'Long Term Measures to Combat Honour-Related Violence in Patriarchal Families', in Mojab, S. and Abdo, N. (eds) *Violence in the Name of Honour: Theoretical and Political Challenges*, Istanbul: Bilgi University Press.
Ålund, A. (1999) 'Feminism, Multiculturalism, Essentialism', in Yuval-Davis, N. and Werbner, P. (eds) *Women, Citizenship and Difference*, London: Zed Books.
An-Na'im, A. A. (2005) 'The Role of "Community Discourse" in Combating "Crimes of Honour": Preliminary Assessment and Prospects', in Welchman, L. and Hossain, S. (eds) *'Honour': Crimes, Paradigms, and Violence Against Women*, London: Zed Books.
Beckett, C. and Macey, M. (2001) 'Race, Gender and Sexuality: The Oppression of Multiculturalism', *Women's Studies International Forum*, Vol. 24, No.3/4, 309.
Berg, L. (2004) 'Swedish Government Initiatives to Help Young People at Risk of Honour Related Violence', in Mojab, S. and Abdo, N. (eds) *Violence in the Name of Honour: Theoretical and Political Challenges*, Istanbul: Bilgi University Press.
Berkowitz, A. D. (2004) *'Working with Men to Prevent Violence Against Women: An Overview'*, VAWnet (National Resource Centre on Domestic Violence), Online. Available at http://www.alanberkowitz.com/articles/VAWNET.pdf.
Campanile, V. and Hernandez, T. (2001) 'Feminism at Work: A Case Study of Transforming Power Relations in Everyday Life: Puentos de Encuentro', in *Institutionalising Gender Equality: Commitment, Policy and Practice, A Global Source Book*, Oxfam, GB, The Netherlands: KIT Publishers.
Crooks, C., Goodall G., Hughes, R., Jaffe, P. and Baker L. (2007) 'Engaging Men and Boys in Preventing Violence Against Women: Applying a Cognitive-Behavioural Model', *Violence Against Women*, Vol. 13, No. 3, 217.
Connell, R. W. (2003) 'The Role of Men and Boys in Achieving Gender Equality', from the Expert Group Meeting on The Role of Men and Boys in Achieving Gender Equality (no.EGM/MEN-boys-GE/2003/bp.10.Brasilia, Brazil: United Nations Division for the Advancement of Women) 21-24 October.
De los Reyes, P. (2003) *Patriarkala enklaver eller ingenmansland: våld, hot och kontroll av unga kvinnor i Sverige*, Integrationsverket, Norrköping.
Daily Mirror (2003), 'Fears Grow for Arranged Marriage Girl', by Jan Disley, 20 November.
Dobash, E. R. and Dobash R. P. (1992) *Women, Violence and Social Change*, London: Routledge.

Elden, Å (2004) 'Life and Death Honour: Young Women's Violent Stories About Reputation, Virginity and Honour – in a Swedish Context', in Mojab, S. and Abdo, N. (eds) *Violence in the Name of Honour: Theoretical and Political Challenges*, Istanbul: Bilgi University Press.

Esplen, E (2006) *Engaging Men in Gender Equality: Positive Strategies and Approaches*, BRIDGE, Sussex: Institute of Development Studies.

Ferguson, H., Hearn, J., Gullvag, O., Holter., J. L. (2004). *Ending Gender-Based Violence: A Call for Global Action to Involve Men*, SIDA.

Galtung, J. (1969) 'Violence, Peace, and Peace Research', *Journal of Peace Research*, Vol. 6, No. 3, 167.

Gupta, R. (2003) 'A Veil Drawn Over Brutal Crimes', available at http://www.guardian.co.uk/comment/story/0,3604,1054858,00.html.

Gupta T. and Hutchinson A. M. (2005) *Honour Based Crimes and Murders*, Law Society, Working Paper.

Hearn, J. (1998) *The Violences of Men: How Men Talk and How Agencies Respond to Men's Violence to Women*, London: Sage.

Hellgren Z. and Hobson B. (2008) 'Cultural Dialogues in the Good Society: The Case of Honour Killings in Sweden', *Ethnicities*, Vol. 8, 385.

Husseini, R. (2004) 'HRV and Human Rights: The Jordanian Experience', in *Honour Related Violence within a Global Perspective: Mitigation and Prevention in Europe*, European Conference Report, Stockholm, 7–8 October.

Johal, A. (2003) 'Struggle not Submission: Domestic Violence in the 1990s', in Gupta, R. (ed.) *From Homebreakers to Jailbreakers,* London: Zed Books.

Kandiyoti, D. (1996) 'The Paradoxes of Masculinity: Some Thoughts on Segregated Societies', in Cornwall, A. and Lindisfarne, N. (eds) *Dislocating Masculinity: Comparative Ethnographies*, London: Routledge.

Kaufman, M. (2001) 'Building a Movement of Men Working to End Violence Against Women', *Development*, Vol. 44, No. 3, 9.

Keeler, L. (ed.) (2001). *Recommendations of the E.U. Expert Meeting on Violence Against Women*, Helsinki, Finland: Ministry of Social Affairs and Health.

Kelly, L. and Lovett, J. (2005) *What a Waste: The Case for an Integrated Violence Against Women Strategy*, Women's National Commission.

Kurkiala, M. (2003) 'Interpreting Honour Killings: The Story of Fadime Sahindal in the Swedish Press (1975–2002)', *Anthropology Today*, Vol. 19, No. 1.

Kymlicka, W. (1995) *Multicultural Citizenship: A Liberal Theory of Minority Rights*, Oxford: Oxford University Press.

Larsson, S. and Englund, C. (eds) (2004) *Debatten om Hedersmord – Feminism eller Rasism* (The Debate on Honour Killings – Feminism or Racism) Stockholm: EXPO Foundation and Svartvitts Forlag.

Mulinari, D. (2004). 'Hon dog for hon ville bli svensk', in S. Larsson (ed.) *Debatten om Hedersmord: Feminism eller Rasism*? Stockholm: EXPO Foundation and Svartvitts Forlag.

Majid, R. and Hanif, S. (2003) *Language, Power and Honour: Using Murder to Demonise Muslims*, Islamic Human Rights Commission, available at http://www.ihrc.org.

Meetoo, V. and Mirza, H. S. (2007) 'There is Nothing "Honourable" About Honour Killings: Gender, Violence and the Limits of Multiculturalism', *Women's Studies International Forum*, Vol. 30, 187.

Narayan, U. (2000) 'Essence of Culture and a Sense of History: A Feminist Critique of Cultural Essentialism', in Narayan, U. and Harding, S. (eds) *Decentering the Centre: Philosophy for a Multicultural, Post-Colonial and Feminist World*, Bloomington, IN: Indiana University Press.

Okin, M. S. (1999) 'Is Multiculturalism Bad for Women?' in Cohen, J., Howard, M. and Nussbaum, M. (eds) *Is Multiculturalism Bad for Women*, Princeton, NJ: Princeton University Press.

Patel, P. (1997) 'Third Wave Feminism and Black Women's Activism', in Mirza, H. S. (ed.) *Black British Feminism*, London: Routledge.

Parekh, B. (2000) *Rethinking Multiculturalism: Cultural Diversity and Political Theory*, Basingstoke: Macmillan.

Pollitt, K. (1999) 'Whose Culture?' in Cohen, J., Howard, M. and Nussbaum, M. (eds) *Is Multiculturalism Bad for Women*, Princeton, NJ: Princeton University Press.

Rao, A (1995) 'The Politics of Gender and Culture in International Human Rights Discourse', in Peters, J. S. and Wolper, A. (eds). *Women's Rights, Human Rights: International Feminist Perspectives*, New York: Routledge.

Razack, H. S. (2008) *The Eviction of Muslims from Western Law and Politics*, Toronto: University of Toronto Press.

Reimers, E. (2007) 'Representations of an Honour Killing', *Feminist Media Studies*, Vol. 7, No. 3, 239.

Rosenberg, T. (2005) 'The Fadime Sahindal Story: Honour Killings as "Death by Culture" in Sweden 2002', in Chaturvedi, R. and Singleton, B. (eds) *Ethnicity and Identity: Global Performance*, Delhi: Rawat Publishers.

Scheinin, M. (2002) 'Universality and Cultural Relativism in the Human Rights Debate – Is Cross-Cultural Dialogue Possible?' in Perheentupa, J. and Karppi, K. (eds) *Cross-Cultural Encounters: Perspectives on Multicultural Europe*, University of Turku.

Siddiqui, H. (2005) 'There is no "honour" in Domestic Violence, Only Shame! Women's Struggles Against "Honour" Crimes in the UK', in Welchman, L. and Hossain, S. (eds) *'Honour': Crimes, Paradigms, and Violence Against Women*, London: Zed Books.

Spinner-Halev, J. (2001) 'Feminism, Multiculturalism, Oppression, and the State', *Ethics*, No. 1, 84.

Sundaram, V. and Jackson, S. (2006) 'Upholding the Myth of Masculinity: The Gendered Production of Violence Victims', in *Violence Victimisation as a Gender Specific Process*, unpublished thesis.

Thapar-Björkert, S. (2006) 'State Policies, Strategies and State Implementation on Honour Based Violence: A Comparative Study of Sweden, United Kingdom and Turkey', Ministry of Justice, Swedish Integration Board, Sweden.

The Independent (2003), 'Execute Me, pleads Muslim who killed his daughter over her Western lifestyle', by Terri Judd, 30 September.

The New York Times (2002), 'Lost in Sweden: A Kurdish Daughter is Sacrificed', by Sarah Lyall, 23 July.

Uguris, T. (2000) 'Gender, Ethnicity and The Community: Locations with Multiple Identities', in Ali, K., Coate, K. and Goro, W.W. (eds) *Global Feminist Politics: Identities in a Changing World*, London: Routledge.

Volpp, L. (2001) 'Feminism Versus Multiculturalism', *Columbia Law Review*, Vol. 101, No. 5, 1181.

Wikan, U. (2005) *The Honour Culture*. Available at http://www.axess.se/english/2005/01/theme_wikan.php.

Chapter 14

Tackling 'crimes of honour'

Evaluating the social and legal responses for combating forced marriages in the UK

Dr Samia Bano
Lecturer in Law, University of Reading

In this chapter the author explores some of the moral, legal and sociological questions that arise from one type of honour crime in the United Kingdom – forced marriage. Focusing on the civil law remedies available under the new Forced Marriage (Civil Protection) Act 2007 the chapter considers how the law in England and Wales deals with tackling forced marriages. In particular, it questions what benefits this new piece of legislation may have for women who may be subject to such practices and questions how this new Act deals with perpetrators of forced marriage. It also discusses the limitations of the Act and examines 'community' concerns about introducing this piece of legislation as a mechanism to tackle forced marriage, and it questions why plans for a specific criminal offence of forced marriage have been abandoned by the government. The chapter also considers why crimes of honour and forced marriage have become emblematic of the problematic nature of one religion – Islam – and its treatment of women. In doing so it considers some of the challenges that the issue of forced marriage poses to secular/liberal notions of law, human rights and gender equality.[1]

Introduction

The practice of forced marriage has over the past decade gained national and international attention, partly due to increased media coverage of high-profile cases,[2] but largely due to the campaigning work of community and feminist activists who have demanded state protection – in all its forms – for victims of forced marriage. Over a long period of time such activists have not only in the name of gender equality organised and represented the experiences of victims of forced marriage but demanded state accountability for failures to tackle the problem. Their most compelling argument is that the state has been reluctant to intervene in internal family and community concerns for fear of being labelled racist. Hannana Siddiqui of Southall Black Sisters points out:

> ... assumptions include the view that it is intolerant, or even racist for a majority community to interfere in minority cultures. Thus respecting

cultural difference means allowing the minority community to govern or police itself. It also seems to mean that any intervention is determined in consultation and agreement with self-styled community and religious leaders, who are seen as gatekeepers and who historically have represented the most powerful patriarchal and conservative forces in the community.

(Siddiqui 2005: 270)

In this way the practice of forced marriage has been closely connected to policing female behaviour in the family and community, as a manifestation of violence against women and a clear violation of human rights. In particular, such analyses have focused on the interrelationship between power, authority and control and the articulation of honour and shame – which define acceptable codes of behaviour for young women and girls and control female sexuality (in the family and community) and are enshrined in cultural practice and religious ideology. It is within this framework that a more thorough and context-specific understanding of forced marriage as a crime of honour allows analysis of law-based strategies to sanction its practice, which is accentuated within some South Asian communities in the United Kingdom. Most recently the issue of forced marriage has been addressed at a national, and increasingly at an international, level.[3] In the United Kingdom the recent murders of young women, who had been killed for refusing to marry,[4] have mobilised a 'multi-agency' approach in tackling the problem. Thus the connection between crimes of honour (for example forced marriage) and honour killings (murder in the name of honour) illustrates the problems in conceptualising differences between consent, coercion and force which can ultimately lead to murder.

In this chapter the author draws upon these debates to evaluate state responses to combating the practice of forced marriage as a crime of honour in the United Kingdom. Today there are a number of legislative and policy initiatives which seek to eradicate its practice, and at the heart of these policy and legal initiatives lies the experience of women as victims of forced marriage – within the wider framework of violence against women. It is interesting to note that strategies to challenge forced marriages also include initiatives designed to explore the psychological motivations for the offenders' behaviours and to understand the complex ways in which forced marriage manifests in the family, home and community, and to understand its relationship to cultural practice and religious ideology (in this case, principally Islam). Yet the wider debates on conceptualising a generic definition of a forced marriage and its articulation within different communities have proved both contentious and problematic. Perhaps more importantly the culturalist approach adopted by the state has led many to argue that the debate on forced marriage stigmatises Islam and Muslim communities as *key* perpetrators of forced marriages, which gives rise to the logic that there is an irreconcilable clash between Islam and the West. For Muslim diasporic communities living in the West such understandings are deeply troubling as they raise fundamental questions of loyalty to the state and the failure of Muslims to integrate within Western democratic societies, and these discourses have become closely linked to debates on immigration and border controls. There is also a growing literature on the experiences of Muslim women as victims of forced marriage, and Razack (2004: 130) describes the 'hypervisibility of the Muslim woman's body' which has led to the extraordinary measures of stigmatisation, surveillance and control (131). With these issues in mind, this chapter draws upon the Forced Marriage (Civil Protection) Act 2007 to consider civil-law remedies available to victims of forced marriage and to question why the state has been reluctant to introduce a specific criminal offence of 'forcing someone to marry'. The author analyses the ways in which this legislation contributes to existing initiatives in tackling the practice of forced marriage in the United Kingdom and questions whether it is possible to acknowledge and confront patriarchal violence within Muslim migrant communities without descending into cultural-deficit explanations ('they are overly patriarchal and inherently uncivilised').

Understanding forced marriage as a crime of 'honour' in Britain

Contemporary discussions on the causes of forced marriage suggest several different, though interrelated, factors, which include the position of women in the family (governed by a social patriarchal order) and the transmission of values, ideas, customs, morals and traditions which remain entrenched within cultural and religious ideology and practice and which place a particular importance on the control of female sexuality. It is generally accepted, however, that the practice of forced marriage falls within the wider spectrum of 'crimes of honour' perpetrated against women. Subsequently, what we understand as honour and crimes committed in the name of honour, such as forced marriage, have given rise to extensive discussions on the difficulties of defining such terms.

A crime of honour has been defined as:

> ... a variety of manifestations of violence against women, including 'honour killings', assault, confinement or imprisonment and interference with choice in marriage where the publicly articulated 'justification' is attributed to a social order claimed to require the preservation of a concept of 'honour' vested in male (family and/or conjugal) control over women and specifically women's sexual conduct: actual, suspected or potential'.

> (Welchman and Hossain 2005: 4)

There is a growing literature which explores the relationship between honour, codes of honour and violence against women. Baker et al. (1999) identifies commonalities in crimes of honour and argues that honour underlies the patriarchal systems of controlling female sexuality related to systems of enhancing and controlling female honour and shame. In this way honour is located within female bodies and closely linked to female sexual regulation and control by male members of the family. This is articulated most succinctly by Purna Sen, who points out that:

> ... codes of honour serve to construct not only what it means to be a woman but also what it means to be a man, and hence are central to social meanings of gender. Honour is thus intrinsically linked to norms of behaviour for both sexes and predicated upon patriarchal notions of ownership and control of women's bodies. Social constraints regulate women's lives in ways that lie beyond statute and codified laws and have significantly more meaning attached.
>
> (Sen 2005: 48)

This also raises questions related to the ways in which the concept of honour can be identified within religious and cultural frameworks. In Britain issues of definition and terminology of honour and crimes of honour have focused largely on discussions of identity, family and community within the British South Asian diaspora and more specially linked to wider questions of the integration of migrant communities and the policies of multiculturalism. The majority of cases of forced marriage in the UK involve South Asian families, yet this does not in itself mean that forced marriage is solely and specifically a South Asian problem; instead the disparity can be explained due to factors such as a large South Asian presence in the UK and the reporting of forced-marriage cases.[5]

Postcolonial migrations have been described as new migrations (Hall 1992: 310) which have led to the creation of diasporic identities which cut across fixed and bounded categories such as 'home' and 'belonging' (Brah 1996). Understanding identity as a process rather than based upon a fixed essence has led to a growing literature on diasporic identities and cultural and religious identifications. However, according to Anthias and Yuval-Davis (1989), much of 'ethnic culture' is organised around rules relating to sexuality, marriage and the family and in this way " ... communal boundaries often use differences in the way women are socially constructed as markers" (1989: 114). Such markers include expectations about honour whereby women are deemed the preservers of 'family honour'. This notion of 'family honour' within South Asian communities has been described as a process used to control female sexuality through restriction of movement (see Afshar 1994; Anthias and Yuval-Davis 1992; Bhopal 1999).

In her study of the structure of female authority within Pakistani households in West Yorkshire, Afshar points out that the significance of *izzat* (honour) is the way in which women are expected to conduct themselves both in the private and public spheres. Wilson describes *izzat* as:

> essentially male but it is women's lives and actions, which affect it most. A woman can have izzat but it is not her own, it is her husband's or father's. Her izzat is a reflection of the male pride of the family as a whole. (What is more) saving her izzat (and through that their own izzat) is perhaps the greatest responsibility for her parents or guardian.
>
> (Wilson 1978: 35)

In this way the role of women as preservers of family honour means that only they can increase the honour of the family through obedience and only they can "lose it" and thus shame the family. As Anthias and Yuval-Davis point out, "A significant element is to be able to control the behaviour of the women in the family, both wives and daughters, for any transgression by them is an imputation of a failure to exercise proper patriarchal control" (1992: 78). Yet the way in which 'family honour' operates within the family, home and community context(s) must also be understood in relation to the specific family and community context(s) to which the women belong. Nevertheless, as existing literature suggests, the significance of family honour to the marriage process raises fundamental questions of human rights and the right to choose a marriage partner based on personal choice, consent and autonomy. It also raises conceptual problems of what we understand as an arranged, forced and own-choice marriage, with the issues of consent and coercion being at the forefront of different interpretations.

A forced marriage has been described as "a marriage without the full and free consent of both parties" and "where people are coerced into a marriage against their will and under duress" (FCO 2005: 3). In this way existing provisions in civil and criminal legislation prohibit the practice of forced marriage. For example, in the United Kingdom the Marriage Act 1949 and the Matrimonial Causes Act 1973 govern the law on the validity of marriages in England and Wales. A forced marriage can be made null and be deemed voidable (civil proceedings for nullity) according to section 12C of the Matrimonial Causes Act 1973 which states that a marriage shall be voidable if "either party to the marriage did not validly consent to it, whether in consequence of duress, mistake, unsoundness of mind or otherwise". The issue of duress has also been extensively addressed by the courts. In *Hirani v. Hirani*,[6] the test of duress for these purposes was whether the mind of the applicant (the victim) had been overborne, howsoever that was caused.[7] Under criminal law, although there is no specific offence of forced marriage, perpetrators can be prosecuted for a range of offences including kidnapping, child abduction, false imprisonment, assault and battery, blackmail and threats to kill.[8]

Interestingly, however, there remains little clarity over the meaning of forced marriage, which has led to criticisms that existing approaches are ineffective. For example, a study on forced marriage by the Council of Europe described it as:

> an umbrella term covering marriage as slavery, arranged marriage, traditional marriage, marriage for reasons of custom expediency or perceived respectability, child marriage, early marriage, fictitious, bogus or sham marriage, marriage of convenience, unconsummated marriage, putative marriage, marriage to acquire nationality and undesirable marriage – in all of which the concept of consent to marriage is at issue.
>
> (Rude-Antoine 2005: 8)

This definition categorises a wide range of practices as amounting to forced marriage. In Britain, however, there has been a deliberate initiative to draw a clear distinction between arranged and forced marriages in order to avoid labelling all arranged marriages as forced marriages. For example the Home Office report, *Forced Marriage: A Wrong Not a Right*, states: "Forced marriages are not arranged marriages. In an arranged marriage the family will take the lead in arranging the match but the couples have a choice as to whether to proceed. In a forced marriage there is no choice" (2005: 4). Yet most commentators also readily accept that there is a narrow distinction between a forced and an arranged marriage, based on difficult issues concerning consent. Thus from the outset the government was clear in its intention not to offend communities who partake in the cultural practice of arranged marriage.

The arranged marriage process can be measured against a set of variables such as individual agency; the process of negotiation; dialogue; and type of family intervention, which for many can produce a positive outcome. In the most 'straightforward' forced marriage cases, the questions of power, authority, coercion and most importantly consent remain paramount, upon which all negotiations are based. In this way, the arranged marriage process often occupies a difficult space between the consensual participation of both parties and family members and the subtle forms of coercion and pressure applied by family members in order for the individual to comply with a marriage proposal. In their research, Stopes-Roe and Cochrane construct a typology of arranged marriages that illustrates the subtle differences inherent within the arranged marriage process and the conceptual problems in clearly demarcating the forced marriage process from the arranged marriage process. They categorise the types of arranged marriage in three ways: the 'traditional pattern', the 'modified traditional pattern' and the 'co-operative traditional pattern', and they point to the underlying tensions of power, dialogue, consent and coercion between all three categories. Furthermore, the values of kinship, matrilineal networks and 'biraderi' which often underpin family and community structures can result in conflicts between

Western ideas of marriage based on individual choice of marriage partner and Asian customs of marriage based on family involvement and parental consent (1990: 95). Bhopal argues that there are profound differences between arranged marriages and Western-inspired notions of marriage, "the most significant being, in the West individuals retain the right to autonomy and personal responsibility for their lives. For South Asians, a lower age of marriage is desirable and customary since individuals have no need for courtship patterns" (Bhopal 1997: 59).[9] This way of understanding the arranged marriage process can be useful as it provides an insight into the different normative criteria attached to the arranged marriage process. Such a view lies at the heart of the paradox of the arranged marriage process, whereby an individual's decision to participate in this process may be influenced by notions of duty, family honour, respect and family expectations. However, it is also important to note that such a paradigmatic approach is unlikely to tease out the tensions and contradictions inherent in the arranged marriage process. Because of issues of honour, conflict, loyalty and belonging in families, marriage cannot be simply understood in an either/or structuralist way.

Forced marriages: state response and legal initiatives

In their study of UK initiatives to combat forced marriage, Phillips and Dustin (2004) point to three broad solutions: regulation, dialogue and exit, of which the British state has favoured the option of exit. This approach seeks to provide vulnerable young women with the support, protection and resources to exit families and local communities who may be instigating and colluding in a forced marriage. Such an approach is based upon the principle of protecting the rights of vulnerable women, rather than challenging internal cultural values. Phillips and Dustin also point out, however, that given the complexities of family honour, duty and respect, coupled with notions of belonging in the family home and local community, women forced into marriage are unlikely to exercise the 'exit option' due to the psychological effects of being ostracised and alienated. In this section the author will outline some of the state initiatives of combating forced marriages, to consider (in the following section) why there was deemed a need to introduce new civil-law remedies in the form of the Forced Marriage (Civil Protection) Act 2007 and to analyse what this legislation entails.

There have been a number of UK initiatives on forced marriages, most recently culminating in the introduction of the Forced Marriage (Civil Protection) Act 2007 (in force from autumn 2008). In 1999 a working group on forced marriage was set up by the home secretary to investigate the extent to which forced marriage was practiced in England and Wales. In the same year the Community Liaison Unit was set up by the Foreign and Commonwealth Office (FCO), which was given responsibility for dealing with the international dimension of forced marriages (see below). In 2000 the report *A Choice by Right* was published by the working group, and this report focused on clarifying the arranged/forced marriage distinction and providing clear guidelines to public bodies such as the police, schools and social services as to what can be deemed a forced marriage. In 2002 police guidelines were issued by the Association of Chief Police Officers to better equip members of the police force in dealing with forced marriages (see Phillips and Dustin 2004: 535). Each of these initiatives focused on the option of exit for vulnerable women forced into marriage. Moreover, community attempts to persuade the state to adopt a dialogue-centred approach via the use of mediation services have been met with resistance from women's organisations.[10] It is argued that, in practice, women's attempts to reconcile with families can lead to undue levels of social pressure to reconcile in the face of a continued threat of being forced into marriage (see Anthia and Gill 2009).

In September 2005 the Foreign and Commonwealth Office (FCO) and the Home Office published a consultation document entitled 'Forced Marriage: A Wrong Not a Right' the aim of which was to consider whether a specific offence on forced marriage would help the state combat the practice. This consultation invited responses from various community and women's groups, as well as faith organisations and victims of forced marriage, in an attempt to provide a comprehensive analysis of the practice of forced marriage and to consider whether the law provides adequate protection from forced marriage, or whether there was a need to introduce a specific criminal offence of forced marriage. This culminated in the Forced Marriage (Civil Protection) Act 2007 (see below).

In recent years, discussions on combating forced marriage have also been accompanied by questioning the commitment of ethnic-minority communities to values such as human rights, democracy and loyalty to the state. For example, Southall Black Sisters point to the culturalist responses to tackling forced marriage, which draw upon a racist logic which condemns immigrant communities for failing to integrate into what are perceived as universal Western principles of justice, equality and human rights – which prohibit forced marriage. In particular, Muslim communities have been targeted as perpetrators of forced marriages, and the Muslim woman is constructed as the 'Other' (Sen 2005: 46). Razack points out that

> The body of the Muslim woman, a body fixed in the western imaginary as confined, mutilated and sometimes murdered in the name of culture, serves to reinforce the threat that the Muslim man is said to possess to the West and is used to justify the extraordinary measures of violence and surveillance required to discipline him and Muslim communities.
>
> (Razack 2004: 130)

Thus debates on challenging forced marriage have been accompanied by a focus on multiculturalism and the failure of Muslims to integrate into British society. These debates have mirrored state policies, with a renewed focus on citizenship, identity and the introduction of citizenship tests for all new migrants. More recently in the United Kingdom, the liberal multi-culturalist model has come under extensive scrutiny and critique with renewed questions about how ethnic diversity should be 'managed' and critiques of multiculturalism's ability to ensure the successful integration of minority ethnic communities into mainstream British society. Unsurprisingly perhaps, this emerging critique specifically targets the integration of Muslims into mainstream British society and questions whether the discursive and practical conditions generated by Islamic religious practice in the United Kingdom serve to undermine social cohesion and lead to the creation of parallel and segregated communities.[11]

The international dimension to tackling forced marriages in the United Kingdom is critical as the majority of cases involve transcontinental marriage. This has, however, led to community tensions within the South Asian diaspora. For example, in their report on community cohesion, Samad and Eade found that older members of the South Asian community in Bradford felt that the primary motivation for tackling forced marriage was "a desire to halt the immigration of spouses" (2002: 105). In the United Kingdom, the government has been vocal in denying this claim, but increasingly European states are regulating the practice of forced marriage as an abuse of human rights, and policies have been closely linked to immigration controls. For example, European countries such as France, Norway, Sweden and Denmark, among others, have introduced legislative measures which include immigration controls to justify strategies to eliminate the practice of forced marriage (see Philips and Dustin 2004).

The Forced Marriage (Civil Protection) Act 2007

In this section the author analyses discussion of some of the key remedies available in The Forced Marriage (Civil Protection) Act 2007 (FMA) and considers how this legislation contributes to state initiatives to combat the practice of forced marriage in the United Kingdom. The Act provides two key remedies: (1) the introduction of an injunction – a court order which aims to prevent the forced marriage from taking place; and (2) civil proceedings which may be brought to obtain compensation where an injunction cannot provide an effective remedy.

The background to this law can be summarized as follows. In 2006, Lord Lester of Herne Hill QC introduced the Forced Marriage (Civil Protection) Bill to the House of Lords as a Private Members Bill. The Bill followed extensive discussions with a wide variety of community and faith organisations and women's groups on ways to tackle forced marriage. The primary objective of the Bill was to provide greater protection for victims of forced marriage by means of civil remedies in the family law courts.[12] At this stage, the Bill included a number of crucial provisions:

1. Prohibition against forcing another into marriage
   A person must not act in a way which he knows amounts to forcing or attempting to force another person to enter into a marriage or a purported marriage without that other person's free and full consent.
2. Unlawful inducement
   It is unlawful knowingly to induce, or attempt to induce, a person to do any act which contravenes section 1 by:
   providing or offering to provide him with any benefit
   subjecting or threatening him to any detriment
3. Aiding unlawful acts
   A person who knowingly aids another person to do an act made unlawful by section 1 or 2 shall be treated for the purposes of this Act himself doing an act of the like description.
4. Orders for Injunction
   The court may by order grant an injunction to prevent an actual or apprehended breach of sections 1, 2 or 3.
   An application for an order under this section may be made by the person who is or may be the victim of the conduct in question or his litigation;
5. Damages
   An actual or apprehended breach of section 1, 2 or 3 may be the subject of a claim in civil proceedings.
   On such a claim damages may be awarded for (among other things) any anxiety, distress, injury to feelings or other detriment caused by the conduct in question.

The Bill as introduced at this stage clearly took into account the need to adopt a broad approach in terms of those who are permitted to access the court to apply for injunctions. As a whole, these clauses go further than any existing legislation which may have been used in cases such as the Family Law Act 1996 and the Protection from Harassment Act 1997. And at this stage although the main aim of the Bill was to offer preventative measures it went a step further in offering victims the opportunity to apply for damages for injury to feelings, anxiety and distress.

At the second reading of the Bill on 26 January 2007, the Bill received cross-party support; however, immediately concerns were raised in relation to the demonising of particular minority communities. For example, Baroness Uddin stated "I fear that a solitary Act may be a symbolic outlawing of forced marriage ... but, without sufficient practical and mainstream support such as education and training for women from specific minority communities, it will not be able to eradicate forced marriage." Lord Plant suggested that critics may feel that Parliament has no place in regulating well-established customs of cultural communities.[13]

The Bill was however completely amended by the House at its committee stage reading on 10 May 2007. One of the main amendments made to the Bill was that instead of being a free-standing piece of legislation, the Bill would insert nineteen new sections into the Family Law Act 1996. The reasons for doing so were twofold: concerns were initially raised that a free-standing Act would demonise particular cultures, as only they would in essence be subject to its provisions, and it may isolate the issue of forced marriage and risk stigmatising certain ethnic-minority groups. In addition, it was argued that incorporating the provisions with those general provisions protecting against domestic violence would be a more effective means of addressing the issue of forced marriage.

The original goal of the Bill remained, but now, although forced marriage would be unlawful, it would not be deemed a criminal offence. Redress to victims would be offered by way of orders made by the courts. Alongside this, the Bill aimed to act as a deterrent to those communities who practice forced marriage, in so far as it would raise public awareness of the issue and send out a clear message that such practices are unacceptable in Western society.

In particular, members of the House were concerned about the possible criminalisation of specific communities. Arguments in favour of criminalisation focused on the need to have in place legislation which acts as a deterrent for future perpetrators – the fear of criminal prosecution could, it was argued, deter potential forced marriages. It was also argued that it would give organisations working to tackle forced marriage a clearer focus on prevention of forced marriage – a clear delineation of boundaries. Arguments against included the view that although there is no specific crime of forced marriage, the practice itself may entail several other offences, including kidnapping, child abduction (under the Child Abduction Act 1984), human trafficking, false imprisonment and various sexual offences, including rape. Baroness Ashton supported the civil route rather than criminal prosecution as she considered the potential to eliminate 'the risk that by coming forward to seek protection, the victim finds that they have driven a wedge between themselves and their family'. Victims of forced marriage are therefore less likely to come forward as they may not be willing to report their family members to the police. There may therefore be evidential problems as victims may be unwilling to give evidence against family members in a criminal prosecution; such hurdles are avoided in civil proceedings.

Since forced marriage is a custom that is most often practiced within minority communities, any offence created would be primarily aimed at those ethnic communities, which could subsequently be viewed by those communities as ethnically or racially motivated. If forced marriage was criminalised, where other forms of violence against women have not been, it may be perceived that violence against women in minority communities where forced marriage does take place is somehow fundamentally different to violence suffered by women in majority communities. As Pragna Patel of SBS argues, 'we do not see the need for criminalisation of forced marriage, which is yet another way of stereotyping and criminalising entire communities at a time when there is heightened racism in this country.'[14] There are other problems such as the basic fact that it would be very difficult to implement such an offence. These include difficulties in having to prove that the perpetrators intended to force the victim into marriage, as well as having to rely heavily on the victim to come forward – this may be difficult due to familial, cultural or other pressures. (The burden of proof is much higher in criminal cases than in civil ones; 'beyond reasonable doubt' versus 'balance of probabilities' suggests the latter will be easier to prove in a case before the courts.) Parents may therefore take their children abroad so as to avoid prosecution in the United Kingdom, and this could mean that the problem is simply being moved elsewhere. It was also feared that criminalisation could simply drive the practice underground.

As a result, the compensation elements of the original Bill were simply dropped. A claim for damages, it was also argued, could prolong the adversarial contact between the victim and the respondent. When criminalisation was abandoned the government promoted the creation of civil remedies as a means of protecting the victims of forced marriage – protect and empower. On 26 July 2007 the Bill received the Royal Assent,[15] and the Forced Marriage (Civil Protection) Act 2007 came into force in November 2008, seeking to take on a 'victim centered human rights approach'.[16]

What are Forced Marriage Protection Orders?

The FMA inserts new provisions into the Family Law Act 1996 by inserting a new part 4A, creating a new Forced Marriage Protection Order (FMPO). Part 4A is issued by both the High Court and the County Courts, with the power to make FMPOs found in Sections 63a–63. The High Court or a County Court can make an FMPO to protect a woman from being forced into a marriage; from any attempt to be forced into a marriage; or to protect a person who has already been forced into a marriage. What can the FMPOs provide? The courts are given wide discretion, and the orders can contain any prohibitions, restrictions or requirements that the courts deem appropriate. An application can be made by a woman, a third party or another person who is given leave by the court to make an application. In this respect, the order differs substantially from other orders such as occupation orders or non-molestation orders as only the party desiring protection can make those orders, and the orders are not restricted to associated persons.

There are four ways in which a court may make an FMPO. First, a person who is the victim of forced marriage may apply to the court for an order.

Second, another person may apply on behalf of the victim if they obtain the permission of the court. Third, the court may make an order without an application if it is already dealing with existing family cases. Finally, the Act also makes provision for a relevant third party who may apply on behalf of the victim without the need to first obtain the permission of the court. A relevant third party does not need to ask the court for permission to apply and may apply on behalf of a victim without being closely connected to her. This last provision raises interesting questions on the nature of third-party intervention, issues of representation and methods of delegation and the fundamental question of *Who should act as a relevant third party?* The focus of such orders is on protecting victims who are not in a position to make an application personally due to personal threats and/or intimidation. On 12 December 2007 the Ministry of Justice published a consultation paper on the role of the relevant third party under the FMA. The consultation asked for responses on the need for relevant third parties, who should act and what safeguards might be needed. At present, the FMPO does have similarities to the occupation orders and non-molestation orders, such as accepted undertakings and making a power of arrest in certain circumstances. Under the 2007 Act the term 'force' has been given a wide meaning to include both being physically and psychologically forced into marriage (s. 63A(6)).

FMPOs can relate to conduct both within and outside of England and Wales, therefore allowing the court to assist British nationals outside of its own jurisdiction. In December 2008 such an order was issued to assist a Bangladeshi woman resident in the UK. In this case Coleridge J issued an FMPO to the applicant, an NHS doctor, Dr Humayra Abedin.[17]

Dr Abedin went on holiday to Bangladesh to visit her sick mother and whilst there was forced to marry an individual whom her parents had chosen for her. The marriage ceremony took place against her will, under duress. She was put under emotional pressure by her parents, who threatened imprisonment if she wanted to return to the United Kingdom. Upon her return she expressed a wish to remain here.[18] Coleridge J, in this case, imposed orders, including an injunction, to protect Dr Abedin so that she could not be forced into marriage and so that she could safely return to the UK. In December 2008, when she arrived back in the United Kingdom, he granted additional orders so that she could not be taken out of the country without first consenting to it. In his judgement he stated that:

> forcing anyone ... to go through a marriage without their consent ... is a complete aberration of the whole concept of marriage. ... the court is now better equipped to tackle these problems by virtue of the new Act ... it is important for the message to be understood in those communities where this kind of behaviour is sanctioned ... this court will act swiftly and decisively wherever this gross abuse of human rights is detected.[19]

As this case illustrates, the FMA therefore can empower victims of forced marriage and offer some protection. However, the effectiveness of the legislation in challenging the practice of forced marriage has yet to be tested, and this assessment can only take place after the Act has been in force for a number of years.[20]

Conclusion

The new FMA marks a fundamental shift in state initiatives from the 'exit' approach to focusing on regulation of forced marriage and the accountability of perpetrators via civil-law remedies. The 2005 Home Office consultation document 'Forced Marriage: A Wrong Not a Right' revealed that community activists and women's organisations were against introducing a specific criminal offence on forced marriage. One of the key concerns against criminalising forced marriages related to the fact that if families are prosecuted, it may stop victims asking for help as they may be reluctant to get members of their families in trouble with the criminal law, and in the longer term this may create difficulties for individuals reconciling with families. Furthermore, prosecutions may also be low due to the problems in collating evidence against family members (and the different burden of proof in civil/criminal proceedings). A primary concern relates to stigmatising large sections of ethnic-minority communities. There remains discussion of the effectiveness of the legislation and whether it can in practice help to tackle forced marriages. For example, it is argued that introducing legislation such as the FMA is a long and expensive process when instead non-legislative measures (such as providing funds for community workers to work within communities) could be a more effective way of challenging such practices. In addition, those in favour of criminalisation argue that creating a specific offence could produce a stronger deterrent and empower victims of forced marriage to challenge parental behaviour. In the long term, it may also relieve pressure on families to continue the practice of forced marriage as a cultural tradition. It is interesting to note that the criminalisation option has not yet been completely shelved, as the Foreign and Commonwealth Offices Forced Marriage Unit announced on 10 May 2007 that it had not ruled out the possibility of creating criminal legislation in the future (and it is to be explored in a two-year strategy on current criminal legislation).[21] Thus, current legal initiatives to tackle the practice of forced marriage focus upon all three key approaches – exit, regulation and dialogue. In this way, the symbiotic relationship between the individual, marriage and family honour reflects how the process of marriage must be understood as a complex and contested issue that raises fundamental questions of consent and coercion, which can ultimately lead to unacceptable levels of compromise and compulsion. Throughout Europe, gender equality has become a critical means of differentiating liberated European and oppressive religious models of family and community life.[22] In the United Kingdom, negative facets of South Asian family life have received wide publicity, with extensive coverage of forced marriages and honour killings. While these problems must be addressed, they have also been utilised to create an unfavourable, often Islamophobic, portrait of South Asian family life that ignores those aspects that do not conform to patriarchal stereotypes.[23] Treating forced marriage and related issues requires care. Pointing to the sensationalism of coverage and its broader function should not mean minimising or ignoring problems, but there remains the danger of legitimising the assumption that family violence, as opposed to its specific cultural manifestations, is more common (and is even paradigmatic) in these communities.

Notes

1 This chapter does not provide a comprehensive analysis of the legal measures available and in particular does not specifically focus on the protections available to children. Children at risk of being forced into a marriage are entitled to the statutory protection afforded by the Children Act 1989. See Harvey (2004).
2 In the United Kingdom the case of Rukhsana Naz is often cited as the catalyst for this interest. There have been a number of high-profile cases, most recently the case of Shafilea Ahmed. For an account of these cases, see Siddiqui (2002).
3 In August 1999, the Home Office established a working group to investigate to what extent forced marriage was a problem in England and Wales and to make proposals for tackling it effectively. In its report, a forced marriage is defined as a marriage conducted without the valid consent of both parties and where duress is a factor. In January 2004, the Metropolitan Police set up a taskforce to deal with the practice of 'Honour Crimes'.
4 Including Rukhsana Naz (1999), Heshu Yones (2003) and Shafilea Ahmed (2007). See *The Guardian*, 17 March 2004.
5 Which raises the possibility of skewed statistical data.
6 (1982) 4 FLR 232.
7 This interpretation of duress can also be found in *P v. R (Forced marriage : Annulment procedure)* [2003] 1 FLR 661 (with short comment in [2003] *Fam Law* 162); see also *Singh v. Singh* [1971] P 226; *Kaur v. Singh* [1972] 1 WLR 105; *NS v MI* [2006] EWHC 1646 (Fam); *Re E (An alleged patient); Sheffield City Council v. E and S* [2004] EWHC 2808 (Fam); *A Local Authority v. N, Y and K* [2005] EWHC 2956 (Fam); *NS v. MI* [2006] EWHC 1646 (Fam).
8 There are also public-order offences according to the Public Order Act 1986 and protection against harassment according to section 2 of the Protection from Harassment Act 1997.
9 In her research, Bhopal found very little evidence which challenged the traditional practice of arranged marriages in South Asian households. Her empirical findings suggest that because women are accorded less power within the family and household, the arranged-marriage process further disadvantages them and creates what she describes as a 'private patriarchy' (1999: 67). The requirement to comply no doubt restricts the terms upon which women are able to develop strategies to challenge parental authority and limits the space upon which they are able to instigate change within the process.
10 For example, the women's organisation Southall Black Sisters resigned from the working group on forced marriage in protest against the recommendation of mediation to reconcile victims of forced marriage with their families.

11 According to current intellectual and political scrutiny, the failure of Muslim integration into British society not only undermines the principle of multiculturalism but also illustrates the need to reject and dispose of it as a policy in its entirety. More worrying still is the rise of anti-Islamic sentiment which underlies many of these arguments.

12 The Parliamentary progress of the Bill can be viewed at http://www.publications. parliament.uk/pa/pabills/200607/forced_marriage_civil_protection.htm.

13 For discussion on the debates generated by this Bill see Odysseus Trust material on forced marriage at http://www.publications.parliament.ik.

14 'Forced marriage law not needed', 17 December 2008. Available at http://www. bbc.co.uk/news.

15 A copy of the Act can be obtained at http://www.opsi.gov.uk/acts/acts2007/ukp-ga_20070020_en.pdf.

16 See Clark and Clark (2008).

17 For a discussion on the facts of this case see http://www.timesonline.co.uk/tol/news/uk/crime/article5340058.ece.

18 *The Guardian*, statement from Humayra Abedin, 19 December 2008, which can be accessed at http://www.guardian.co.uk/world/2008/dec/19/statement.

19 Walsh (2009).

20 The MOJ published a report in 2009 which outlined the effectiveness of this piece of legislation in its first year of inception. The figures provided in the report appear to indicate that more forced marriage protection orders were made by the courts than actual applications. The report noted that although more judicial training was required the courts have taken a responsible approach in attempting to prevent a potential forced marriage from taking place. See Ministry of Justice (November 2009).

21 This can be viewed at http://www.fco.gov.uk/Files/kfile/FMU/20Two-Year20/Strategy.pdf.

22 See, for example, Roggeband and Verloo (2007).

23 Ibid.

Bibliography

Afshar, H. (1994) 'Muslim Women in West Yorkshire: Growing Up with Real and Imaginary Values Amidst Conflicting Views on Self and Society', in Afshar, H. and Maynard, M. (eds) *The Dynamics of Race and Gender*, London: Taylor and Francis.

Anthia, S. and Gill, A. (2009) 'The Illusion of Protection? An Analysis of Forced Marriage Policy and Legislation in the UK', *Journal of Social Welfare and Family Law*, Vol. 31, No. 3, 262.

Anthias, F. (2002) 'Beyond Feminism and Mutliculturalism: Locating Difference and the Politics of Location', *Women's Studies International Forum*, Vol. 25, No. 3, 275.

Anthias, F. and Yuval-Davis, N. (1989) 'Introduction', in Anthias, F. and Yuval-Davis, N. (eds) *Woman-Nation-State*, Macmillan: London.

——(1992) *Racialized Boundaries: Race, Nation, Gender, Colour and Class and the Anti-Racist Struggle*, London: Routledge.

Baker, N.V., Gregware, P.R. and Cassidy, M.A. (1999) 'Family Killing Fields', *Violence Against Women*, Vol. 5, 164–184.

Bhopal, K. (1999) 'South Asian Women and Arranged Marriages in East London', in Barot, R., Bradley, H. and Fenton, S. (eds) *Ethnicity, Gender and Social Change*, Basingstoke: Macmillan.

Bradby, H. (1999) 'Negotiating Marriage: Young Punjabi Women's Assessment of their Individual and Family Interests', Barot, R., Bradley, H. and Fenton, S. (eds) *Ethnicity, Gender and Social Change*, Basingstoke: Macmillan.

Brah, A. (1996) *Cartographies of Diaspora: Contesting Identities*, London: Routledge.

Clark, B. and Richards, C. (2008) 'The Prevention and Prohibition of Forced Marriages: A Comparative Approach', *International and Comparative Law Quarterly*, Vol. 57, No. 3, 501.

Enright, M. (2009) 'Choice and Culture and the Politics of Belonging: The Emerging Law of Forced and Arranged Marriage', *Modern Law Review*, Vol. 72, No. 3.

Foreign and Commonwealth Office and Home Office Consultation on Forced Marriage: 'Forced Marriage: A Wrong Not a Right', September 2005.

Hall, S. (1992) 'The Question of Cultural Identity', in Hall, S., Held, D. and McGrew, T. (eds) *Modernity and Its Future*, Cambridge: Polity Press.

——(1999) 'Life for Honour Killing of Pregnant Teenager by Mother and Brother', *The Guardian*, May 26 2009. Available at http://www.guardian.co.uk.

Harvey, H. (2002) 'Forced Marriage: The Work of the Foreign and Commonwealth Office', *Childright*, Issue, 189, 14.

——(2004) 'Teachers and Social Workers: Guidance on Forced Marriage', *Childright*, Issue 209, 19.

Hutchinson, A. M. (2002) 'Forced Marriage and Multiculturalism – Recent Developments', *Family Law,* Issue 32(Oct) 728.

Ministry of Justice (2009) 'One Year On: The Initial Impact of the Forced Marriage (Civil Protection) Act 2007 in its first year of operation'.

Philips, A. and Dustin, M. (2004) 'UK Initiatives on Forced Marriage: Regulation, Dialogue and Exit', *Political Studies*, Vol. 52, 531.

Razack, S. H. (2004) 'Imperilled Muslim Women, Dangerous Muslim Men and Civilized Europeans: Legal and Social Responses to Forced Marriages', *Feminist Legal Studies*, Vol. 12, Issue 2, 129.

Roggeband, C. and Verloo, M. (2007) 'Dutch Women are Liberated, Migrant Women are a Problem: The Evolution of Policy Frames on Gender and Migration in the Netherlands 1995–2005', *Social Policy and Administration,* Vol. 41, No. 3, 271.

Rude-Antoine, E. (2005) 'Forced Marriages in Council of Europe Member States: A Comparative Study of Legislation and Political Initiatives', Strasbourg: Council of Europe.

Samad, Y. and Eade, J. (2002) *Community Perceptions of Forced Marriage*, London: FCO.

Sen, P. (2005) '"Crimes of Honour", Value and Meaning', in Welchmen, L. and Hossain, S. (eds) *Honour: Crimes Paradigms and Violence Against Women*, London: Zed Books.

Siddiqui, H. (2002) 'Forced Marriage: An Abuse of Women's Human Rights', *ROW Bulletin*, Spring, 2.

Stopes-Roe, M. and Cochrane R. (1990) *Citizens of this Country: the Asian-British*, Clevedon: Multilingual Matters.

Walsh, E. (2009) 'Newsline Extra: Forced Marriage Action', *Family Law*, Vol. 39, No. 2.

Welchmen, L. and Hossain, S. (2005) *'Honour': Crimes Paradigms and Violence Against Women*, London: Zed Books.

Wilson, A. (1978) *Finding a Voice: Asian Women in Britain*, London: Virago.

——(2006) *Dreams, Questions, Struggles: South Asian Women in Britain*, London: Pluto Press.

Chapter 15

Reconfiguring 'honour'-based violence as a form of gendered violence

Dr Aisha Gill

Senior Lecturer in Criminology, Roehampton University

Over the last three decades, violence against women (VAW) has become a matter of major public and academic interest (Gangoli, Razack and McCarry 2007; Hester, Kelly and Radford 1995; Thiara and Gill 2010). Investigative work has started to reveal the extent to which various forms of violence – ranging from domestic violence to sexual violence, and from culturally sanctioned forced marriages to female genital mutilation (FGM) – are inflicted on women around the world (Horvath and Kelly 2007). However, although considerable progress has been made toward understanding the nature of VAW, much remains to be done, both to address its consequences and to prevent it from occurring. In the UK, there has been little empirical research into a particular form of VAW: so-called honour crimes. The concept of 'honour' crimes includes all forms of violence directed towards individuals (almost always women) in the name of honour.[1] There is an urgent need for research in this field to focus on Iranian/Iraqi Kurdish communities, where the incidence of honour crimes is increasing (Begihkani 2005). Criticisms have also been made about the paucity and ineffectiveness of measures designed to reduce and, ideally, eradicate such crimes (Baxi, Rai and Ali 2008).

Progress towards greater understanding has partly been impeded by semantic wrangling over the use of the term 'honour' in relation to VAW. Critics suggest that the concept places undue emphasis on male honour, and argue that the term encourages the widespread incidence of non-fatal violence to be discounted. The Council of Europe's definition (2002) does recognise some of the complexities of the issue, but it does not consider the spectrum of behaviours focused on maintaining and restoring honour that is directed at vulnerable and relatively powerless individuals, usually women and children. These behaviours may involve control, domination and intimidation, as well as physical violence; however, definitions and remedies focus solely on physical force, ignoring the other types of harm that may be inflicted through other means. The lack of consensus over the definition of honour crimes has led to countless debates about what actually constitutes honour-based violence (HBV); as yet, these debates have not produced an accepted working definition or understanding which would advance efforts to tackle and prevent these abuses (Welchman and Hossain 2005).

For the purposes of this chapter, a working definition is required. Although HBV does affect men from time to time, male cases represent a tiny minority; thus, this chapter will focus on the crime as it affects women. HBV is a highly gendered form of violence, both in terms of its victims and in terms of its perpetrators; men are generally only targeted through their association with 'transgressive' women. Thus HBV is usually an expression of patriarchal power, with women as its victims. HBV is thus considered to constitute any form of violence perpetrated against females within the framework of patriarchal family structures, communities and/or societies where the main justification for the perpetration of violence is the protection of a social construction of honour as a value system, norm or tradition. This parallels the Council of Europe definition, but encompasses more of the specific injuries or wrongs enacted against women within patriarchal cultures. Crucially, this leads to the radical suggestion that the notion of HBV should be overthrown entirely, and that the problem should be seen as a specific manifestation of VAW. Only by seeing honour crimes as part of the VAW paradigm can the situation be freed from notions that treat cultural values as a justification for these crimes.

The role of culture and gender in HBV

The term 'honour-based violence' should be abandoned, in favour of situating violence committed in the name of honour within the wider context of VAW.[2] One reason for this proceeds from the understanding that there is no honour involved in these crimes, and that referring to them as 'honour killings' or HBV plays down their severity and belittles their victims. Another reason for rejecting the term in favour of VAW is socio-political: these are crimes of violence committed predominantly by men, and against women. This form of VAW is a means of establishing boundaries between the gendered cultural codes of family and local community and the gendered norms and values of the dominant society. Honour is less important within these crimes than the desire, on the part of male leaders within the patriarchal social groups where honour-based crimes are common, to retain their political and cultural authority by reinforcing established gender roles and expectations. This strategy revolves around social control concerned with how individuals and their families attain or forfeit honour.

Shame (Urdu: *sharam*) is often associated with transgressions of personal honour, and functions as the opposite to honour: honour is valued highly, whereas shame is to be avoided at all costs. Fears about the loss of personal or family honour shape how individuals act; shame is therefore an effective tool for curbing the behaviour of individuals, and operates as a threatened sanction imposed by a community on those who transgress against the community's norms, traditions and values.

Appeals to cultural relativism should no longer be used to preserve cultural values in minority communities when those cultural values are fundamentally at odds with concepts of equality, and human rights, held by mainstream society. Patriarchal communities often seek to establish their own autonomy, with their own laws, within (or even apart from) UK society; however, these communities should be governed by the laws and principles of the wider society of which they are a part. Most importantly, women in these communities must not be victimised for adopting norms and behaviours that are accepted, and even endorsed, in the wider community.

In an honour-based society, the man is defined as the head of the family, irrespective of how much value is attached to female activities. The man is the defender of his and his family's honour: it is his duty to protect his and his family's honour against any behaviour that might be seen as shameful or humiliating by the community. He is expected to protect 'his' women; they are regarded as his property and effectively function as symbols of honour; as such, it is through the conduct, actions and social performances of women that families attain honour and prestige. As honour relies on the behaviour of women, safeguarding family honour can also be viewed as a means of exercising social control over women's bodies and behaviour. Thus, in patriarchal societies, women are invested with immense negative power: any misbehaviour on their part can bring shame and dishonour to the male members of an entire community or lineage (Kandiyoti 1988). Female chastity and modesty, in particular, are considered to be essential components of the family's honour (Derne 1994), which results in the systematic control of women's social and sexual behaviour (Ortner 1978).

This system of belief is not restricted to the South Asian context, but functions wherever shame and honour are used to coerce and victimise women. To illustrate this by example, in some honour-based cultures, the woman's hymen (a symbol of female chastity) is regarded as a key element in defining the family's honour; for this reason, some communities (especially, although not exclusively, in certain parts of Africa) practice FGM on the grounds that this activity is done in order to protects the family's honour (Peristiany and Pitt-Rivers 1992). In this, as in other cases of HBV, a cultural tradition is used to justify violence against women; the woman's health, well-being and interests are subordinated to notions of family honour and, thus, the family's interests. It is precisely because the notion of honour underlies so many forms of gender-based violence across the world that HBV cannot be studied, or even understood, in isolation from other forms of VAW and the particular societal contexts in which such violence occurs.

This argument marks a significant departure from scholarly tradition, because HBV has historically been defined as a category of violence quite distinct from VAW. HBV is usually differentiated from other forms of domestic violence on the grounds that it (a) occurs within the framework of collective family structures, communities and societies; (b) involves a pre-meditated act, designed to restore a societal construction of honour as a value system, norm or tradition; and (c) is based on men's putative right to control women's sexual and social choices, with a concomitant perception of women as the property of men (Sen 2003; Welchman and Hossain 2005). Forced marriage and FGM are often conceptualised as closely related to other honour crimes, such as honour killings, forced virginity, forced hymen repair, forced abortion, imprisonment of partners and other forms of coercion and abuse (Dustin 2006). The assumption is that because honour-based crimes are culturally mandated they are quite distinct from VAW.

The problem is further compounded by the fact that often the victims of these crimes do not recognise that they are victims of gender-based violence, but interpret their treatment as an intrinsic part of their culture. Typically, a woman who lives in an honour-based society learns either that she is not regarded as a human being or that she is not equal to her male counterparts. The socialisation of young women in such societies revolves around notions of family honour; the cultural norms and traditions which support the honour-based value system are often so deeply internalised that women find it difficult not to accept the need to uphold these values. As a result of this socialisation, many women feel that they are to blame for the emotional and physical abuse they suffer, and so become complicit in their own subjugation.

Within the family, mothers, mothers-in-law and older siblings are often also involved, both directly and indirectly, in the perpetration of HBV. Although male control and dominance of women is the main underlying cause of VAW in South Asian communities, the involvement of female family members in the violence is a by-product of the interlocking systems of gender roles and life-cycle-based hierarchies that characterise the South Asian family (Gill 2004).

The interdependencies between family members in patriarchal systems are explicitly hierarchical: the woman's role within the family is defined in relation to men. According to Sangari (1999), when they become involved in the socialisation of other women (particularly their daughters) women in these communities comply with patriarchal ideologies because their multilayered identities are rooted in class, caste and familial notions of status. Furthermore, just as the family subsumes a woman's identity, so it also defines her position in society; acquiescing to such ideologies becomes, for many women, their way of justifying their own self-worth and their status in the community. Consent to the patriarchal norms of religion, culture and class is strongly encouraged, and the degree to which each woman conforms to the value systems embedded in these institutions is reflected in the way she is perceived by her marital and blood families. This complicity with patriarchal structures legitimises VAW, as a necessary force for sustaining the social order, in the eyes of women as well as men (Kandiyoti 1988).

HBV is a fundamental part of the patriarchal order in these societies: it is designed to control women in order to maintain the patriarchal status quo (Kandiyoti 1988) – men victimize and abuse women in their communities in order to sustain their dominance within the social system. HBV is thus implicitly gendered and is, therefore, merely one form of VAW.

Honour killings

At the extreme end of the HBV spectrum are so-called honour killings: acts that seems to have a culturally specific basis. And yet these too are an explicitly gendered form of violence, better seen as an expression of VAW rather than as possessing a unique signature. Only by seeing VAW as a continuum of gender-based violence can the issue be properly addressed; claims that honour killings have no parallel, and that they are unique, dismiss these crimes as cultural aberrations, rather than understanding them as an aspect of a wider social problem.

The term 'honour killing' typically refers to the murder (or attempted murder) of a woman by members of her family who do not approve of her sexual behaviour (Abu-Odeh 1996; Werbner 2007). Perpetrators can include a woman's female family members (most often her mother or mother-in-law). As with less extreme forms of HBV, the murder is intended to restore the family's social reputation: the use of the word 'honour' disguises the fact that 'honour killings' are almost always premeditated crimes. Furthermore, the notion that a woman has been killed because of honour implies that she has brought the crime upon herself by besmirching her own honour and that of her family.

One of the most frequently cited cases of HBV exhibits a number of characteristics typical of family honour killings: in 1998, Rukhsana Naz, a woman from Derby who had been forced into marriage at the age of 16, was murdered by her family because they thought she had become pregnant as the result of an adulterous affair. She was judged to have been in contravention of her community's laws and deemed sexually deviant; her behaviour represented a violation of fundamental Pakistani norms and values and so brought shame upon her family. Once a family's reputation is thought to have been 'dishonoured' in this way, the 'culpable' woman – whether she be a sister, daughter or daughter-in-law – is in danger of being killed. The killer or killers then treat this act as a form of 'honour cleansing': as a way of wiping away a stain on the family honour. Ironically, this cleansing process is accomplished through the spilling of blood.

Honour killings cut across ethnic, class and religious lines. Despite the meagre amount of academic literature on honour killings in the Punjab, Kurdistan, Turkey and Pakistan, a number of studies have come to the conclusion that these practices are fundamentally Islamic (Ginat 1979; Kressel 1981). In fact, honour killings are perpetrated not only by Muslims, but also by Druze, Christians and occasionally Jews (of Sephardic backgrounds, primarily in Greek and Latin American societies). Honour killing transcends cultural boundaries, though laws governing specific cultures are often invoked to support the practice.

Honour killings are transcultural crimes committed by men (and sometimes women) who use the trappings of culture and tradition to justify the violence they perpetrate against women.

The scope of the problem

The United Nations Population Fund estimates that 5,000 women are killed in the name of honour each year worldwide, though the majority of these crimes are committed in the Middle East and Asia. It is impossible to know the exact number of women killed, or to determine how widespread HBV is, as reports to the police are rare and sporadic: both male and female family members typically try to cover up these crimes. Many victims of honour killings are abducted: they disappear and are never reported missing (Dustin 2006). To date, the few honour killings reported in Europe have occurred in migrant communities, and have mainly involved South Asian, Turkish or Kurdish communities. The victims, in many of these cases, have also experienced forced marriage.

Although there are no official statistics on honour killings in the UK, an incomplete survey of the cases that received coverage in the national media reveals that during the period 1998–2007 an average of 12 honour killings were investigated by the police each year (Metropolitan Police Service 2007). The Criminal Prosecution Service (CPS) figures are very similar, indicating that approximately 12 honour killings take place in the UK every year. However, it is generally agreed that honour killings represent a fraction of the number of honour-based crimes (of all types) in the UK, the majority of which, according to police records, occur in South Asian communities.

The response in the UK and Europe

Governments and non-state actors throughout the world have identified HBV, including honour killings, as a growing problem which requires urgent attention in the establishment of both short- and long-term preventative and educational initiatives. For example, in 2004 the Dutch NGO TransAct launched a National Platform against Honour-Related Violence to facilitate the exchange of information and expertise, and to develop collaborative endeavours between European countries aimed at eradicating such crimes. In November 2003, the Swedish Minister of Democracy and Integration Issues convened an expert panel on HBV; Sweden is also the base of a cross-European project on HBV, initiated by an NGO called Kvinnoforum and supported by the European Union (as the Daphne Project). These initiatives were established in an attempt to create a knowledge base about HBV and to promote the sharing of good practice across Europe. In 2004, Stockholm hosted an international conference which culminated in The Stockholm Declaration to Combat Honour-related Violence in Europe. The strategies outlined in the declaration consist of both preventative and punitive measures that recognise that awareness-raising in the communities concerned will play a key role in tackling the issue.

Although none of these countries have suggested that honour crimes should comprise a specific category within the legal system, in policy terms honour crimes tend to be treated as distinct from non-honour-based VAW. Yet, in the UK, many NGOs focused on women's causes use the term VAW, rather than domestic violence or HBV, to define these crimes, because VAW encompasses the range of violence that women from both majority and minority communities experience (Dustin 2006).

However, if we examine the number of honour killings that have been prosecuted in the UK, it emerges that almost all the defendants (who were mostly from Pakistani, Sikh and Kurdish backgrounds) offered a cultural defence. These perpetrators claimed that the victim had dishonoured the family and so killing her was an obligation imposed by their culture, tradition and moral values. This allowed them to distance their behaviour from any association with VAW. Throughout the 1980s, UK judges accepted this cultural defence, especially in domestic violence cases involving South Asian communities, and, in consequence, the courts imposed reduced sentences, usually for manslaughter instead of premeditated murder (for a critique of the admission of cultural evidence, see Carline in this collection). Such leniency, Southall Black Sisters argue, offers an incentive for patriarchal communities predicated on honour systems to continue to commit HBV; moreover, these rulings suggest that men have the right to monitor, punish and even kill female relatives in order to moderate these women's culturally 'deviant' behaviour (CPS 2007; Gupta 2003).

Until recently, the main government initiative on HBV in the UK was aimed at forced marriage; as such, the government focused on a small subset (of a distinct legal category) of victims, rather than attempting to understand the wider context of HBV and VAW. Consequently, most of the more general work on HBV has been carried out by academics and groups focused on women's rights. One of the key UK initiatives was the Project on Strategies to Address Crimes of Honour, which was set up in 1999 in coordination with the Centre of Islamic and Middle Eastern Laws (CIMEL) at the School of Oriental and African Studies, University of London and the International Centre for the Legal Protection of Rights (INTERIGHTS). At a grass-roots casework level, there are a number of community and women's groups, including Newham Asian Women's Project, Southall Black Sisters and Kurdish Women's Action against Honour Killings, that have been campaigning for many years to bring the true incidence of HBV to light and to work to address such crimes in their many guises.

More recently, the Metropolitan Police Service (MPS) has taken the lead in efforts to prevent HBV. The immediate catalyst for this was the extensive media coverage, in 2002, of the murder of a 16-year-old Turkish Kurd named Heshu Yones, who was killed by her father after he learnt of her affair with a Lebanese Christian man. In line with the general belief that honour crimes are simply a matter of cultural difference, the judge, on sentencing the father to life imprisonment, described the case as 'a tragic story arising out of irreconcilable cultural differences between traditional Kurdish values and the values of Western society' (Abdulla and Yones 2003). Two other high-profile cases occurred in 2003: Anita Gindha was strangled and Sajhda Bibi died of stab wounds on her wedding day. The extensive reporting of these honour killings helped to make this form of VAW visible to the wider public for the first time, and provoked the police service to take action.

In January 2003, in response to pressure from women's organisations, and following the publication of an MPS report on domestic violence (which identified honour killings as an important area for future work), the MPS set up the Strategic Homicide Prevention Working Group on Honour Killings to cover the London area. A second, national group was developed to deliver a training package to all police forces in the country. In June 2004, Scotland Yard announced that it was re-examining 109 possible honour killings from the period 1993–2003, many involving women from South Asian communities. Although many of these cases had already been closed, one of the purposes of the initiative was to look at the motivations behind these crimes, with a view to developing risk-assessment indicators and a national police database to monitor and record such cases more effectively. In June 2007, the CPS began piloting a scheme to track HBV cases as part of a wider HBV project, which also involved training 25 specialist prosecutors to work in HBV hotspots in the UK, as well as instituting a system for flagging forced marriage and HBV cases (CPS 2007).

Although there have been more focused and determined efforts to tackle HBV in recent years, both by the criminal justice system and by related agencies, there is general agreement among those working to combat the problem that much remains to be done to improve the quality of policing in the private sphere (Welchman and Hossain 2005). In 2003, the then head of the Serious Crime Directorate (the lead senior police officer dealing with honour killings), Commander Andy Baker, stated, at a European seminar on the issue, that the police remained ignorant of many honour-related crimes and admitted that honour killings were 'not on the police radar' (Baker 2003). Six years on, it seems as though the police service still lacks a solid, basic understanding of the problem; thus the police remain unable to offer an adequate response to women experiencing HBV.

The case of Banaz Mahmod

This is reflected in the way in which the MPS and West Midlands Police handled the case of Banaz Mahmod. This case exemplifies both the patriarchal underpinnings of HBV and the relative inadequacy of the state response to the problem. In 2005, 20-year-old Banaz Mahmod tried to escape from family members who were threatening to kill her. Her family had recently arranged her marriage to a cousin in the family clan group. Shortly after this, Banaz sought a divorce on the grounds that her husband was abusing her, but her desire to dissolve the marriage was regarded, by the senior male members of the family, as a betrayal of the family's honour.

Banaz (an Iraqi Kurd) met her lover, Rahmat Sulemani (an Iranian Kurd), at a family gathering; they fell in love and decided to elope. In Kurdish society, however, elopement (particularly with someone of a different class) is considered *haram* (forbidden) (Begikhani 2005). Banaz's behaviour was perceived as scandalous by the family; her actions became known throughout the tight-knit Kurdish community in South West London, where it is said that 'nothing is secret' (Kurdish: *hich shtek nheni*). When the family became aware of her intention to elope, Banaz's father held a family meeting; at the insistence of her uncle it was decided that her punishment would be death.

Her father's first attempt on her life took place on New Year's Eve 2005. When her father forced her to drink alcohol, Banaz realised that she was in danger and attempted to flee the house; although she managed to break a window and escape, she could not find a safe place to evade her family and eventually called the police. Despite the fact that her hands were bleeding (she had cut them when escaping via the broken window), the police treated her plea for help as mere attention-seeking in the aftermath of a private family argument. The female police officer she talked to dismissed her claims as 'dramatic and calculating' (Barton and Wright 2007); the policewoman later admitted that she had made a terrible mistake. In fact, the police even considered charging Banaz with criminal damage over the broken window. She later recorded a telephone video message on her boyfriend's mobile phone about the police's refusal to help her; this message was used in evidence against her father and uncle in their trial for her murder in January 2006. Banaz had been strangled; her body had been stuffed into a suitcase and buried in a Birmingham garden.

The perpetrators in this case believed that their acts of violence against Banaz were a justified response to her 'dishonourable behaviour', which they saw as affecting the honour of the whole family; this view was supported by other family members and the Kurdish community as a whole. In this community, honour depends not on an individual's own behaviour (in the case of men) but on the behaviour of the women in their family. Societies in which these traditional (mis)conceptions of honour and shame govern the behaviour of members sanction honour killings because the 'aberrant behaviour' of one woman is thought to affect the social status of everyone connected to her (Gill 2004). In such cases, it is men who decide when honour has been besmirched, and it is women who are the victims when men decide to restore that honour.

Shortcomings of current responses to HBV

HBV is clearly a complex and multifaceted issue, but it encompasses a manifestation of VAW and so should not be viewed as distinct from other forms of gendered violence. HBV can (and usually does) involve people other than spouses and partners, as the Banaz Mahmod case showed: HBV tends to be perpetrated not only by husbands and sexual intimates, but also by family members and even members of the wider community. However, Welchman and Hossain (2005) insist that HBV should be seen as a particular form of VAW because it is only *cosmetically* dissimilar to domestic violence and other forms of VAW. Only by seeing it as one manifestation of the wider problem of VAW can HBV be properly understood as a human-rights violation.

It is difficult to be optimistic about the possibilities for a speedy elimination of HBV in the UK. Crimes of honour are the product of long-standing cultural practices designed to control and subordinate women by whatever means necessary. Although local and international activists continue to work to eradicate HBV, there is still a lot to be done. For example, current UK asylum and immigration law is often interpreted in such a way that gender-based persecution is not recognised as a legitimate reason for granting asylum (Siddique, Ismail and Allen 2008). This must change. Until the problem of gender-based persecution is confronted at its source, society must ensure that its victims are granted the right to live in a safe place.

Yet programmes for the prevention of VAW cannot succeed without challenging the unequal power structures governing relationships between women and men: that is, by confronting the root cause of the problem. As UN Special Rapporteur on Violence Against Women Yakin Erturk has argued (2007), a gender-sensitive response must be adopted in order to end all forms of VAW. Honour-based crimes must be recognised for what they are: crimes against women that are the products of societies structured along explicitly patriarchal lines. There must be cultural sensitivity to the context in which these crimes take place when working to help the victims of these crimes. Cultural 'sensitivity' must not be used to excuse these crimes, either in terms of reducing sentences for perpetrators or in terms of allowing minority communities to adopt and enforce 'laws' and values that support the abuse of women.

It is also essential that the historical inaction of police officers and criminal-justice professionals is confronted, and also their failures to deal appropriately and compassionately with victims of HBV. Research has shown that women often move back and forth between the public and private realms when attempting to stop the violence they are experiencing (Hester, Kelly and Radford 1995). Banaz appealed to the authorities long before her murder, but her treatment by the investigating officers led to her being handed back to the men who eventually killed her. Due to the fact that VAW is viewed as a matter of public concern, if women do not seek to remedy their problem through public means (i.e. in the manner dictated by the state), then they are accused of manipulating the system for private ends; this means that they are often denied assistance. Thus, they are forced back into the private realm, where they are susceptible to further violence.

The high-profile case of Banaz Mahmod (as well as evidence disseminated by the CPS in 2007) shows that the police now view honour killings as serious crimes that require a policy of deterrence and also harsh punishment for offenders. The fact that there have been discussions about producing national guidelines, and also training for all police officers, shows that the police and CPS are now taking the issue of honour killings increasingly seriously. Nevertheless, the situation is mired in discussions about how to move forward. This has hindered the implementation of changes on the ground that are intended to make women feel safe enough to report the violence perpetrated against them by their families.

There is a growing sense of uncertainty as to whether or not the push towards the greater criminalisation of HBV is actually a victory; there is even some doubt as to whether it is appropriate in all cases. For example, recent research on forced marriage has questioned whether criminalisation alone can address the root causes of the problem (Gill and Anitha 2010). Although it is clear that the police are trying to adapt to meet the growing demands for a solution, their response to recent cases of forced marriage and honour killing represent a myriad of competing rationales that are simultaneously both progressive and paternalistic. Too often they either minimise the severity of the violence in their reports and responses or implicitly blame the victim for not leaving her family.

Moreover, despite years of training initiatives, police officers do not always believe women's stories as they do not adequately understand how to weigh and analyse personal testimony in HBV cases. The issue of victim credibility was particularly evident in the Banaz Mahmod case, but it is an endemic problem. Often, when police condemnation of HBV occurs, it derives from the notion that South Asian/Kurdish women are a vulnerable group in need of protection; this belief tacitly reinforces the subordinate status of women by promoting the view that the police need to provide legal protection for this vulnerable group, rather than ensuring the personal safety of individual women.

There is a growing consensus on the urgent need for policing and criminal-justice efforts to go beyond policy and push towards broader social change. Improving specialist services, designed to respond to different types of VAW, is part of the solution. There must also be a change in what Scheppele (1992) refers to as the 'habits of belief' (124) that persist across the criminal justice system and result in women always being treated in the same way. For instance, black and minority ethnic and refugee (BMER) women who suffer domestic violence do not get help until they have had, on average, 17 contacts with agencies; for white women, it takes 11 contacts on average (Brittain 2005). Only once these habits of belief change will the discourse on VAW in BMER communities evolve and the overarching quest for justice in cases of VAW will contribute to, or at least not undermine, the continued emancipation of women.

The heart of the issue is this: without a long-term plan for preventing all forms of VAW, and a pragmatic sequencing of sustainable interventions aimed at challenging the normalised acceptance of VAW, interventions to prevent the killing and abuse of women in the name of honour are likely to have little long-term impact.

Notes

1 'Honour' (*izzat*) has multiple connotations and overlapping meanings relating to respect, esteem, dignity, reputation and virtue, all of which are equated with the regulation of women's sexuality and the avoidance of social deviation. Inherent in this code of honour is the need to constantly strive to maintain it and avoid shame. However, even among communities which subscribe to this code, the specific acts that are deemed to increase or erode *izzat* are subject to constant contestation and change, and vary between particular groups within patriarchal communities in both the diasporic context and in South Asia (Gill 2009).
2 VAW has received greater political attention in the UK in recent years. This has led to changes in the way that VAW is conceptualised. Until recently, domestic violence has been used as a 'catch all' term, subsuming different forms of gendered violence. Many feminists are now arguing that the term 'violence against women' promotes a more integrated approach and illustrates the gendered nature of the types of violence under consideration (Horvath and Kelly 2007). The concept of VAW looks beyond the physical and psychological harm that women suffer in order to examine the systems of inequality that support such violence: as such, VAW encompasses a plethora of discrete influences. Women's experiences of violence cannot be treated in a piecemeal way, as though each axis of injustice exists in isolation: VAW is the consequence of many colliding and interconnecting elements. It is part of the widespread, systemic abuse of women – the result of multiple, intersecting types of inequality – and can only be properly understood in this context (Horvath and Kelly 2007).

Bibliography

Abdulla, R. and Yones, M. (2003) Central Criminal Court, 27 September 2003, London, Transcript: Smith Bernal.

Abu-Odeh, L. (1996) 'Crimes of Honour and the Construction of Gender in Arab Societies,' in Yamani, M. (ed.) *Feminism and Islam*, New York: New York University Press.

Baker, A. (2003) *The Hague Conference on Violence Against Women in the Name of 'Honour,'* 20–21 June 2004, The Hague: Metropolitan Police Service.

Barton, F. and Wright, S. (2007) *Murder Girl's Five Cries for Help That Were Ignored.* Retrieved 31 July 2008, from http://www.dailymail.co.uk/news/chapter-461280/Murder-girls-cries-help-ignored.html.

Baxi, P., Rai, S., and Ali. S. (2008) 'Legacies of Common Law: "Crimes of Honour"', in Cornwall, A. and Molyneux, M. (eds) *The Politics of Rights: Dilemmas for Feminist Praxis,* London and New York: Routledge.

Begikhani, N. (2005) 'Honour-Based Violence: The Case of Iraqi Kurdistan', in Welchman, L. and Hussain, S. (eds) *'Honour': Crimes, Paradigms and Violence Against Women,* London: Zed Books.

Brittain, E. (2005) *Black and Minority Ethnic Women in the UK,* London: Fawcett Society.

Crown Prosecution Service (CPS) (2007) *Forced Marriage and Honour Crimes Pilot Study in the UK,* London.

Council of Europe (2002) *Crimes of Honour,* Stockholm: Council of Europe Publications.

Derne, S. (1994) 'Hindu Men Talk About Controlling Women: Cultural Ideas as a Tool of the Powerful', *Sociological Perspectives,* Vol. 37, 203.

Dustin, M. (2006) *Gender Equality, Cultural Diversity: European Comparisons and Lessons,* London: London School of Economics.

Erturk, Y. (2007) *Elimination of all Forms of Violence Against Women: Follow-up to the Secretary-General's In-Depth Study at National and International Levels,* 1 March 2007, Retrieved 28 January 2008, from http://www.un.org/womenwatch/daw/csw/csw51/panelvaw/YE_CSW_Statement_07.pdf.

Gangoli, G., Razak, A. and McCarry, M. (2006) *Forced Marriage and Domestic Violence Among South Asian Communities in North East England,* Bristol, UK: University of Bristol.

Gill, A. (2004) 'Voicing the Silent Fear: South Asian Women's Experiences of Domestic Violence', *Howard Journal of Criminal Justice,* Vol. 4, No. 5, 465.

——(2009) 'South Asian Women's Experiences of Rape: Analysis of the Narrative of Survival', in Horvath, M. and Brown, J. (eds) *Rape: Challenging Contemporary Thinking.* Devon: Willan Publishing.

Gill, A. and Anitha, S. (2010) 'The Illusion of Protection? An Analysis of Forced Marriage Legislation and Policy in the UK', *Journal of Social Welfare and Family Law,* Vol. 31, No. 3, 257–269.

Gupta, R. (ed.) (2003) *From Homebreakers to Jailbreakers: Southall Black Sisters,* London: Zed Books.

Ginat, J. (1979) 'Illicit Sexual Relationships and Family Honour in Arab Society', *Israeli Studies in Criminology,* Vol. 10, 179.

Hester, M., Kelly, L. and Radford, J. (1995) *Women, Violence and Male Power,* Buckingham, UK: Open University Press.

Horvath, M. and Kelly, L. (2007) *From the Outset: Why Violence Should be a Priority for the Commission for Equality and Human Rights,* London: CSWASU.

Kandiyoti, D. (1988) 'Bargaining with Patriarchy', *Gender and Society,* Vol. 2, 274.

Kressel, G. (1981) 'Sororicide/Filiacide/Homicide for Family Honour', *Current Anthropology,* Vol. 22, 141.

Metropolitan Service Police (MPS) (2007) *Honour-Based Violence Action Plan and MPS Strategy*, London: MPS.

Ortner, S. (1978) 'The Virgin and the State', *Feminist Studies*, Vol. 4, 19.

Peristiany, J. and Pitt-Rivers, J. (1992) *Honour and Grace in Anthropology*, Cambridge: Cambridge University Press.

Sangari, K. (1999) *Consent, Agency, and the Rhetoric of Incitement: Politics of Possible Essays on Gender, History, Narratives, Colonial English*, Delhi: Tulika Press.

Scheppele, K. (1992) 'Just the Facts, Ma'am: Sexualised Violence, Evidentiary Habits and the Revision of Truths', *New York Law School Law Review*, Vol. 37, 123.

Sen, P. (2003) 'Successes and Challenges: Understanding the Global Movement to End Violence Against Women', in Kaldor, M., Anheier, H. K. and Glasius, M. (eds) *Global Civil Society*, London: Oxford University Press.

Siddique, N., Ismail, S. and Allen, M. (2008) *Safe to Return: Pakistani Women, Domestic Violence and Access to Refugee Protection – A Report on a Transnational Research Project Conducted in the UK and Pakistan*, Manchester, UK: South Manchester Law Centre.

Thiara, R. and Gill, A. (eds) (2010) *Violence Against South Asian Women: Issues for Policy and Practice*, London: Jessica Kingsley.

Welchman, L. and Hossain, S. (eds) (2005) *'Honour': Crimes, Paradigms and Violence Against Women*, London: Zed Press.

Werbner, P. (2007) 'Veiled Interventions in Pure Space: Honour, Shame and Embodied Struggles Among Muslims', *Theory Culture Society*, Vol. 24, 161.

Index

HRV = honour related violence